OPERATION

Captain M.N.R. Samant is a recipient of India's second-highest gallantry award, the Maha Vir Chakra, for conspicuous gallantry in the face of enemy fire during the 1971 India–Pakistan War.

Sandeep Unnithan is an executive editor with *India Today* where he writes on security-related issues. He is the author of *Black Tornado: The Three Sieges of Mumbai 26/11.*

THE UNTOLD STORY OF INDIA'S COVERT NAVAL WAR IN EAST PAKISTAN, 1971

OPERATION

CAPTAIN M.N.R. SAMANT

AND

SANDEEP UNNITHAN

HarperCollins *Publishers* India

First published in India by
HarperCollins *Publishers* in 2019
A-75, Sector 57, Noida, Uttar Pradesh 201301, India
www.harpercollins.co.in

2 4 6 8 10 9 7 5 3 1

P-ISBN: 978-93-5357-019-4
E-ISBN: 978-93-5357-020-0

Typeset in 11.5/15.2 Adobe Garamond at
Manipal Digital Systems, Manipal

Printed and bound at
Thomson Press (India) Ltd

MIX
Paper
FSC FSC® C010615

To the people of Bangladesh, who fought and won a heroic battle against extinction. The inheritors of Sonar Bangla, the land of Bangabandhu Sheikh Mujibur Rahman's dreams.

In Memoriam

**Captain M.N.R. Samant, Maha Vir Chakra
(1930–2019)**

Sailor, submariner, covert warrior, war hero

CONTENTS

FOREWORD

Much is known about the excesses of the Pakistan Army in 1971 in what was then the eastern half of the country. This was a period when an estimated three million Bangladeshis were killed during the Pakistan Army's onslaught on its own citizens in East Pakistan. The Bangladesh military conflict between India and Pakistan in 1971 was the inevitable consequence of this genocide and the pressure of tending to the over eight million refugees who had fled to India. The war finally resulted in the formal surrender by the Pakistan Army on 16 December 1971, and close to 93,000 Pakistani nationals surrendering as Prisoners of War to a joint command of the Indian Army and the 'Mukti Bahini' Bangladesh freedom fighters.

While much has been written about the land and air battles that led to the liberation of Bangladesh, there has been an impression that, except for operations by carrier-based aircraft in the Bay of Bengal and an attack on Karachi during the conflict, the Indian Navy had little or no role in the developments leading to the liberation of Bangladesh. More than four decades after Bangladesh was liberated, this impression has finally been corrected, thanks to this book written by Captain M.N.R Samant, who was awarded the Maha Vir Chakra for exceptional bravery in the conduct of covert commando operations in Bangladesh. These operations were undertaken well before the actual declaration of war in December 1971. The book is co-authored by Sandeep Unnithan, who has been one of India's foremost writers on issues related to defence and national security. It also sheds light on how Prime Minister Indira Gandhi personally approved and regularly monitored the covert naval operations in Bangladesh, which were undertaken under the supervision of the then naval chief, Admiral S.M. Nanda and the director of naval intelligence, Captain (later Vice Admiral) M.K. Roy.

The case for a naval role in the developments within Bangladesh emerged on humanitarian grounds. But what gave the idea impetus was a virtual rebellion within the Pakistan Navy just after the Bangladesh uprising commenced. Eight Bengali naval personnel deployed in a recently acquired French built submarine, the *PNS Mangro*, decided to desert the Pakistan Navy and join the freedom struggle after hearing horrific details of the Pakistan Army's brutal killings in East Pakistan. The submariners found their way to the Indian Embassy in Madrid, seeking India's help in returning to their homeland. These sailors formed the base upon which the Indian Navy built its whole offensive, and played a key role in contacting and providing local support for the covert Indian operations that were aimed at destroying logistical facilities across the coastal areas of Bangladesh, weeks before actual military operations by India began.

The book spells out how covert operations on foreign soil are conducted and the constant danger that those involved in these operations face to their lives, every moment they are operating on foreign soil. That, for me, is what makes this book such a gripping read. I was also happy to see that it is able to place the whole situation in an international setting by defining the contours of the difficult diplomatic situation that India's leadership faced in dealing with the emergence of a virtual US–China alliance which had been built with Pakistan acting as the intermediary. US President Richard Nixon's aversion for India and its leadership, and the US's keenness to turn a blind eye to the brutal suppression of the Bangladeshis – despite the superpower's avowed love for democracy as well as Sheikh Mujibur Rehman's rightful claim to power – failed to make matters easier for India.

The entire strategic scenario across India's eastern borders has changed after the epochal conflict of 1971. Bangladesh, which was then virtually written off as a potential economic basket case, forever leaning on international aid for its existence, has proved the sceptics wrong. Largely self- sufficient in meeting its food needs, the country has now emerged as a leading player in exports worldwide of textiles and textile products. While its military did play a role in the initial years after independence, Bangladesh is today a vibrant democracy. Even long-standing differences with India over its land and maritime borders have been amicably resolved.

The reality today is that it is not Bangladesh, but Pakistan that has emerged as an 'international basket case', heavily dependent on foreign aid to make both ends meet. Already one of the world's fastest-growing major economies, Bangladesh is poised to overtake Pakistan's GDP in the next few years.

Captain Samant was given a hero's welcome whenever he visited Bangladesh and met friends and admirers who looked back on what happened in 1971 with justifiable pride. He lived a full, heroic life, and it pains me immensely that he could not be here to witness the adulation this wonderful book would receive. However, it gives me satisfaction that he was able to recount to readers the real story of the covert naval operation that birthed Bangladesh, and to finally give us a glimpse into the lives of the unknown heroes who made the bigger campaign possible.

While this book is a celebration of the Indian heroes, it would be remiss of us if we forgot the role of the eight brave Bangladeshi submariners – M. Rahmatulla, S.M. Hussain, Aminullah Sheikh, A.W. Chowdhury, M.B. Alam, M.A. Rehman, A.R. Mian and M. Ahasanullah – who were prepared to sacrifice their lives for the cause of freedom and dignity of their fellow countrymen.

G. Parthasarathy

New Delhi
May 2019

DRAMATIS PERSONAE

INDIAN NAVY

OFFICER	DESIGNATION
Admiral Sardarilal Mathradas 'Charles' Nanda	Chief of the Naval Staff
Capt Mihir Kumar 'Micky' Roy	Director Naval Intelligence
Commander M.N.R. 'Sammy' Samant	Staff Officer (Naval Operations X)
Lt Cdr George Martis	Officer in Charge, C2P, Plassey (June–Nov 1971)
Lt Vijai Prakash Kapil	Officer in charge, C2P (April– June), Second-in-Command (June– Dec 1971)
Lt Samir Das	Instructor, Training Coordinator C2P Plassey
Lt Cdr Ashok 'Aku' Roy	Officer in Charge Naval Detachment, Delta Sector (July– Oct 1971)
Lt Cdr Jayanto Kumar Roy Choudhury	Commanding Officer *MV Palash*, Squadron Commander C2H

OFFICER	DESIGNATION
Lt Suvesh Kumar Mitter	Commanding Officer *MV Padma*
Lt Cdr Vishnu Kumar Raizada	Chief Squadron Technical Officer, C2H (Electrical)
Lt Cdr C.S. Menon	Staff Officer to Cdr Samant (May– Oct 1971)
Lt Cdr G.D. Mukherjee	Staff Officer to Cdr Samant (Oct– Dec 1971)
Commodore R.P. 'Squeaky' Khanna	Naval Officer in Charge (NOIC) Calcutta
Lt J.V. Natu	Squadron Engineer Officer C2H
Sub Lt A.K. Bandopadhyay	Junior staff officer to Cdr Samant (November-December 1971)
Sub Lt B.S. Thakur	Replaced Lt Samir Das as instructor, training coordinator in C2P, October 1971
Vice Admiral N. Krishnan	Commander-in-Chief Eastern Naval Command, Visakhapatnam
Vice Admiral S.N. Kohli	Commander-in-Chief Western Naval Command, Bombay
Pandurang K. Dhole	Petty Officer, CD-3, Chief Instructor C2P
Madhusudhan Gupta	Leading Seaman, CD-3, Senior Instructor C2P
Karan Singh	Leading Seaman CD-2, Instructor C2P
E.J. Princhan	Leading Seaman, CD-2, Instructor C2P
Chiman Singh	Leading Seaman, CD-2, Instructor C2P
Lt S.V. Chitale	Fleet Air Arm Engineer, Air-dropped ordnance specialist

INDIAN ARMY

OFFICER	DESIGNATION
Lt General Jagjit Singh Aurora	General Officer Commanding-in-Chief Eastern Army Command
Major General J.F.R. Jacob	Chief of Staff, Eastern Command , Director Ops (X) Oct-Dec 1971
Major General B.M. 'Jimmy' Sarkar	Director Ops (X) August- Oct 1971
Brigadier N.A. Salik	Sector Commander, Charlie Sector, West Bengal
Brigadier Shabeg Singh	Sector Commender, Delta Sector, Tripura
Brigadier Joginder Singh Gharaya	Brigade Commander, 42nd Brigade, Krishnanagar
Lt Col A.B.C. D'Mello	C.O. 2 Sikh LI, Krishnanagar

MUKTI BAHINI

OFFICER	DESIGNATION
Colonel M.A.G. Osmani	Commander-in-Chief Bangladesh Armed Forces
Abdul Wahed Chowdhury	Leading Telegraphist PNS Mangro, later Commander Task Unit 54.1.2 Chittagong
Mohammad Jalaluddin	Leading Seaman, Pakistan Navy; Later chief bosun mate MV Padma
Captain Rafiqul Islam	Commander, Mukti Bahini Sector One

OFFICER	DESIGNATION
Badiul Alam	Petty Officer *PNS Mangro*, Commander Task Unit 54.1.2 Chandpur
Mohammad Ahsanullah	Ex-*PNS Mangro*, Commander Task Unit 54.1.3 Narayanganj
Mohammad Rahmatulla	Ex-*PNS Mangro*, Commander Task Unit 54.1.14 Khulna
Atharuddin Talukder	Naval Commando
Humayun Kabir	Naval Commando

PAKISTAN NAVY

OFFICER	DESIGNATION
Rear Admiral Muhammad Shariff	Flag Officer Commanding East Pakistan (FOCEP), Dacca.
Captain Zamir Ahmed	Chief of Staff, Eastern Naval Command, Dacca

PROLOGUE

PLASSEY, 23 June 1757

Plassey. A nondescript village on the banks of the Bhagirathi, named for *Butea monosperma*, the bright orange–red spring flower native to the region. The red bloom on the riverbank that day, however, wasn't from 'The Flame of the Forest' Palashi flowers. It was from the scarlet woollen coats of the over 2,100 infantrymen of Colonel Robert Clive, commander of the ground forces of the East India Company. The sepoys cradled their long Brown Bess muskets tipped with gleaming socket bayonets as they found shelter in the mango grove sprawled along the riverbank. The Laksha Bagh, as the grove was called, brought temporary relief from the damp, enervating Bengal heat. Perspiration trickled down the backs of the sepoys, while the wet mud sucked greedily at their boots – the woollen uniforms were meant for the cold plains of Britain, not the oppressive heat of the Indian summer. The orchard was also a natural stockade that would shelter the sepoys from the enemy's cannonade. The white puffs of smoke in the distance were a sign that Siraj-ud-Daulah's gunners had commenced their bombardment. Cannon balls hit the trees, scattering leaves and splintering wood. But the sepoys were safe. The Nawab's army, which they counted as 50,000 strong – 35,000 foot soldiers and 15,000 cavalry waited in the distance to overwhelm them, just as they had the English garrison at Fort William the previous year. That campaign led to the infamous Black Hole of Calcutta, where some 146 English prisoners were confined to a tiny twenty-square metre dungeon by the Nawab's men, with only twenty-three emerging alive the next morning.

Clive's army had been sent to re-establish the British factories in Bengal. In January, he had recaptured Calcutta (Kolkata now) and, by March, captured Chandernagore from the French. Now he marched to face Siraj-ud-Daulah who had set out at the head of a huge army from his capital Murshidabad, determined to teach the British another lesson. Clive's infantry – 600 Europeans and over 2000 native infantry drawn from Bombay, Madras (Mumbai and Chennai now) and Bengal – had marched through heavy rain and flooded fields to reach Plassey. The colonel had turned the Nawab's impressive brick hunting lodge, surrounded by a high wall, into his field headquarters – Plassey House. At sunrise, he had watched, from atop the roof of the lodge, all three divisions of the Nawab's army encircle his position. The battle had started at around 8 a.m., when the Nawab's French gunners opened fire on his positions. Clive ordered his men to take shelter behind a mud bank in front of the grove.

The stench of impending defeat hung on the riverbank, but whose defeat, it wouldn't become clear until a few hours later. The treacherous, shape-shifting sandbanks, which could alter the course of the deceptively calm Bhagirathi river twisting through the Bengal plain, held a clue. Mir Jafar, who commanded a third division of the Nawab's army, watched impassively, opting not to join the battle.

The Nawab's guns continued firing for nearly four hours and a worried Clive gathered his men around for a war council when a thundercloud and the Bengal monsoon beat down on the battlefield and soaked Siraj-ud-Daulah's ammunition. The British were better prepared. They had brought tarpaulins which they threw over their guns and ammunition. With their artillery rendered useless, Siraj-ud-Daulah's army began an orderly retreat to their camps by 3 p.m. Clive spotted his opportunity and ordered an advance. His artillery began taking a toll on the Nawab's army. Bakshi Mir Madan, the Nawab's most trusted general and chief of the artillery, was killed, as was Bahadur Ali Khan, chief of the musketeers, and captain of the artillery, Nauwe Singh Hazari.

As the British infantry surged forward by 5 p.m., their Brown Bess muskets discharging volleys of shot, it was all over. The twenty-four-year-old Nawab, his worst nightmares having come true, mounted a camel and fled the battlefield. His army followed suit. Siraj-ud-Daulah was captured and executed days later, and his treacherous general, Mir Jafar, was appointed the puppet Nawab of Bengal.

Neither Clive nor the hapless Siraj would realize the significance of that battle. Palashi – like the hot, dusty village of Panipat, where Mughal invader Babar routed the forces of Ibrahim Lodhi on the north Indian plains on 21 April 1526, would be a pivot in world history. It marked the birth of an empire. With the defeat of Mir Jafar's successor, Mir Qasim, in the Battle of Buxar in 1764, Clive had unlocked a booty beyond the wildest dreams of the board of directors ensconced in East India House on London's Leadenhall Street. The Company transitioned from being merchants to conquerors and administrators of a province that was created by geographical features. The landmass bound by the Himalayas in the north, the province of Bihar in the west and the Purvanchal mountains in the east, was born out of the massive silt and debris – flowing down from the mighty Himalayas mountain range that had risen thanks to the collision of the Indian and the Eurasian plates – carried down over millennia by the Ganges and the Brahmaputra.

Towards the south, the confluence of the two rivers in the province created the world's largest delta – approximately 354 kilometres wide – as they emptied into the Bay of Bengal. The year-round irrigation and fertile soil saw agricultural surpluses that led to prosperity and a geopolitical maxim, voiced succinctly by historian Vincent Smith in *The Oxford History of India*: 'Whichever power controls the lower Gangetic valley, ultimately rules north India.'

Before Clive's victory, Bengal was the richest Mughal suba or province, delivering nearly half of the empire's revenues. The military occupation of the province in 1576 allowed Babur's progeny to tighten their grip over India. Now, over two centuries later, Bengal was once again a war chest, open to conquest. Less than a century after Plassey, the British would – using a combination of intrigue, infantry and incomes from a province the combined size of Germany and France – grind down the empires of the Sikhs and Marathas. The other native princes meekly fell in line. Plassey ushered in a hundred-year reign of the Company.

Calcutta, which grew around their walled trading settlement, Fort William, became the Company's capital for 132 years. From their three bastions – Calcutta, Bombay and Madras – the Company's armies engulfed the Indo-Gangetic plains, the land of five rivers and the Deccan, in a spate of conquest until the mutiny by the scarlet-coated sepoys of the Bengal Army in Kanpur in 1857 rang the curtains down on it. Company rule was followed by ninety-nine years of Crown Rule, when India glittered as the Jewel in the Crown.

After the political awakening among the Hindu Bengali middle class in the late 19th century challenged British rule, the province also became the laboratory for another British tool of subjugation – divide and rule. In 1905, Bengal was partitioned between the Muslim majority eastern part and the Hindu-dominated west, an event that would be mourned with the immortal words 'Amar *shonar Bangla'* (my Golden Bengal), by the anguished poet and Nobel laureate, Rabindranath Tagore.

The British undid the partition in 1911 even as they shifted their capital to New Delhi. But Tagore would not live to see the single worst depredation of colonial rule – the starvation deaths of three million Bengalis in 1943, when the British stockpiled rice and wheat to feed themselves through World War II, even as they continued to export rice from Bengal. The food shortage led to India's worst famine. Millions swarmed the cities of Bengal looking for food. British Prime Minister Winston Churchill blamed Indians for the famine. It was their fault, he said at a briefing of the war cabinet 'for breeding like rabbits'. He later told Secretary of State for India, Leopold Amery, that he hated Indians because 'they are a beastly people with a beastly religion'.

For many Indians, the Bengal Famine was the proverbial last straw. The twist of the knife that had been plunged in at Plassey. Sheikh Mujibur Rahman, the future prime minister of Bengal recounted in his memoirs in the 1960s:

When the East India company had annexed Bengal following Mir Zafar's betrayal in the 18th century, Bengal was so rich that a wealthy businessman of Murshidabad had enough money to buy the city of London … And now I saw what we were reduced to: mothers dying in the streets while their babies still suckled; dogs competing with people for leftovers in garbage dumps; children abandoned by their mothers who had run away or sold them, driven by hunger. At times, they failed to do even that since there would be no buyers.

After the famine came the bloodbath.

The savage riots that followed the 'Direct Action Day' – called by S.H. Suhrawardy, the Muslim League chief minister of the Bengal

Province in 1946 – finally led to the province being cleaved away in 1947 to make the eastern wing of Pakistan, the new homeland for Indian Muslims. Nearly a quarter century after Partition, the sleepy village of Palashi on the Bhagirathi awaited its role in another battle for Bengal.

1
GENERAL GENOCIDE

Sporting a full-sleeved cream safari shirt, khaki Jodhpurs, and a natty crimson cravat around his neck, General Aga Muhammad Yahya Khan slid off his open jeep and strode around the photo opportunity with panache. Gelled hair slicked back and covered by a Panama hat, a gleaming silver-knobbed baton in his left hand, right hand raised Caesar-like to acknowledge the masses around him, Khan certainly bore more titles than a Roman potentate. He was president of Pakistan, chief martial law administrator, commander-in-chief of the Pakistan Army, and supreme commander of the armed forces.

The miserable knots of humanity who sat huddled on the ground, palms outstretched for aid, gave the event a distinctly feudal air, and Yahya, the look of a landlord touring his estates.

East Pakistan had been hit by a tragedy far greater than the bloody Partition riots. Just four days earlier, on 12 November 1970, Cyclone Bhola – the deadliest cyclone in human history – had ripped through the coast, killing over 3,00,000 persons, leaving millions homeless and causing damage worth $86.4 million.[1]

---

1   Calculated as per 1970 US dollar rates

Eyebrows poised above his heavy-lidded eyes like angry caterpillars, the president shot his bites out in staccato bursts into a forest of waiting microphones: 'I am satisfied and I am going to satisfy myself more. If I am not satisfied on this tour, then I shall do something about it … but so far, they are doing their damndest!'

Yahya's inaction in East Pakistan fuelled public anger. The international community, including India, had moved in with aid faster than the Pakistani authorities had. Khan's visit was meant to be a public relations salve, but turned out to be a disaster.

Two years ago, on 25 March 1968, Field Marshal Ayub Khan had handed power over to Yahya, 'a much smaller Pathan and a heavier drinker', as historian Stanley Wolpert described him.

Both generals had seen military service in the British Indian Army during the Second World War that ended with the atomic incineration of Hiroshima and Nagasaki on 18 August 1945. Two empires, German and Japanese, built in a little over a decade of swift military conquests, collapsed. A third – Great Britain's colonial possessions acquired over two centuries of conquest – had begun to rapidly unravel. The deceptive lull that followed the end of the Second World War had turned into bitter recrimination as the Congress and the Muslim League battled over the partition of the subcontinent. The League's two-nation theory held that Hindus and Muslims were separate nations and became the basis for the creation of Pakistan.

The non-cooperation movement and the Indian freedom struggle launched by Mahatma Gandhi had been non-violent. But, by 1946, India was perched on a precipice of violence. The spark to set the tinder on fire came from an unexpected source – the trials of the Indian National Army (INA). The INA had been founded by the firebrand young nationalist Subhas Chandra Bose. Bose had parted ways with the Congress and staged a dramatic escape from house arrest in Calcutta, travelling to Afghanistan, then to Soviet Russia and finally to Nazi Germany, hoping that his enemy's enemy would help him achieve Indian independence. In the winter of 1943, the invading German columns had halted in the Russian winter and India was too distant in Germany's war plans. So, Bose made another dramatic voyage – a U-boat ride took him from Germany to Japan, where he raised the Indian National Army from the thousands of Indian Army personnel taken prisoner by the Japanese during the invasion of Malaya and Singapore. The INA would fight alongside the Imperial Japanese Army as it swept through Burma, right up to the doorsteps of north-eastern India.

The defeat of the Japanese Army and the tragic death of Bose in an air accident in Formosa (Taiwan) seemed like the last chapter in India's armed struggle for freedom, but it was not. Bose was the Samson of India's freedom struggle, a freedom fighter who was convinced that only violence could force the British out of India. In his fiery death, he had shaken Britain's faith in one of the pillars of British rule: the military. The public trial of the defeated INA sparked off further unrest and a mutiny among the ratings of the Royal Indian Navy hastened the transfer of power from Great Britain to the dominions of India. On 14 August 1947, Pakistan, the land of the pure, was birthed from the chaos of this hasty exit, accompanied by the largest migration – of ten million people – in all of human history. The savage riots that followed bloodied the non-violent freedom struggle, leading to one of the century's bloodiest civil wars.

When the dust had settled, 390 million people, or nearly one-fifth of humanity, were divided into two countries – India and Pakistan. The latter was a geographical oddity, its two wings – East and West – separated by 1,600 km of Indian territory, which is more than the distance between Berlin and Moscow.

On 22 October 1947, thousands of tribal raiders poured into Jammu and Kashmir to forcibly annex the state whose ruler

Maharaja Hari Singh was undecided on joining either country. The raiders – Pathans from the NWFP – had been gathered and sent by Brigadier Akbar Khan of the Pakistan Army. They were defeated by the Indian Army, which flew into the state after Maharaja Singh signed an instrument of accession. The defeat of the raiders drew the Pakistan Army into the conflict in May 1948, until the United Nations called for a ceasefire on 1 January 1949.

Pakistan lurched between a series of political crises through the 1950s before President Iskander Mirza, Mir Jafar's great-grandson, was overthrown in a bloodless coup by Field Marshal Ayub Khan in September 1958. The Sandhurst-trained Ayub had overruled his own order – issued after he took over as Pakistan's first chief of army staff in 1951 – to keep the army out of politics. The disastrous war that he launched in 1965 to try and take Jammu and Kashmir by force ended with a counter move which took the Pakistan Army by surprise – Indian tanks at the gates of Lahore. The Tashkent Declaration which he signed in January 1966 with his Indian counterpart, Prime Minister Lal Bahadur Shastri, marked the decline of his fortunes. Pakistani politicians blamed Ayub for the capitulation.

An economic downturn triggered by the war and mounting internal unrest saw Ayub make way in 1969 for his ambitious army chief, General Aga Muhammad Yahya Khan. Yahya, a graduate of the Indian Military Academy, Dehra Dun, appeared in the living rooms of Pakistani families on 25 March 1969 with a finger-wagging televised address. 'I will not tolerate disorder,' he said in a clipped British accent as he announced the imposition of martial law in Pakistan.

Yahya abrogated the 1962 constitution, dissolved the parliament, and dismissed all of President Ayub Khan's civilian officials. Yahya's arrival was proof of the wildly different trajectories taken by the two armies that shared a common heritage.

In India, politicians decide their army chiefs. In Pakistan, it was the other way around. And so it was with Yahya Khan, who had begun his term with a sense of purpose, of shaping Pakistan's polity. On 28 November 1969, he had clarified that he did not want to make martial law a permanent feature in Pakistan and that his intent was to create 'conditions conducive to the establishment of constitutional government'. He called for general elections towards the end of 1970.

Elections announced by a general would normally be taken with a pinch of salt. But there were no strings attached. The elections, Yahya said, would be based on universal suffrage. They would be Pakistan's first elections based on the one person-one-vote principle.

On 1 July 1970, he dissolved the 'One Unit' that had existed since 1954 and reinstated Pakistan's four original provinces. The elections were going to be the field marshal's attempt at a legacy which had eluded his predecessor. The elections were to have been held in October, but the cyclone in East Pakistan saw them being pushed to December.

Meanwhile, across the borders in New Delhi, a guardedly ambitious political figure had begun her struggle for pre-eminence. India had lost two prime ministers in just nineteen months when Indira Gandhi took over. The daughter of India's first Prime Minister Jawaharlal Nehru might have appeared unthreatening to her father's powerful party colleagues, the collegium of satraps often referred to as the 'Syndicate' – Congress President K. Kamaraj, Bengal Pradesh Congress Committee President Atulya Ghosh, S.K. Patil from Bombay, and S. Nijalingappa, the chief minister of Mysore – who controlled the Indian National Congress after the demise of the colossus-like Nehru. One of Gandhi's opponents, the socialist Ram Manohar Lohia dismissed her as a 'goongi gudiya' (dumb doll) when she was elected PM in 1966. The line stuck. It echoed the Syndicate's reasons for appointing her. When India's second Prime

Minister Lal Bahadur Shastri died suddenly in Tashkent soon after signing an agreement with Ayub Khan, they pitted Indira against Morarji Desai, the man who ought to have been the automatic successor to Shastri. In the party elections, Indira defeated Desai, 359–169 votes, to take oath as India's first woman prime minister. She was a third-generation politician, but possessed seemingly none of the charisma of her father's towering personality. Against the powerful lobby that controlled the party, she appeared helpless.

India's fourth general elections in February 1967 saw the Indian National Congress under Indira Gandhi win its lowest tally since Independence – 283 seats. The verdict suited the Syndicate. Gandhi would remain the puppet that Lohia had said she was, tethered to their strings.

Meanwhile, another powerful force – Bengali nationalism – which predated the idea of an independent Pakistan, was brewing in cyclone-hit East Pakistan. The sentiment of Bengalis sharing a common cultural bond had first found expression after Lord Curzon's partition of Bengal, and later in influential leaders like Abul Kasem Fazlul Haq. Mohammed Ali Jinnah's new nation had only briefly papered over Bengali nationalism, and it now simmered beneath the surface, fuelled by the brazen neglect of the eastern wing by the west. Fifty-six per cent of Pakistan's population lived in its eastern province in 1971 and had a greater share of exportable commodities – mainly jute and tea – which fetched precious foreign exchange. East Pakistan's share in the country's foreign export was about 50 per cent (sometimes even 70 per cent), but its share in foreign imports seldom exceeded 33 per cent. East Pakistanis made up only 5 per cent of the Pakistan Army's officer corps in 1963, and the province got only 4 per cent of foreign aid and 34 per cent of US aid. These unfair allocations saw the phenomenal growth of industries in West Pakistan, which also used East Pakistan as a captive market for its finished products.

For the third time in five centuries, Bengalis felt as if they had been colonized. Cracks in the edifice had appeared soon after partition in 1948 when Jinnah announced that Urdu alone would be the lingua franca of the new nation. Nationalist forces had been uncorked and swirled around the emerald green Bengal countryside, looking for a nucleus. They found it in the charismatic leader Sheikh Mujibur Rahman. Mujib, as he was known, was a towering personality, literally and metaphorically. Just under six feet tall, his thick black hair streaked with grey, sporting a dark moustache and thick rimmed spectacles, he stood out in a crowd. He was born into an aristocratic Muslim family in Tungipara village in Faridpur district and had started as a Muslim Students League leader during the independence movement and spearheaded the language agitation, even heckling the governor general, Mohammed Ali Jinnah, on 19 March 1948 in Dacca (Dhaka now) when he announced that Urdu would be the only national language of Pakistan. Bengali was eventually recognized as a state language in 1954. In 1955, Mujib's party, the Awami Muslim League dropped the 'Muslim' to mark the birth of a secular democratic political party.

In 1966, Mujib, as the leader of a coalition of Bengali parties, had launched an agitation for greater autonomy for East Pakistan under the 'Six Point programme' that, among others, called for a Federation of Pakistan with the federal government dealing only with defence and foreign affairs. East Pakistan would have a separate military or paramilitary force, Naval Headquarters (NHQ), the power to collect taxes and revenue, its own account for foreign exchange earnings, and trade links with foreign countries.

For Field Marshal Ayub Khan the six points appeared treasonous and an attempt at secession. In 1967, Mujib and others were implicated in what came to be known as the Agartala Conspiracy Case, and charged by Pakistani authorities with fomenting a secessionist movement and colluding with Indian intelligence agents in Agartala, the capital of the Indian state of Tripura. The trial which began in 1968 made Mujib a Bengali hero. Faced by mass public protests, the Pakistani authorities dropped the charges against him in 1969. Soon after his release, the Awami League chief received a tumultuous welcome at Dacca's Race Course Maidan, where he was first addressed by the honorific 'Bangabandhu' (Bengali brother). The movement for an independent Bangla Desh (Bangladesh now) now had a symbol, but it still had to reckon with a recalcitrant Pakistan. East Pakistan was lightly guarded. Internal security duties were handled by the 10,000-strong paramilitary, the East Pakistan Rifles. The military garrison there comprised only one division of 12,000 soldiers, four naval gunboats and one squadron of eighteen F-86 Sabre jets because General Headquarters (GHQ), Rawalpindi, believed that, 'the defence of East Pakistan lay in the west'. This essentially meant that Pakistan would attack from the west and grab territory, diverting India's attention from the east.

In India, meanwhile, Indira Gandhi had begun her collision course with the Syndicate. In July, she announced the nationalization of fourteen private banks (which accounted for nearly 70 per cent of India's deposits) and divested Finance Minister Morarji Desai of his portfolio, which led to his resignation as deputy prime minister and the breakup of the Congress into Indira's Indian National Congress (Requisitionists) and the INC (Organisation) led by Kamaraj.

At the same time, Yahya was intent on taking Pakistan towards democracy, or at least guide it towards a space where the army's position was maintained and he could continue as president. On 31 March 1970, his decree of a Legal Framework Order (LFO) dissolved the 'One Unit' geopolitical programme begun in 1954 by PM Mohammed Ali Bogra. The One Unit programme was a ploy to diminish the differences in population between the two wings of the country. Yahya called for direct elections to a 300-seat National Assembly of Pakistan, based on proportional representation. This general election, Pakistan's first ever, held on 7 December 1970, triggered off a political tsunami. Mujib's Awami League swept the elections, winning 160 of 162 seats in East Pakistan. Bhutto's Pakistan People's Party could win only eighty-one of 138 seats in West Pakistan. For the first time in its brief existence, West Pakistan faced the prospect of being ruled by a party from the East. A fact that discomfited the West Pakistani ruling elite.

Meanwhile, in India, Indira Gandhi dissolved the Lok Sabha and called for fresh elections nearly a year ahead of schedule. The elections, she told the nation on radio and TV, would be held in mid-February 1971.

By 1971, the Cold War was in its twenty-sixth year. In Washington, President Richard Nixon, now into his second year in office, had begun implementing his campaign promise of extricating the United States from the quagmire of Vietnam. Over 50,000 American soldiers had died in the Vietnam War – more than the number of US troops that had perished in the Korean War or in World War I – which saw the United States at its most polarized since the Civil War. The Soviet Union under Leonid Brezhnev had begun diverting more resources towards a massive military build-up to globally challenge the United States. The Soviet Navy's 'Exercise Okean' in 1970 saw over 200 warships, submarines and aircraft manoeuvring in the Indian, Pacific and Atlantic Oceans, and in the Mediterranean and Baltic Seas.

In China, Chairman Mao's giant wrecking ball, the Cultural Revolution, swung unabated in its fifth year, battering institutions and people. It was the Great Helmsman's[2] third disastrous grasp at relevance. Britain had a wary eye on the third year of 'The Troubles',

---

2　Mao was often called the Great Helmsman

a home-grown insurgency where the British troops battled the Irish Republican Army in Northern Ireland.

On the verge of being declared an economic basket case, India had concerns of its own. Inflation was high; foreign exchange reserves barely enough to cover two months of imports; the worst droughts in a century had ravaged the country in 1965 and 1966, exacerbated by the 1965 war; there was a crippling 'ship to mouth' dependence on Public Law 480[3] wheat imports from the US, on which the Lyndon B. Johnson administration had begun to turn the tap down for India, since India disapproved of the ongoing US war in Vietnam. The Five-Year plans were temporarily discarded between 1966 and 1969 as the government went into economic fire-fighting mode. Prime Minister Shastri's slogan 'Jai Jawan, Jai Kisan' in 1965 thus underlined the dilemma of a non-aligned state that had to defend its borders, expand its military and feed its people by increasing crop yields through the 'Green Revolution'. Armed internal insurgencies continued to simmer in Nagaland, Mizoram and Manipur and among the peasantry of West Bengal in the late 1960s.

In January 1971, as campaigning started for the fifth Indian general elections, Indira Gandhi hit the campaign trail with her shrill 'Garibi hatao' (remove poverty) battle cry. These two words summed up her party's socialist tilt too, and she criss-crossed the countryside chanting what would become the Congress party's mantra for the next two decades.

In East Pakistan, meanwhile, President Yahya Khan met Mujib in Dacca and described him as the future prime minister of Pakistan but vacillated over convening the National Assembly.

Things would have continued uninterrupted but for a tape which unspooled in General Headquarters (GHQ), Rawalpindi. In

---

3   The US food aid programme, under which India imported wheat

the tape, purportedly recorded by a Bengali journalist interviewing Sheikh Mujib, Bangabandhu had laid out his plans for the independence of Bangla Desh.

Yahya was apoplectic with rage when he heard about this. GHQ began secretly reinforcing the East with the Pakistan Army troops flown via Sri Lanka. On 30 January that year, an Indian aircraft was hijacked to Lahore by two Kashmiri separatists. India suspended all Pakistani overflights over its territory. The air bridge between the two wings of Pakistan shifted thousands of kilometres down south, via Colombo. A showdown was inevitable.

On 22 February, Yahya met with the provincial governors in Islamabad. The meeting was also attended by Lt General Sahabzada Yaqub Khan, commander, eastern command. In this conference, Yahya approved the plan for military operations. Yaqub was given carte blanche to execute plan 'Blitz' in case Mujib failed to toe their line.

Five days after the meeting, two infantry battalions were flown into Dacca by PIA commercial airliners flying via Colombo.

The rapid-fire events of March altered the course of history. On 1 March, Yahya Khan announced the postponement, sine die, of the national assembly meeting. Mujib responded with a call for a general strike and a civil disobedience movement of the kind that the country had last seen against the British in the 1940s. The Awami League went on the rampage, targeting those whom it saw as collaborators with the West Pakistani regime. On 7 March, Sheikh Mujibur Rahman, sporting a white kurta-pyjama and a black half-sleeved jacket, ascended the stage at Dacca's Ramna Race Course. The throaty cries of 'Amar Desh, Tomar Desh, Bangla Desh, Bangla Desh' (My country, your country, Bangla Desh, Bangla Desh) and 'Swadhin Karo, Swadhin Karo, Bangla Desh Swadhin Karo' (Liberate, liberate, liberate Bangla Desh) from a surging crowd of tens of thousands of people rent the air. Bangabandhu put his thick black spectacles on the wooden rostrum, held his hands behind his back and gently pivoted on his feet to address the sea of humanity with one of the most important words he had ever spoken: 'Our struggle, this time, is a struggle for freedom. Our struggle, this time, is a struggle for our independence. Joy Bangla.'

That day, a PIA flight from Islamabad brought in another man who would forever change the destiny of East Pakistan – Lt General Tikka Khan, a man who was the exact opposite of his suave aristocratic predecessor, Lt General Yakub Khan. Known as the Butcher of Balochistan for brutally putting down an insurrection in that province in 1970, Tikka's infamy preceded him. He was presented a garland of shoes at Dacca airport by the Bangla Deshis, while the chief justice refused to swear him in as governor. When he was finally sworn in, he directed the army to disarm the East Bengal regiment, battalions of the East Pakistan Rifles, and the East Pakistan police.

India's politics, meanwhile, had undergone a dramatic shift with Indira Gandhi registering a landslide victory in the general elections, winning 325 of 515 Lok Sabha seats in the results announced on 17 March. She now stood unchallenged on the Indian political landscape.

On 22 March, Yahya indefinitely postponed the meeting of the National Assembly. Mujib hit back by declaring that 23 March, which was observed as Pakistan National Day commemorating the Lahore Declaration, would now be observed as Resistance Day.

This greatly rattled West Pakistan's military rulers. Students marched holding aloft green flags with a red circle – symbolizing Bangla Desh – even as they trampled on the Pakistani flag. Awami Leaguers thronged towards Mujib's house in the Dhanmandi area of Dacca waving Bangla Deshi flags. The stage was set for a confrontation. On the afternoon of 25 March, Yahya Khan secretly left Dacca via Colombo.

Four months after Cyclone Bhola, a manmade catastrophe was to hit East Pakistan. On Thursday, 25 March, West Pakistan declared war on its Eastern wing. Just an hour short of midnight, General Tikka Khan turned on Operation Searchlight. It was code for a massive military crackdown, which would catch thousands of hapless Bengalis in its searing glare.

Troops fanned out into Dacca from the cantonment and descended on Dacca University, firing tanks, rocket launchers, recoilless guns and mortars at the university building. Hundreds of students were murdered in cold blood.

By the time the first Martial Law proclamation was issued by Tikka Khan the next morning, some 50,000 people had been butchered, most of them without offering any resistance. On the morning of 27 March, when the curfew was lifted after thirty-three hours, the flight began. Within the next twenty-four hours, about 80 per cent of the population had left the capital city. The massacre continued with accompanying arson, loot and rape. The people killed in and around Dacca alone numbered around 150,000, for the instruction from Tikka Khan to his troops was: 'I want the land and not the people.'

'The military action was a display of stark cruelty,' Lt General A.A.K. Niazi wrote in his memoirs, 'more merciless than the massacres at Bukhara and Baghdad by Changez Khan and Hulagu Khan or at Jallianwala Bagh by the British general, Dyer.' At 1 a.m., Special Services Group (SSG) commandos swarmed Mujib's residence in Dhanmandi. 'Big bird in the cage ... others not in their nests ... over' the special services group major reported after the mission. Mujib was bundled into an aircraft and flown to Karachi three days later.

The same day, a message from Sheikh Mujibur Rehman played over the airwaves:

This may be my last message. From today, Bangla Desh is independent. I call upon the people of Bangla Desh to resist the army of occupation to the last. Your fight must go on until the last soldier of the Pakistan Occupation Army is expelled from the soil of Bangla Desh and final victory is achieved.

Hundreds of Bengali leaders melted into India, crossing the vast border, into states like Meghalaya, Assam, Tripura and West Bengal. In Dacca, foreign journalists were confined to their hotel rooms to be deported the following day as the Pakistan Army tightened its grip on the renegade province.

On 26 March, General Yahya Khan in his speech banned the Awami League and declared Mujib a traitor. Lt General Tikka Khan imposed martial law in East Pakistan and executed orders for military action to 'reinstate public order and central authority'. These orders had been approved by Yahya on 20 March, when he was talking to Bhutto and Mujib.

The following day, a Friday, Major Siddiq Salik, the public relations officer of the Inter-Services Public Relations (ISPR) East Pakistan of the Eastern Command and sympathetic to the Bengali cause, reported to the cantonment for lunch. Salik found the atmosphere very different: 'They felt that the storm, after a long lull, had finally blown past, leaving the horizon clear.' The officers chatted in the mess with a visible sense of relaxation. Peeling an orange, one of the officers, Captain Chaudhry, said, 'The Bengalis have been sorted out well and proper – at least for a generation.' Another, Major Malik added, 'Yes, they only know the language of force; their history says so.'

Meanwhile, in response to Mujib's message, the Bengali soldiers mutinied. On the same day, Major Ziaur Rahman, the second-in-command of the East Bengal regiment raised the banner of revolt. Major Rahman took command over his forces, seized the transmitting station and broadcast his declaration of independence.

The regiment, comprising five infantry battalions, had been raised by Pakistan in 1948 to balance a predominantly West Pakistan army.

Chittagong had already been simmering for the past few days. In mid-March, Bengali port workers had refused to offload the arms and ammunition from the *MV Swat*, because word was that this would be used against Bengalis. They had heard right. The Pakistan Army, having realized the imbalance in Chittagong – there were 5,000 Bengali troops in Chittagong and only 600 West Pakistani troops – had begun a military build-up. The East Bengal Regiment was now the nucleus of the armed resistance against West Pakistan.

At 9.59 a.m., local time, on 28 March, Archer Blood, the US consul general in Dacca sent out the first of what would come to be known as the 'Blood Telegrams', a ringside view of the unfolding genocide. The series of confidential missives he sent out to the US Secretary of State were copied to the embassies in New Delhi, Islamabad, London and Bangkok. The telegrams were a damning account of how the US administration stood mute witness to the carnage.[4]

> Here in Dacca we are mute and horrified witness to a reign of terror by the Pak military. Evidence continues to mount that the Martial Law Authorities (MLA) have a list of Awami League supporters whom they are systematically eliminating by seeking them out in their homes and shooting them.
> 'Among those marked for extinction in addition to the Awami League hierarchy, are student leaders and university faculty.
> 'Moreover, with the support of Pakistan military, non-Bengali Muslims are systematically attacking poor people's quarters and murdering Bengalis and Hindus. Streets of Dacca are aflood with Hindus and others seeking to get out of Dacca. Many Bengalis have

---

4   Consulate General, Dacca, to the Department of State, Telegram 959, 28 March 1971

sought refuge in home of Americans, many of whom are extending shelter.

'Tightening of curfew today (it is being re-imposed at noon) seems designed to facilitate Pak military's search and destroy operations. There is no, repeat, no resistance being offered in Dacca to military.'[5]

On 31 March, the Pakistan Army attacked Chittagong using tanks, aircraft, artillery, gunboats and a naval destroyer. Leading Seaman Mohammed Jalaluddin instantly recognized the distinctive multiple thumps of naval artillery in the distance as the 4.5-inch guns of the *PNS Jahangir*, a World War II-era Royal Navy destroyer. They were blasting the headquarters of the East Pakistan Rifles in Chittagong.

Jalaluddin had been captain of the turret on the *PNS Babur*, flagship of a seven-warship flotilla that included the *Jahangir*, which had shelled the Indian port town of Dwarka during the 1965 India–Pakistan war.

Now, these guns were being turned inwards. The last few days had been a blur of revolution and then, finally, liberation. The short and swarthy sailor knew that naval artillery signalled the end of liberty was nigh. The .303 rifles carried by the East Pakistan Rifles who were barricaded would not hold out for long against the might of the Pakistan army, navy and air force, who had been building up their strength to retake the vital port city.

Jalaluddin had responded to Sheikh Mujibur Rahman's call for independence. The thirty-five-year-old sailor had deserted his post at the *PNS Bakhtiar*, Pakistan Navy's largest base in the eastern wing. Days before that, on 23 March, all the Bengali sailors on the base had been disarmed and confined to their barracks. Three days later,

---

5   Declassified US State Department cables, 2003

Jalaluddin slipped out of the base at night, shed his khaki rig for a lungi and shirt, and went to the local Awami League office to enrol himself in the fight for freedom. He then visited his family – his wife Shireen, son Bilaluddin, daughter Nargis and niece Siyarun. A sea of humanity had flowed through Chittagong's streets for the next few days, waving Awami League flags and shouting 'Joy Bangla'. Now, just five days later, the streets were deserted and the atmosphere fearful. At 5 p.m. on 31 March, the guns stopped firing. 'We can't fight them,' Jalaluddin said. 'They will advance in the morning and kill us all.' He advised his comrades to retreat towards India.

He ran to his home in the naval accommodation for married sailors, woke up his family and asked them to start walking. They left everything behind, except a transistor radio – their sole link to the outside world.

Among the multitudes fleeing towards India was a slim, bespectacled Awami League student activist Atharuddin Talukder. The nineteen-year-old engineering student from the Chittagong University of Engineering and Technology had fled the port city for his native village in Patuakhali district when the crackdown began. Accompanied by his friends K.M. Nurool Huda and Yusuf Ali, he crossed over into India. They reached Hingalganj in West Bengal's 24 Parganas on 25 May and stayed at the Takipur transit camp for nearly a month.

Chittagong fell to the Pakistan Army and Major Zia. The remnants of the Bengali resistance retreated into Belonia, a town in southern Tripura. For many who fled, the resistance was as short-lived as the 18 April 1930 Chittagong uprising against the British, led by school teacher Surya Sen.

On 31 March, India threw its weight behind the people of East Pakistan. 'The people of East Bengal are being sought to be suppressed by the naked use of force, by bayonets, machine guns, tanks, artillery and aircraft,' read a resolution in Parliament moved by

Indira Gandhi. 'This House calls upon all peoples and Government of the world to take urgent and constructive steps to prevail upon the Government of Pakistan to put an end immediately to the systematic decimation of people, which amounts to genocide.' The resolution was in the true spirit of Ashoka, a 4th BCE Indian emperor who, after witnessing the horrors of his wars, set up a benevolent welfare state and from whom the young Indian republic borrowed its emblems – the four Sarnath Lions and the Dharma Chakra.

What the Indian government also did, unobtrusively, was to hark back to the time of Ashoka's grandfather, Chandragupta Maurya and his brilliant political adviser Kautilya. In Arthashastra his influential treatise on statecraft, Kautilya listed three types of warfare – open war, silent war and the concealed or guerrilla war. In the months that followed, the Indian state showed itself adept at all three.

Military assistance to the Bengali freedom fighters began a few days before Indira Gandhi moved the resolution. India's Border Security Force (BSF), a paramilitary force raised after the 1965 war, was given this task. On 28 March, the Indian home ministry asked Director General BSF K.F. Rustamji to divide the border with East Pakistan into sectors and put key senior staff in charge of training the Mukti Bahini in Agartala in Tripura, and Cooch Behar, Balurghat and Bangaon in West Bengal. On 29 March, the Indian Army – then deployed to West Bengal to ensure peaceful elections – also agreed to provide limited assistance.

In the months that followed, India demonstrated that it was no stranger to the use of irregular forces when no formal war had been declared. Irregular forces or 'non-state actors' had been used by Pakistan in both of its wars with India until then. They allowed the state to deny direct involvement even as they advanced Pakistan's politico-military objectives. The raiders of 1947–48 were followed in 1965 by thousands of Pakistani soldiers disguised as raiders and led by a major general, hoping to spark off an uprising in the Valley.

This was Operation Gibraltar – named for the Ummayad conquest of Hispania – routed by the Indian Army and which marked the beginning of the second Indo–Pak War.

By 31 March, Indira Gandhi's evocative address to Parliament signalled that the boot was on the other foot and that the Indian political leadership would provide covert support for the arming and training of the Mukti Fauj (Liberation Force), its core drawn from the estimated 20,000 men of the East Pakistan Rifles and the East Bengal Regiment who had now taken shelter in India.

Mrs Gandhi's decision was also influenced by one of her closest security advisors, Rameshwar Nath 'Ramji' Kao. In 1968, India's newly created Research & Analysis Wing (RAW/R&AW), set up just three years before under the enigmatic Imperial Police officer R.N. Kao, had identified East Pakistan as a thorn in India's flesh. It was a base from where Pakistan's Inter-Services Intelligence (ISI) infiltrated Naga and Mizo insurgent groups inside India. The Mizo National Front's Pu Laldenga and his men were based in the Chittagong Hill Tracts that abutted Mizoram. The ISI had supported India's oldest insurgency, the Naga insurrection, since the 1950s. Gangs of Nagas routinely crossed over into the Chittagong Hill Tracts where they were trained, armed and equipped by the ISI.

The Directorate General of Security (DGS) a special para-military outfit set up with CIA assistance after the 1962 war with China, specialized in covert warfare. It trained men to operate behind enemy lines, blow up bridges and communications, and to assassinate enemy leadership. The organization, operating under the Cabinet Secretariat, had three arms – the Special Frontier Force, a guerrilla army of Tibetan refugees officered by the Indian Army; the Aviation Research Centre, a small air force for transporting the commandos; and the Special Services Bureau, a unit to impart guerrilla training to civilians on the border, and to fight and coordinate a resistance movement behind enemy lines in case of another Chinese invasion. After 1968, the DGS was subsumed by RAW. The RAW chief, known as 'Secretary (R)', also wore an additional hat of director general, security.

Now, nearly a decade after India's China war, Pakistan would bear the full brunt of India's newly acquired hard power capabilities, both overt and covert.

On 10 April, the provisional government of Bangla Desh was established as an independent sovereign people's republic, with Sheikh Mujibur Rahman as its president-in-absentia and Syed Nazrul Islam as acting president, vice-president and supreme commander of the armed forces. The proclamation of independence, deemed to have come into effect from 26 March, was made from the border town of Baidyanathtala in East Pakistan, renamed Mujibnagar. On 11 April, Defence Minister Colonel Muhammad Ataul Gani Osmani took command as the first commander-in-chief of the Bangla Deshi forces – the Mukti Bahini or Liberation Force. Short and wiry, with an impressive snow-white handlebar moustache, Osmani had been commissioned into the British Indian Army and opted for the Pakistan Army after Partition, where he rose to become a colonel, serving as deputy director of military operations during the 1965 Indo-Pakistan war. Colonel Osmani had joined the Awami League after his retirement, had contested and won a seat to the now suspended National Assembly in the 1970 elections.

A day later, on 12 April, Lt General Tikka Khan, the architect of Operation Searchlight, was appointed governor and martial law administrator of East Pakistan. The army had, by now, re-established control over East Pakistan, the armed insurrection was faltering, and most Bengali soldiers were joining the trickle of refugees from East Pakistan across the 2600-km unguarded border into India.

West Pakistan quietly began a policy of segregation after 26 March. Bengali officers in the armed forces of West Pakistan were kept under watch. Bengali flying crew in the PIA were grounded. In the Pakistan Navy, particularly after 7 April, all Bengali officers and sailors were taken off ships and transferred to shore establishments. This was because of an incident in France.

THE *MANGRO* EIGHT

The spark from the atrocities of Operation Searchlight travelled across the world on a cordite line to the French naval base of Toulon, where the *PNS Mangro* – the third of the Pakistan Navy's French-built Daphné-class submarines – was undergoing sea trials.

The most dangerous man in the Pakistan Navy in 1971 was a lanky twenty-six-year-old leading submarine telegraphist named Abdul Wahed Chowdhury. 'Abu' to his family and 'Chow' to his friends, he didn't have a clue about his destiny, for in his estimation, he was just another homesick sailor, eager to get back home.

On July 1970, after a visit to Paris from Le Trait where he was posted for submarine training, he posted back a colour photograph – a novelty in those days – to his father back in Dacca. There was a message on the obverse side: 'It is very difficult to have lonely snaps in Paris ... especially near the Eiffel Tower'. The snap had a lanky young sailor in tight brown trousers and a checked polyester shirt, alone in a sea of laughing couples in the rain-swept French capital. Chowdhury rarely spent any time ashore or in his native East Pakistan ever since he had run away from Dacca to join the navy as an eighteen-year-old. Beginning with a war patrol on the *PNS Ghazi* during the 1965 war when its skipper Cdr Karamat Rahman Niazi prowled the Arabian Sea off Bombay looking for the Indian Navy's aircraft carrier *INS Vikrant*. Soon after, the young radio operator he was one of only four Pakistani submariners sent to Surabaya to sail back with the *Brahmastra*, one of two Soviet-built Whiskey-class submarines that Indonesia's dictator Sukarno had offered Pakistan in its ongoing war against India. The war had ended by the time the boat arrived after a fortnight-long passage. From then on, it was one foreign deployment after the other, first to Turkey for the *Ghazi*'s refit and then to France in 1970 where he was one of fifty-four crew of the Pakistani submarine the *PNS Mangro*, third of a batch of submarines ordered from France in February 1966. The *Mangro*, like her sister subs the *Hangor* and *Shushuk*, were built with a Rs 150 million loan from the French government in the state-owned shipyard Direction des Construction Naval (DCN) in Brest.

Compared to the lumbering 95-metre 1,570-ton *Ghazi*, the Daphnés handled like race cars. Smaller (just 57 metres long), lighter (displacing 860 tonnes) and nimbler, it could dart about underwater at 15 knot speeds like the coastal sharks they had been named for. Each boasted a maximum range of 10,000 nautical miles, diving depth of 500 metres, and a formidable weapon load – a dozen E14 550 mm anti-ship torpedoes, eight in forward tubes and four in aft tubes, each one a potential ship-killer. The *Hangor* and the *Shushuk* were already in Pakistan. On 2 December 1970, the *Mangro*, under the command of Lt Cdr S.A. Khalid, left her shipyard in Brest on the Atlantic coast of Britanny. She stopped at the giant naval base at Toulon in the Mediterranean, where she would conduct her final pre-sea trials before leaving for Karachi. The submarine set out for her sea sorties each morning and returned in the evening.

The crew who had been away from home for nearly two years, longed to see the lights of Karachi's Manora Island. Most had already purchased their refrigerators and TV sets and had shipped them back. March was also the month that the fourteen Bengali submariners on board had started tuning in to the news from home in East Pakistan, and this was when Chowdhury heard the charismatic Sheikh Mujibur Rahman's thunderous speech calling the Bengali people to join the struggle for independence. Every word of what Bangabandhu spoke struck a deep chord within the young sailor. And on 25 March, when the tanks, armoured personnel carriers and troops began their rampage through Dacca, something inside snapped: 'How could they use the military against us?' Submariner Chow had to join the struggle for liberating Bangla Desh. But he wouldn't do it alone. He was the commanding officer's (CO) secretary and had the combination to the submarine's safe where the *Mangro*'s confidential papers and all the forty-five crew passports were kept. He nimbly selected fourteen of those passports and kept them in his cupboard in the mess ashore. Then he started looking for accomplices. 'I am planning to leave to fight for Bangla Desh. Will you join me?' he called each of the thirteen Bengali crewmen aside and whispered. Eight sailors agreed to make a break for it.

Chow was committing high treason. If the group was caught, they could expect severe punishment. The ring leader was sure to face execution.

The mutineers hailed from different districts of the Eastern province. The senior most, Chief Electrical Artificer (Power) Mohammad Rahmatulla, chief petty officer and in charge of the *Mangro*'s sonar was from Khulna. Syed Mosharraf Hussain, the engine room artificer, was from Faridpur; Aminullah Sheikh, petty officer, electrical (power) from Chandpur; Mohammad Ahsanullah, leading seaman (mechanical) from Feni. The three youngest crewmen were Alhaz Badiul Alam from Rangpur division, Abdur Rakib Mian, electrical mechanic and M. Abdur Rehman from the supply and secretariat branch. Mian and Alam were both from Tangail.

They would not serve in a military that crushed its own people. They only awaited Chowdhury's signal. Time was running out. The *Mangro* was set to sail on 1 April. She was now dry-docked one last time to get her underside cleaned for the long passage to Karachi around the Cape of Good Hope. This was the moment Chowdhury had been waiting for. He asked each of his fellow mutineers to meet him at the Marseilles train station at a half past midnight. Only he knew of the escape route that lay ahead.

After sunset on Monday, 29 March 1971, nine *Mangro* crew left the naval base in Toulon and headed for Marseille, 48 km away. They headed out individually so as not to attract suspicion, taking taxis and trains to reach their destination. Chowdhury had already left, carrying nine passports with him, his plan already in place. By then he knew of India's role in supporting the freedom struggle and decided to head for the nearest Indian mission – not in France, which might hand the crew back to Pakistan – but in neighbouring Switzerland. Chowdhury heaved a sigh of relief when all eight crew arrived at the train station. Around midnight, the *Mangro* eight boarded the train to Geneva and sat away from each other, even though their thick black naval-issue coats gave them away. They were already one crewman less – a ninth crewman, Abdul Mannan, had taken his passport and gone in the other direction, to his relatives in Great Britain.

When the train arrived in Switzerland six hours later, the crew were in for a disappointment. They could not enter without valid Swiss visas. The escape route to Switzerland was closed. Chowdhury swallowed his disappointment and cheerfully told the lady at the immigration counter that they were on their way to Paris to get their visas. He booked a fresh set of tickets and boarded the train to Paris. But they alighted in Lyon, just 100 kilometres away, to throw any would-be pursuers off their tail. They checked into a hotel in Lyon and, on March 31, they boarded a train to Barcelona, five hours away, for they found out that they didn't need visas to enter Spain. The Indian consulate in Barcelona directed them to the Indian embassy in Madrid.

Escape from Madrid

It was around 5.30 p.m. on Wednesday, 31 March. Gurdip Bedi, Second Secretary in the Indian Embassy in Madrid was ready to leave for the day. Bedi, nearly six feet tall, with a heavy black beard and neatly tied turban, was the scion of landed Sikh gentry who traced their roots to Sargodha, West Punjab. The 1964 batch IFS officer was now charge d' affairs at the embassy as the ambassador, Bikram Shah, was in India on a month's leave of absence.

The Indian Embassy on Velazquez overlooked one of the Spanish capital's major thoroughfares. The 30-year-old IFS officer had only three other junior staffers to man the mission. Not that there was much to do, apart from the usual political and economic reporting. The only Indian nationals in Spain were the tiny Sindhi community, based mainly in the Canary Islands.

That evening, Bedi's Spanish idyll was interrupted by a knock on the embassy door – Chowdhury and Rahmatullah. The two crewmen entered nervously and narrated the incredible story of their escape from Toulon two days earlier. They wanted asylum in India so they could go back home and join the struggle for freedom.

Bedi sized up the situation as he examined their passports. This was clearly a matter well above his pay grade. He would have to seek counsel from the Ministry of External Affairs in Delhi. But that did not prevent him from playing good host. Where were the rest of the crew? Sightseeing around the city, Chowdhury told him. Did they have enough money? Enough for food, but not for a hotel stay. Bedi instructed his staff to put them up in a nearby pension – a cheap Spanish hotel – two to a room. 'Lie low,' he instructed them as he dictated an urgent telegram to New Delhi. The reply came back the next morning, a speed that surprised Bedi. The message was terse: 'Immediately arrange for them to fly to India.'

Immediately. That word suggested an urgency that could only mean his cable had been on a top-secret distribution list – from the Prime Minister's Office to the MEA. Bedi could expect no cooperation from the Spanish authorities. Formal ties between the two countries had been established only in 1956 and a resident ambassador appointed in 1965. Relations were frosty.

The young diplomat now had to orchestrate the escape of the men under his charge. Every hour the crew spent in Madrid only increased their chances of being caught.

Bedi worked the telephones. His first call was to Pablo Olmeda who ran Air India's offline office in the Spanish capital. Offline because the national carrier didn't fly into the country. Bedi directed Olmeda to block eight seats on the Alitalia flight to Rome the next morning, from where the East Pakistani crewmen would catch the Rome–New Delhi flight. But there was still Spanish immigration to deal with.

His next step was to get them temporary travel papers. He took the crew's Pakistani passports even as his staff sat through the night getting the crew photographed and putting their faces on a fresh set of travel documents. They gave the eight crew fake Hindu names, affixing the commonest surnames they could think of. Ram, Kumar, Singh, Dutt … They worked their imagination as they transformed the eight Pakistani submariners into Indian nationals.

The young diplomat had already wrapped a cloak of deniability around the operation by ensuring he would not be seen with any of the crew again and minimising contact with them. It was left to his staff to escort the crew on their final hurdle.

The next morning Chowdhury, Rahmatullah and the six submariners were at the Madrid–Barajas airport, fourteen kilometres away from the city centre, waiting to stage another act in their great European escape.

One of the Indian handlers escorting them walked up ahead past immigration and stood on the other side. Chowdhury and the *Mangro* crew then lined up at immigration and got exit stamps on their Pakistani passports. Their exit from Spain cleared without a fuss, the men crossed the immigration line and walked up to the diplomat, who slipped them their temporary travel papers. Eight Indians who had ostensibly lost their papers while on holiday in Spain were soon on the flight to Rome.

Bedi had ensured they exited from Spain as Pakistanis and entered Rome as Indians. The New York–Bombay Air India flight, due to stopover in the Italian capital, would be the crew's route into India. But there was a change of plan. News of their arrival had leaked to the media. The Italian press were at the airport, waiting for the crew to arrive – and so were officials from the Pakistan embassy. The *Mangro* had by now sounded the alarm about its missing crew. Pakistan wanted the men back. The crew resisted. There was a brief scuffle at the airport as Chowdhury told one of the Pakistani diplomats who had come to fetch them: 'We were born afresh on 26 March. We are going to fight for our country.'

A labour strike in New York had delayed the Air India flight. Waiting for the next flight would have meant a ten-hour layover in Rome, which would give the Pakistani authorities, now on full alert, the chance to make another grab for the crew. So the eight crewmen were put on a flight to Geneva.

Back in the Indian embassy, the man who had orchestrated their escape received a call from the Spanish foreign office. The director general, the second most important official in the foreign office, had summoned Bedi for a meeting. At 6.30 p.m. that day, just hours after the *Mangro* crew had flown out of Madrid, the young charge d' affairs was sitting before the DG.

'Have you any knowledge of a group of Pakistani sailors travelling from Switzerland to Portugal?' the DG asked him pointedly. Bedi was surprised, but his face betrayed none of it. 'I can tell you with all honesty and sincerity,' he replied calmly in Spanish, 'I have no knowledge of any Pakistani sailors travelling from Switzerland to Portugal.' He was correct. Technically.

The DG didn't seem convinced. He reminded the young diplomat of international law and that the Indian embassy was obligated to hand the escapees over to the Pakistani authorities. The Spanish police were on the lookout for these crewmen, the official said. The hunt was on.

On his lonely drive back to the embassy, Bedi perhaps recalled what the 17th century English politician Sir Henry Wotton had said about ambassadors – honest men sent abroad to lie for the good of their country. He sent out a top secret 'crash telegram' to New Delhi, explaining what was going on. The answer, which he received in a few days, was brief. 'Keep Denying. Don't admit.' At Geneva, the eight fearless men from the *Mangro* crew boarded an Air India flight to Bombay, one step closer in their long walk to freedom.

2

THE EMPEROR, KING COBRA
AND THE WATER RAT

'Admiral,' Prime Minister Indira Gandhi asked hurriedly, looking at her watch, 'do you have anything to say?' Mrs Gandhi had finished speaking with the flamboyant army chief, General SHFJ 'Sam' Maneckshaw and the suave air force chief, P.C. Lal. Now she turned to the bulldog-jowled navy chief, Admiral Sardarilal Matharadas Nanda. The navy chief was by now used to this. As were all the chiefs who preceded him. The navy figured at the bottom of the government's list of priorities. And this became painfully evident during the frequent strategy meetings the PM held in March 1971 in her sparsely furnished office in Room 152 of South Block to review the calamitous events in East Pakistan.

The navy was the Cinderella service, drawing just Rs 106.12 crore or 4 per cent of the defence budget. It was also the smallest – just 3,500 officers and 27,000 sailors. Barring the shelling of the Portuguese frigate, the *Afonso de Albuquerque* during the liberation of Goa in 1961, it had never seen war.

'Charles' to his friends, Nanda had been raised on Manora, an island south of Karachi port. His father Mathra Das had migrated there from Gujranwala, Pakistan's Punjab province, and was employed there as an office superintendent. The eldest of seven children, Nanda had started out as a clerk in the Manora Port and Pilotage department. During the Second World War, he was commissioned into the Royal Indian Navy Volunteer Reserve (RINVR) as a sub-lieutenant on 11 October 1941, around the time when Hitler's armies were poised at the gates of Moscow. Post-independence, he rose to the top with prestigious billets like the commissioning CO of the light cruiser *INS Mysore* in 1957. It was Nanda's executive officer Cdr Rustom Nanavati who brought the navy nationwide attention when he shot and killed his wife's lover in 1959. Its British acquisitions like the *Mysore*, frigates of the *Talwar*, *Khukri* and *Brahmaputra* class, and a newly refurbished aircraft carrier *Vikrant*, were proof that, despite not having an imminent seaborne threat, the fledgling republic had one of the most impressive navies east of the Suez. But there was a twist.

Some of these acquisitions, Admiral Nanda was to later note in his autobiography, reflected British priorities of preserving order in the Sea Lanes of Communication (SLOCs) between the Gulf of Aden and the Malacca Straits, and did not reflect an independent naval strategy for the new republic. 'Of the eight new frigates acquired from the UK, five were anti-submarine and three were anti-aircraft escorts. These frigates were acquired at a time when there was no submarine or air threat in the Indian seas.'[6]

The Indian staff manual, as Admiral Nanda noted, was dictated by the priorities set by the British Naval War Manual and emphasized the importance of those SLOCS purely from the British point of survival in a long war.

The lack of attention the political class gave to the navy ought to have been surprising for a country that had been enslaved from

---

6   Admiral S.M. Nanda, *The Man Who Bombed Karachi* (New Delhi: HarperCollins *Publishers* India), 2004

the sea by merchants turned conquerors. Newly independent India's territorial threats, however, were preponderantly land-based. The 1947 invasion of the kingdom of Jammu and Kashmir by tribal raiders organized by the Pakistan Army; the first India–Pakistan war in 1948 and the resolution that followed, which resulted in the Ceasefire Line, an unresolved boundary – all of these meant that the perceived threat was always from land.

In 1962, the landward focus was exacerbated when China's People's Liberation Army (PLA) poured across a disputed land boundary to administer a shock military defeat on India's unprepared army. The IAF was kept out of offensive air operations in the month-long border war, even as the Indian Army was being mauled. In Ladakh in the north, the army fought ferociously, with one post fighting to the last man. In the North-East Frontier Agency, as Arunachal Pradesh was then called, swarmed and routed an entire division.

Limited military objectives, a severely stretched logistics line, and the approaching winter kept the PLA from advancing to sever India's north-east away from the rest of the subcontinent. Only a veiled warning from the US had kept Pakistan's President Ayub Khan from moving his army into Jammu and Kashmir.

India's stated policy of not being aligned to either superpower block of the era – the US or Soviet Russia – made sense only if it had a strong military to defend its contested borders. And so, in 1963, the Indian state began diverting its scare resources towards its military, doubling defence spending to nearly 3 per cent of the GDP and doubling the army from 5,25,000 to 8,25,000 soldiers.[7]

It was a re-invigorated Indian Army that faced up to Ayub Khan's attempt in 1965 to seize Jammu and Kashmir by force. The war's naval component, a 7 September gun raid by the seven-warship

---

7   Vivek Chadha, *Even if it Ain't Broke Yet Do Fix It: Enhancing Effectiveness through Military Change* (New Delhi: Pentagon Press), 2016, p. 35

Pakistani naval flotilla on the port town of Dwarka, did not see an Indian naval riposte. As the brief attack unfolded, the *INS Talwar*, a spanking new British-built Leopard-class frigate with radar-directed 4.5 inch guns, detected the Pakistani task group from its anchorage in Okha, less than 30 kilometres away, but for reasons that would become clear only later, did not challenge them.

Many of the shells failed to explode. The ones that did, killed a cow. Where the shells did make an impact was in the mind of Rear Admiral Nanda, then managing director of the Mazagon Docks Ltd in Bombay. He was then supervising a milestone – the building of India's first indigenously built frigate, the *Nilgiri*. India's first warship with anti-aircraft missiles and an embarked helicopter. But, as the *Talwar* incident had proved, 'ships of the line' were useless if there was no naval strategy or, more importantly, the political sanction to deploy them offensively.

Why the navy sat out of the 1965 war quickly became evident to him during a debrief of the war in the spring of 1966. In room 129D, the impressive conference room in the heart of South Block, a representative from NHQ said the navy had met all the operational war directives given to it. The navy was to ensure 'the safety of Indian merchant shipping, the sanctity of the Indian coast and not 'widen' the war.

Nanda seethed as he recalled the frustration and anger his sailors and officers felt in Bombay in 1965. The navy would seize the initiative in any future conflict, he vowed, somewhat rashly, for it was done in public. 'And if war comes again, I assure you that we shall carry it right into the enemy's biggest ports like Karachi,' Nanda, the C-in-C of the Western Naval Command then, told the Bombay-based news weekly *Blitz* in a March 1969 interview. 'I know this harbour quite well, for I started my career working there. And you have my word that given the opportunity, the Indian Navy will make the world's biggest bonfire of it.'

The comment might have sounded like the vain boast of a force that had never seen action. But those who knew Nanda intimately knew this was anything but. In 1971, he was deep within the labyrinthine corridors of India's capital, trying to get the attention of the political leadership.

By April, it had become clear that war with Pakistan was not a question of if, but when. Earlier, on 26 March, Indira Gandhi had directed the Border Security Force (BSF) to assist the East Pakistani forces who had revolted, but the personnel had been beaten back by the Pakistan Army. If the government was to go ahead with its plans, the Indian Army would have to move in, and that meant war. November seemed like the earliest date when a military campaign could be conducted. The services were asked to prepare their plans for war. This was the navy's moment and Charles Nanda rushed headlong into it.

Never before had the independent Indian state prepared to wage war. The economic reasons against going to war were compelling. India was a developing country with a feeble economy and sluggish growth of 3.3 per cent per annum.

Military spending had been accelerated after the 1962 war and, interestingly, India was now becoming a major buyer of Soviet hardware. The tack towards Moscow had been accelerated by the refusal of the US and UK to supply modern military hardware to the country. The Pakistan Navy had leapt ahead of the Indian Navy by loaning a refurbished World War II-era, Tench-class long-range fleet submarine from the US in 1963. The Indian Navy's attempts to acquire a modern submarine from its traditional supplier Britain were rebuffed. The IAF found the US unwilling to sell F-104 Starfighter supersonic jets to it. The Soviet Union tactfully filled the hardware gap. In September 1964, Defence Minister Yashwantrao Chavan returned from Moscow with an off-the-shelf buy of 40 MiG-21 supersonic fighter aircraft and agreement to license-produce 400

more in India. Three years later, in 1967, Moscow sold the Indian
Navy four top-of-the-line Foxtrot-class diesel-electric submarines
with a 20,000-km patrol range; Petya-class ASW corvettes –
torpedo- and rocket-carrying submarine hunters; and, finally, eight
missile boats, each armed with four radar-directed anti-ship missiles
to protect its harbours from Dwarka-style raids. As Nanda went on
to discover in the months ahead, these new platforms ushered in
dramatic new capabilities and allowed the Indian Navy to rewrite
its staid Royal Navy-inspired battle precis. Not that conventions
bothered him. 'Damn the rules,' he had once bellowed when a young
lieutenant had approached him to complain about regulations that
limited rent allowances for young officers. 'That's my business, not
yours.' Sure enough, the rent limit was quadrupled within a week.
As Lieutenant Suresh Nanda later told the young officer: 'My father
can do anything. He's the Emperor.'

In April 1971, Emperor Charles, a man in search of redemption
for his neglected service, saw a convergence of interesting events – an
official government sanction for the armed forces to train the Mukti
Bahini and the arrival of the eight *Mangro* escapees in New Delhi.
He saw the series of events for what it was: the opportunity he had
been waiting for. And for this, he needed an ally. And he turned to
the man who sat on the ground floor, just below his office – Captain
Mihir Kumar Roy.

The King Cobra

They called him Micky. All Royal Navy-trained officers had a
nickname. Captain Roy's came from his initials. Lean, of medium
height and build, an aquiline nose and a smile that lit up his face,
Roy was the scion of an aristocratic family of zamindars from East
Pakistan. His father Bijoy Kumar Roy had been an Imperial Forest
Service officer who rose to become deputy conservator of the entire

Madras Province. Roy Senior took his son on camping tours through the jungles of the Western Ghats, where the young Roy was required to, in the manner of naturalists, maintain log books and diaries with illustrations.

Roy Junior had been commissioned into the Indian Navy in 1946 after four years at the Royal Navy College at Dartmouth. His affable demeanour never betrayed the razor-sharp military mind or the wicked sense of humour. As a young lieutenant and air observer with the navy's first air wing – the Fleet Requirements Unit Squadron – which flew amphibious Sea Lands in 1953, he had narrowly escaped arrest after an April fools' day prank went awry. Roy and a fellow aviator had released bugs and beetles collected from the runway into the Command Staff briefing room at the *INS Garuda* airbase in Cochin. There was panic at the meeting. An infuriated Commodore B.S. Soman eventually spared the culprits, which was just as well – Roy was selected the first squadron commander of one of two air squadrons that embarked on the *INS Vikrant* when it was acquired from the UK in 1956.

'Mother', as the navy's first aircraft carrier *INS Vikrant* was affectionately called, carried two sets of 'children' – the gun- and rocket-armed Hawker Sea Hawks, which were sleek, fast jets with clean lines; and the French-built Breguet Alizés which were slower turboprops. When the Alizé, French for 'tradewind', was not in flight, it squatted at an incline on its tricycle undercarriage, wings folded up in a yogic tree pose. But appearances were deceptive. The aircraft was a specialist submarine hunter and was packed with gadgetry possessed by any contemporary Indian military aircraft – a Thomson-CSF DRAA-2B retractable radar to detect masts of snorting submarines, ESM sensors which could sniff their transmissions, drop sonabuoys to ping them, and finally destroy them by firing rockets from six underwing pylons or dropping torpedoes and depth charges from a weapons bay in the belly. Roy, the hunter and jungle tracker, saw the aircraft for what it was – a Cobra. His aunt Meena Gupta painted the squadron crest for him, a coiled black cobra rearing to strike. Roy the squadron commander adopted the moniker of another snake species for himself, *Ophiophagus Hannah* – the King Cobra.

Roy went on to command the *INS Ranjit* and the 16th Frigate Squadron – the three Leopard-class frigates *INS Brahmaputra, Beas* and *Betwa*. 'F-16', as the squadron commander was called, already had a vision that extended beyond the horizon. He could often be spotted standing on the *Brahmaputra's* forecastle, lecturing his bewildered command on the importance of sea power and India's maritime destiny. He was a fast riser, and so, eyebrows were raised when he was appointed Nanda's Director Naval Intelligence (DNI) in 1970. Often derisively expanded as 'Director of Naval Invitations', this was a largely ceremonial post, with incumbents regularly spotted at the capital's diplomatic parties. Roy's appointment marked Nanda's revamp of the DNI into a cutting-edge intelligence organization.

The Directorate now had around nineteen officers and a hundred men divided into four wings, each under a lieutenant commander (Lt Cdr) – 'general division', which gathered open-source intelligence and controlled spies; 'foreign division', which collected intelligence from overseas; 'protocol', that liaised with embassies and high commissions for clearances; and 'security', which handled counter-intelligence and manned the interrogation cell inside the Red Fort. The *Mangro* crew, by now in a RAW safe house in Delhi were handed over to Roy.

Meanwhile, a plan had begun taking shape in the mind of a man who shared a deep connect with East Pakistan. His father's zamindar family hailed from Barisal, an ancient port city in south-central East Pakistan.

By an amazing coincidence, it was also a region that his boss, Admiral Nanda, had operated in. Lieutenant S.M. Nanda had patrolled the Sundarbans at Khulna in a motor launch, accompanied by a platoon of Indian Army soldiers in 1942. His four-month–long deployment was meant to warn of the possible advance of the Japanese towards the erstwhile British capital, Calcutta. Those months taught Nanda about the lifelines of the Bengal province – the bustling riverine waterways which covered 24,000 kilometres, around 11 per cent of her total area. The network of broad, shallow river valleys and extensive deltas, the largest of which – the Jamuna – was formed by the confluence of the Ganga and the Brahmaputra. The ocean-like, over 200 km long Jamuna had an average width of ten kilometres. As Nanda wrote in his autobiography, 'For centuries, an elaborate network of boats, barges and ferries were the only way to transport people and commodities across these formidable rivers.'

Admiral Nanda and Captain Roy no doubt also studied with interest the Sea Lanes of Communication (SLOCs) which had become even more vital for resupplying Pakistan's eastern garrison by April 1971 after India closed its airspace to Pakistani aircraft.

The entire military garrison – the cantonments of Dacca, Comilla, Sylhet, Jessore, Rangpur, Rajshahi, Bogra, Khulna and Chittagong – had to be sustained from the sea. Jet fuel for its F-86 Sabre jets, gasoline for its M24 Chaffee tanks, ammunition for its guns and even wheat to make rotis for the West Pakistani soldiers flowed into the province's only deepwater port, Chittagong. From here, they were unloaded onto smaller boats and transhipped into Chalna and other inland ports deep inside East Pakistan. In mid-1971, the military's requirements of transporting 200,000 tons of cargo and 1,50,000 personnel doubled after Yahya Khan despatched two additional infantry divisions from West Pakistan.[8]

---

8   Vice Admiral M.K. Roy, *War in the Indian Ocean* (New Delhi: Lancer Publishers), 1995

It became very clear to Charles and the King Cobra that these waterways would have to be disrupted if India had to realize her maritime military objectives in East Pakistan.

But how? Regular forces could not do it because war had not been formally declared. Hence they looked at a more cost-effective method.

The eight *Mangro* crew could form the nucleus of a Mukti Bahini naval commando team, based in India, to strike in the riverine areas of East Pakistan. But the Bengali sailors only knew how to run engines, torpedoes and radios of submarines. They did not have the endurance swimming, diving and explosive handling expertise needed by marine commandos.

The Indian Navy lacked an equivalent of Pakistan's Special Service Unit (SSU) frogmen. NHQ hence decided to make do with their closest special forces equivalent: a small corps of 'clearance divers' – eight officers, fifty CD sailors and 150 ship divers – a diving school in Kochi and clearance diver teams in Bombay and Visakhapatnam. Clearance divers or CDs removed underwater obstacles and sea mines from harbours and anchorages. They had originated as a class thanks to a set of inventions in the early 20th century – a self-contained breathing apparatus using a cylinder of compressed air as well as a full-face mask invented by a French naval officer, Commander Yves Le Prieur, in 1924. Le Prieur later combined this with another French naval officer Louis Marie de Corlieu's 1934 invention – diving fins. The modern free-swimming scuba diver, thus born, went on to replace the diver in the ponderous canvas suit, weighted boots and copper helmets. Clearance divers proved their military utility during World War II when Royal Navy CDs cleared harbours and anchorages of underwater obstacles and sea mines prior to the 1944 Allied landings on the beaches of Normandy.

Indian naval divers were trained in the Naval Diving School in Cochin. The school was housed on Willingdon Island, India's largest manmade isle. The 7.7 km island, located at the centre of the 96-kilometre–long Vembanad Lake, India's longest, was reclaimed during the Second World War. The island housed a naval air station, INS Garuda, and four schools to train sub lieutenants in their specializations – basic & division, gunnery; navigation; and torpedo and anti-Submarine (TAS). The diving school was a wing of the TAS school. It was a block of six rooms – five classrooms and the officer-in-charge's room near the diving tower. This thirty-foot–high 9.4-foot-wide cylindrical concret tank, nearly filled to the brim with fresh water, was where rookie divers were dunked for training sessions as their instructors watched from above. The school's crest was an old brass diving helmet with the silhouette of a plunging frogman, with the motto emblazoned on the scroll below the crest – 'Service Most Silent'.

In early April, the school was missing its chief instructor Lieutenant Samir Das. The lean, swarthy, Royal Navy-trained instructor had quietly vanished over the weekend, leaving his six young trainee officers wondering about his whereabouts. 'He's away on temporary duty,' the school's officer-in-charge (O-i-C) Lt Cdr James Gill laconically informed the curious sub lieutenants Arun Saigal and B.S. Thakur. But the grapevine had a juicier story – Das had been flown out by Admiral Nanda over the weekend in his official aircraft for a hush-hush mission.

Das was the answer to Roy's riddle on who would train the *Mangro* escapees. He ticked all the boxes. Not only was he an outstanding instructor, he was Bengali, spoke the language fluently, and had his roots in East Pakistan, though he had never lived there thanks to his parents migrating to Sibsagar, Assam, in the 1930s from their village in central Dacca province.

Das was summoned to New Delhi to induct the eight sailors into naval training for possible underwater and clandestine warfare. He set to work almost immediately, putting the men through a short, intensive introductory module in swimming and explosive-handling training in the Yamuna near the national capital. He was assisted by only one other diver, Madhusudhan Gupta, clearance diver III from the diving school.

But the Indian Navy was not the only one looking at the offensive use of naval divers. Roy had inputs that the Pakistani navy was planning and training for a lightning, surprise attack that could turn Bombay into a Pearl Harbour.

Pakistan, the navy feared, might launch simultaneous attacks on its warships with submarines, midgets and chariots, and also infiltrate saboteurs on beaches near sensitive areas at the outbreak of hostilities. The Pakistan Navy, naval intelligence said, would position a mothership within 100 nautical miles of the Indian coast by last light to launch small underwater craft and their commandos.

Water Rat[9]

Sometime in April, Captain Roy sat down at his study table in New Delhi to write out one of the most significant concept notes written by an Indian military officer. In a handwriting almost as inscrutable as his own persona, Captain Roy scrawled out a paper titled 'Jackpot: underwater guerrilla forces' – six-pages in blue fountain ink.

The note was precise in its aims and objectives, meticulous in its approach, and ambitious in its goals. Captain Roy aimed 'to train raw but physically strong and mentally stubborn Bangla Desh personnel to launch surface and subsurface raids on ports, shipping and inland waterways.'

The objectives would be met by training the personnel in batches of thirty personnel for day and night operations. They would be trained in the use of explosives to destroy vital infrastructure in port

9   This section is courtesy the Vice Admiral M.K. Roy family archive

and inland waterways; ship damage; in the destruction of ferries, pontoons and barges; blocking waterways and channels; removing navigation aids in channels; cutting anchors and cables; setting up underwater obstacles/ traps; destruction of port communications; and damaging fuel installations.

These underwater guerrilla forces would complement the army-run Operation Jackpot's covert training of the Mukti Bahini, which aimed to secretly train and field a force of 100,000 Mukti Bahini fighters over the next few months. The *Mangro* deserters were to form the core of a distinct naval wing.

Roy's 'Water Rat' concept note, envisaged Bengali naval commandos to be like the semi-aquatic carnivore – small, aggressive predators who would swarm the enemy from hideouts in estuaries, mangroves and coastal areas.

Under 'selection of personnel', Roy listed the qualitative requirements for his recruiters – 'good swimmers who have physical stamina and mental strength, between the ages of 18 to 30. The selected personnel had to preferably be from different sectors of Bangla Desh, so that there was local knowledge of terrain and installations.' He wanted the ex-*Mangro* crew to help recruit 'former Pakistan merchant servicemen who had defected', 'Mukti Fauj forces, particularly from the coastal sectors of Chalna, Khulna, Chittagong/Sylhet, Dacca/Chandpur and Barisal' and 'refugees who have crossed into India'.

The numbers he had in mind were large – 200 teams or nearly 600 commandos to be trained over several months. These were deemed sufficient for the world's largest delta, the extensive riverine network of Bangla Desh and critical if the navy had to achieve its 'Stage III' objectives – the complete paralysis of ports, harbours and inland waterways inside East Pakistan.

Operations would unfold in three distinct phases. It would begin by targeting ports and harbours. As more commandos became available, they could gradually fan out to target the province's entire inland waterway network. He drew up the requirements for each stage:

1st stage (50 teams; concentrated in ports and harbours)
D-Day for the first stage should be selected to cause maximum damage to the ports of Chalna/Khulna and Mongla through a saturated attack of coordinated strikes to effectively block the harbours by sinking ships, barges and river steamers.

2nd stage (100 teams; divided into sector foot-groups and subdivided into task units)
They will move up inland from the ports to suspend movement in the inland waterway system, the rivers and channels.
This will involve sinking ships and obstructing channels, removing navigational marks, planting underwater obstructions, rendering ineffective riverine tankers and exploding pontoons or ferries.

3rd stage (200 teams)
To paralyze ports, harbours, communications and the entire inland waterways system.

Roy scrawled a set of names on the back of the note – Lt Cdr Martis, Lt Cdr Sajjan Kumar, Lt Cdr James Gill, Lt Das, Lt George Duke, Lt Vijai Kapil, Bhattacharjee, C. Singh, M.S. Gupta and P.K. Dhole, all clearance divers. He also scribbled a separate list of four senior naval officers, commanders with eighteen years of service – Nadkarni, H.M.L. Saxena, Almeida, T.N. Singhal and Samant.

The key pieces in a jigsaw had been assembled.

3

CAMP PLASSEY

The jangle of the telephone echoed down the deserted corridors of the Western Naval Command mess, Colaba. The lodgings for young officers were built near Prong's Reef, where Bombay's tailbone vanished into the Arabian Sea. It was past midnight. A sleepy hand darted out from under a sheet and scooped up the black Bakelite receiver. The voice at the other end sounded urgent: 'Lieutenant Kapil, this is the Maritime Operations Room (MOR). There's been an alert in the naval dockyard. We are on State I.'

In a flash the slim, bearded twenty-nine-year-old boss of the Fleet Clearance Diving Team (FCDT) shot out of bed and into his trousers and shoes. State 1 meant an enemy frogman had been sighted.

Kapil sprinted down the deserted mess corridor towards the 'purple peacemaker' – his Vespa scooter with a large black-and-yellow peace sign decal – and sped towards the naval dockyard ten kilometres away. The dockyard berthed the Indian Navy's crown jewels – the *INS Vikrant,* Asia's sole aircraft carrier and its escorts, the six-inch gun cruisers *Delhi* and *Mysore.* As the FCDT boss, their bottoms were in his care. His current agony had to do with a British and Italian military innovation in the 1930s – deadly explosives

43

with timers which could be stuck on the side of warships using magnets. The inventors called their deadly little inventions limpet mine after the mollusc family that anchored itself to objects with its powerful muscular foot. Divers could swim away to safety after planting limpets, and this was what bothered Kapil.

It was April 1971. The genocide in East Pakistan and the refugee influx that followed had turned the subcontinent into a tinderbox. A third Indo-Pakistan war seemed imminent and the Directorate of Naval Intelligence in NHQ anticipated a first strike from the frogmen of Pakistan's SSU. Like submarines, frogmen were a weaker navy's weapon of choice. The Italian Navy's Decima Flottiglia MAS (Tenth Assault Boat Squadron) frogmen riding 'chariots' and 'Gamma Group' assault swimmers) had sunk or disabled 73,000 tons of Allied warships and 128,000 tons of merchant shipping between 1940 and Italy's surrender in 1943. Decima Flottiglia's frogmen caught warships with their fearsome combination of belted steel armour, big guns, torpedoes and aircraft at their most vulnerable: resting in the harbour. Their mascot – a skull with a red rose clenched in its teeth – promised a deadly tango.

In April 1971, the Indian Navy believed the Pakistan Navy would strike first. Intelligence flowing out of Captain Roy's directorate suggested that warships of the western fleet were vulnerable to a 'Pearl Harbour-type pre-emptive attack'. The Pakistan Navy would strike Indian Navy installations just like the Imperial Japanese Navy that had, three decades ago, caught the US Pacific Fleet off-guard. Local police, fishermen and port authorities were looking out for midget submarines that could be carried on board merchant ships, warships or large dhows and released in the vicinity of the target. Kapil and his team were the only ones who stood between the warships and saboteurs.

The dockyard was in a frenzy when the young officer arrived. Operation Awkward – as the navy's counter-sabotage drill was called

– was on in full swing. The waters resounded with the dull underwater pop of explosives as harbour patrol craft chugged about, dropping special two-pound explosive charges to incapacitate frogmen. All the major warships had lit up their sides and switched their engines on, with their propellers churning froth in the harbour and their sonars pinging to disorient frogmen. It was a State 1 standard operating procedure (SOP). Even aircraft carriers were not believed to be safe. Just seven years ago, a Vietcong saboteur had sunk a 9,800-ton US Navy aircraft carrier, the USNS Card, in Port Saigon.

Lt Kapil reached the quay where the aircraft carrier *INS Vikrant* was berthed. His team was waiting. He kicked off his shoes and slipped into his blue hosiery Admiralty pattern diving suit, and donned the air bottles and face mask of his Surface Air Breathing Apparatus (SABA) set. Then, looking more fish than human, he hit the water, leaving a trail of bubbles, like James Bond. Just six years ago, he had marvelled at a scuba-diving

Sean Connery in *Thunderball*, Hollywood's first big movie extensively shot underwater. Bombay harbour, alas, wasn't the Bahamas. The water was inky black, a mixture of furnace fuel oil and flotsam. Near-nil visibility meant manual searches done by hand in all the places a saboteur was likely to target.

Trained by the Royal Navy on the art and science of disabling a warship using explosives, Kapil knew all these vulnerable spots. He groped in all the places a diver could place a limpet mine – the stern gland where the propeller shafts exited the warship; and the engine room, the biggest non-watertight compartment which could rapidly flood the ship. He mentally ticked off these boxes as he swam under the carrier. He felt the finger-sized link chains wrapped around ship's bottom up to the deck level – meant to give divers reference points.

Enemy frogmen would come to their target riding a two-ton 'manned torpedo' like the CE2F/X30 craft Pakistan had acquired from Italy in the late 1960s. The evolutionary descendants of Decima MAS' chariots, these battery-operated torpedo-shaped craft had a range of only sixty nautical miles and were operated by two frogmen. Besides the limpets, a frogman could use the 200-kg high explosive charge carried by his six-metre-long chariot. This charge could break a ship's keel and sink it.

How effective the strike was depended on what the warship was doing when the charge went off. If it was in harbour, the ship would take in water and sink to the bottom of the harbour, not more than 20 feet. Disabled, but still salvageable. But if it was out in deeper waters when the charges went off, the chances of survival were bleak.

Kapil ran his hand down the side of the ship, looking for the tell-tale blister of a limpet mine. It was the underwater equivalent of an airline security pat-down search on the ship's bottom, but far, far more rigorous. He had learnt the drill in the chilly waters of the Portsmouth channel, feeling the moss-encrusted undersides of the mothballed Royal naval fleet. The moss often hid angry electric eels which gave intruders a jolt, which felt much like touching a live wire. Startled trainee divers were always a source of perverse delight for course instructor Petty Officer J.G. Miller. There were no eels here in the dockyard and, as he discovered to his relief four hours later, no limpet mines under *Vikrant*.

The fleet divers and their colleagues in the command clearance diving team then moved on to the other capital ships – the *Delhi* and *Mysore*. The smaller frigates and missile boats, they reckoned, could wait until dawn.

The underwater searches were a routine ever since the C-in-C Western Naval Command Vice Admiral N. Krishnan had put his whole command and all the warships on 'alert', one step short of 'precautionary'. All commanding officers of ships and establishments had to be within arm's length of a telephone day and night.

Frogmen, it seemed, were everywhere. Sentries posted at the jettyside and fleet warships saw black phantoms. The sightings shot up after sunset, when fear spread faster than an oil slick on the dark harbour waters. Every black ripple, it seemed, hid the enemy who could punch a hole in their shipside. The brass, Kapil suspected, didn't mind the false alarms – they didn't want the vigil to slacken.

After the *INS Mysore* and *Delhi*, the team moved on to submarine tender *INS Amba* and the fleet tanker *INS Deepak*. Kapil knew all these ships by touch. It would be 4 a.m. when his Purple Peacemaker would make its journey back to the mess. It was usually a few hours' rest and then back to the dockyard grind. Divers were the navy's Cinderfellas. Kapil couldn't get a store house for his human minesweepers to deposit their equipment. After months of temporary lodgings in warships, which eventually sailed away, they finally found refuge – inside a pontoon used to moor the navy's patrol boats. The diving compressor went atop, and the diving sets beneath, in the hollow metal dock which was also used as a resting room.

The only relief from this drudgery was Cabin Number 411, which, as was whispered, was the Western Naval Command's most happening room. Its occupant was the WNC's junior-most officer with a telephone, thanks to Operation Awkward. The centrepiece in the living room was a Philips 4408 reel-to-reel tape recorder with detachable speakers and eight hours of Leonard Cohen, Nana Mouskuri, Joan Baez, Bee Gees, The Beatles and Jethro Tull on its spools. From the balcony, you could sit on the low white chairs, sip your tea and take in a stunning, uninterrupted view of the Arabian Sea.

It was the crash-out place for the Young Officers (YOs) – partying in South Mumbai's discotheques such as 'Hell' in Worli, 'Slip Disc' near the Radio Club and 'Blow Up' at the Taj – if they missed the last motor launch to their ships moored in the harbour. It was the rendezvous for roaring all-nighters with Kapil and his wild bachelor pals Franklin, Bhende and Ashok 'Daffy' Mehta, and Lt Cdr Ashok 'Aku' Roy, an Alizé pilot from 310 Squadron.

Aku was a loner with few friends in the navy – six feet tall, well built, dark haired, his angular face offset by a pointed beard, the son of a major general in the Army Medical Corps and his Estonian wife,

Aku was five years senior to Kapil in service and their friendship seemed like an unusual one because officers rarely fraternized with their juniors.

Roy and Kapil had met as drinking buddies at the Cochin Club, the thatch-roofed watering hole for all naval officers in the naval base where Kapil was doing his sub-lieutenants' courses in INS Venduruthy. During the early days of their friendship, they took weekend excursions to Munnar and Thekaddy in Aku Roy's Red Standard 10. In an explosive conclusion to an evening, a tipsy Aku staggered into his cabin, blasting his 12 bore shotgun at house lizards, peppering his startled drinking buddies with lead shot. With Aku around, you could never be sure how things would end.

Back in Bombay, Roy now posted as torpedo anti-submarine (TAS) officer of the *INS Ranjit,* was one of the privileged few to have all access to Room 411 because Kapil had asked the mess steward to let him have the keys whenever he wanted.

One sultry April day brought some respite from Operation Awkward. Commodore B.N. Thapar, the chief staff officer (operations), asked Kapil to fly to Calcutta to meet the DNI captain, M.K. Roy. That's all Commodore Thapar knew, or cared to share. INS Hooghly (INS Netaji Subhas now) in Calcutta housed the naval officer in charge (NOIC), Calcutta, but he had no warships, so the possibility of counter-sabotage drills was ruled out. It was, perhaps, an 'aid to civil authority' mission, Kapil thought as he packed a change of clothes into his airbag and drove to the airport. The navy was the sole repository of the country's diving expertise. Naval divers jetted across the country like medical specialists. Their time-critical missions ensured they flew Indian Airlines, a privilege reserved only for ranks above naval captains.

Kapil landed into the thrum of Calcutta, a sea of people, trams, hand-pulled rickshaws and yellow Ambassador taxis. He was back in the city where he had worked as a management trainee for Usha

Martin Black in 1965. The company made wire ropes, automobile parts and carbon black in the metropolis during the Swinging Sixties. The flat he shared with a friend in trendy Park Street floated above the epicentre, jiving to the beat. Beer in the afternoons in Firpos, and drinks at the Blue Fox where Kapil had celeb-spotted Shirley Maclaine and her friend, Bhutan's acting prime minister, Lehndup Dorji.

It was a world of privilege, a bastion of the Brown Sahebs, where business deals were discussed at race courses and finalized in golf courses. A life not very different from that of the business executive in *Seemabaddha* which was lensed by auteur Satyajit Ray in 1971. This world was movie-like and almost unreal, insulated from the rural tumult that marked the rise of the Communist Party of India. Interrupted only by the sight of IAF jets doing barrel rolls over the skies during the 1965 war. And this ended his life as a business executive. Kapil signed up to join the navy in 1966 as an emergency commission officer – a job that would fetch him half his 700-rupee-a-month salary. Why did he join? It was perhaps an unrequited passion – he had been ejected from the 86th General Duty Pilot course in 1963 after flying fifteen hours in HT-2 trainers in Jodhpur. He refused an offer of doing the navigator's course. It was either full wings or nothing. Five years later, he was back in Calcutta. A series of surprises awaited Kapil as he wound his way to the INS Hooghly, the British-era naval establishment along the river it was named after.

'Das!'

Kapil was surprised to spot his CD course batchmate from *HMS Vernon*. After exchanging pleasantries, Das got down to business – stay away from the navy mess and stay in the officers' mess in Fort William instead. To Kapil, both options were dreary. Military messes were bare and unfurnished and a reminder of the hardscrabble service life. Residents had to bring their own mattress rolls, towels and toiletries. Kapil only had a change of clothing. The prospect of sleeping on a bare wooden cot pained him. But when Das spoke of the unusual operation, his thoughts receded rapidly. The deserters from the *Mangro*, their amazing flight out of France and, finally, Operation Jackpot. The operation was part of India's 29 April directive formally ordering the Eastern Army Command to guide the government of Bangla Desh – housed in a bungalow on 8, Theatre Road, in Calcutta – in exile on its guerrilla warfare campaign in East Pakistan.

Where did the Indian Navy divers fit into Roy's scheme of things, Kapil wanted to know. As trainers of the naval saboteurs, Das said. He revealed how he and Seaman Madhusudhan Gupta, his assistant from the diving school, had given them lessons in swimming and underwater sabotage in Delhi.

Underwater sabotage? In Delhi? Kapil thought Das was joking.

He wasn't. The crew had been trained in an isolated part of the Yamuna river that flowed through the national capital. The NHQ had pulled the plug on the course after a week, for training saboteurs in the open wasn't a good idea. Besides, the navy reasoned, the crew were too far away from their intended battle theatre – the rivers of East Pakistan.

Now, Das said, the rest of his queries would be answered by the architect himself. He drove Kapil to the Eastern Command Officers' Mess less than a kilometre away.

The Director of Naval Intelligence (DNI) sat in his sparsely furnished mess room, waiting for them. In his civilian rig, Roy could have passed off for a city bureaucrat. After a brief round of introductions, he swiftly spelt out his plan: the *Mangro* crew would only be the nucleus; the force would be bigger. More recruits would join to form a special force of at least thirty saboteurs. The Indian Navy would train them in clandestine warfare – to use diving sets, limpet mines, and plastic explosives. They would then be infiltrated across the border to wage clandestine naval warfare inside East

Pakistan. Some Bengali nationals overseas had donated scuba diving sets, fins and equipment – gear that wasn't easy to come by in India – to the Indian Navy for use by the naval wing of the Mukti Bahini. It wasn't quite then clear to Kapil how those nationals knew of this clandestine naval effort. NHQ was shipping the sets to Calcutta in a few days, Roy told them.

Kapil disagreed over the use of scuba sets. Air sets looked good in the movies, Kapil explained to Roy, but were impractical for combat use because they discharged gases into the water. And that left a trail of bubbles – as stealthy as a commando on a mission walking about with a burning torch. The only option was to get stealthier closed-circuit diving sets used by frogmen, which recycled a diver's exhaled gases. These rebreather sets, however, were expensive and in short supply for the navy's diving teams.

What would the frogmen attack their targets with? Kapil wanted to know. Limpet mines were the obvious answer but there was a problem here too. The navy's fledgling diving branch was defensively focused, used primarily for clearing harbours, removing wrecks and underwater obstacles and, of course, protecting warships from saboteurs. Limpet mines – the primary weapons of an offensive underwater unit – were low priority and used primarily as training aids, in the manner of a bomb-disposal squad using bombs as an instruction tool. The Indian Naval Ordnance depots held less than a hundred Mark III limpet mines, which were all wartime stocks, imported from British Royal Ordnance. But even these had never been used operationally. A clandestine operation using naval divers wasn't even considered. The navy had no specialist vessels to launch them from, and only a tiny number of diving officers. Most, including lieutenants Sajjan Kumar and George Duke, had trained with Kapil in the nine-month intensive Overseas Long Mine Clearance and Diving course at the *HMS Vernon* in 1969.

Covert, deniable missions would need large inventories of ordnance which could not be traced back to India.

Roy revealed a Naval Armament Inspection Organisation (NAIO) project – being executed at top speed at Admiral Nanda's directives – to fabricate limpet mines.

Roy's immediate priority was to assemble the teams to train his water rats. The mission, he told the young officers, was hazardous and might even involve operations behind enemy lines.

'Are you ready to volunteer?'

'Yes, sir', the officers spoke, almost in unison.

'Hand me your resignations.' Roy had kept this request for last. The young officers dutifully scrawled out what they were told to write – they were resigning their commissions to pursue their own interests – and handed the notes to the DNI. Roy carefully kept it away. With that, the Das and Kapil shed their naval whites to enter a dark netherworld, one where their service and country would deny any knowledge of their existence in case they were exposed or captured. The rush of participating in a unique mission had overpowered their doubts.

Kapil had only one question: how long would he stay in Calcutta? Four, maybe five months, the DNI shrugged. The lieutenant wrangled a deal. He would be allowed to go to Bombay every month. 'Don't worry about it. The navy will pay your fare,' Captain Roy sniffed, perhaps mentally deducting the amount from his secret funds. Kapil had another request.

'A bedding roll?' Roy looked at him quizzically. 'Done!'

A week later, an unmarked grey Willys jeep hurtled across the green Bengali countryside down the narrow National Highway 12, snaking northwards along the East Pakistan border. In the front, next to the driver, sat Major Shankar Roychowdhury. The clean-shaven Bengali officer, freshly minted from Staff College Wellington, exchanged wisecracks with lieutenants Kapil and Das sitting in the rear. The trio were in plain clothes.

Roychowdhury, an armoured corps officer, was among several of the army's Bengali-speaking officers swept up from the far corners of the country and posted into Operation Jackpot, the Eastern Command's covert training and equipping of the Mukti Bahini. It operated directly under the General Officer Commanding-in-Chief (GOC-in-C) Lt General J.S. Aurora and Major General O.S. Kalkat.

The secret operation had strung five operational sectors, Alpha, Bravo, Charlie, Delta and Echo (a sixth, Echo-1 in Masimpur, Assam, would be added a few months later), each under a brigadier. These sectors, dealing with East Pakistan, coordinated the logistics and training of the Mukti Bahini. Roychowdhury was brigade major or BM of Charlie Sector, earlier, the 32 Infantry Brigade with its peacetime locations in Barrackpore and Kanchrapara near Calcutta. His sector commander, Brigadier Nasim Arthur Salick, a tough, chain-smoking officer from the Kumaon regiment, had deputed him help the naval element of the operation locate a camp site.

Das and Kapil had worked out the basic criteria for the camp – training had to be done in secret and, hence, far from an inquisitive civilian population. The site had to be on the waterfront to impart day- and night-swimming training. The camp not only needed space to accommodate, train and protect a lot of trainees, it also needed room for expansion in case more volunteers came.

Roychowdhury had accompanied the duo in his Willys for over a week now and watched as they crossed out a number of locations. Diamond Harbour – strong currents, too many civilians around; the Sundarbans – no secluded spots, strong currents and too far away from the support system in Calcutta.

Time was running out, and back in Delhi, Captain Roy was getting impatient. When finally, the brigade major mentioned some promising sites north of Charlie Sector, near the banks of the Bhagirathi river.

The jeep left the highway and drove down a small fork through endless rows of jute, paddy and sugarcane fields. They had entered the village of Palashi, where, over two centuries ago, the history of the subcontinent had taken a decisive turn. The Bhagirathi, a distributary of the Ganga, branched off from its parent river near Murshidabad and flowed lazily southwards through the plains of Bengal into East Pakistan. On the eastern riverbank, giant brown chimneys of a sugar factory soared above the low-lying land, partly hidden by endlessly swaying fields of young sugarcane.

The factory was empty and its smokestacks stood like stubbed-out cigars because all the cane had been crushed the previous month. It would be another eight months before its giant rollers would start turning again.

The heat was stifling as Kapil, Das and Roychowdhury entered the factory. Here, they met a short and stocky, bespectacled S.N. Mehra, a man who had spent a lifetime in the factory as chief agricultural officer and now held additional charge as the general manager. Kapil and Das introduced themselves as BSF officers looking for a spot to set up a training camp. Mehra bought their story. The border was less than 40 kilometres east of Plassey and everyone knew about the crisis in East Pakistan. He was happy to be of help. He escorted them around the Ramnugger Cane and Sugar Company Limited and told them about its history. The factory, built in 1936, he informed them, was unique. It was West Bengal's only mill that harvested, crushed and processed cane grown on its own farms. In the season, it harvested 1,800 tonnes of sugarcane each day from its 1,54,313-hectare plantation on either bank of the Bhagirathi.

Kapil and Das were more interested in the waterfront. They walked towards it and assessed the river. The water was five feet deep and had a current of up to three knots, just right to support training in the water. If the current had been any faster, trainees would have found underwater swimming difficult.

The fallow fields from where the sugarcane had been harvested offered plenty of open ground where they could pitch tents and set up training facilities. A sufficiently wooded orchard was ideal for explosives training. Ramnugger ticked all the boxes. The quest for a camp had finally ended.

Roychowdhury then dropped the naval officers off at Pagla Chandi, five kilometres away from Plassey, where the Second Battalion of the Sikh Light Infantry (LI) was encamped. The army had attached the tiny naval unit to the Second Battalion of the Sikh LI. The Mazhabi and Ramdasia Regiment, named for the Sikh communities it recruited from, was disbanded in 1935 and then, re-raised during the Second World War as the Sikh Light Infantry Regiment. It had moved into West Bengal from its peace station in Ranchi, Bihar, just before the 1971 general elections.

The Sikh LI officers' mess was a large house, requisitioned from a local politician. The commanding officer, Lt Colonel A.B.C. D'Mello was away on leave. His second-in-command, Major G.S. Sharma, hosted the young officers for the next few days. The unit had been deployed in the varied terrain of nearly every war since Independence – Goa in 1961, the heights of Se La during the 1962 Indo–China war, and the salt desert of the Rann of Kutch in the 1965 war. In 1971, after supervising the elections, the unit had continued to stay on, attached to the Krishnangar-based 42nd Brigade.

A few days later, the naval officials shifted to the Central Public Works Department (CPWD) guest house built next to a war memorial commemorating the fallen soldiers of Plassey. The Plassey Monument, as it was called, was a cement obelisk erected by the British over a century ago. A circular plaque that read 'Battle field of Plassey, June 23, 1757', marked the exact spot where Clive's redcoats had faced Siraj-ud-Daulah's troops over two centuries ago.

The inspection bungalow right next to the monument was more recent – a quaint, colonial structure with wide open verandas, shuttered doors and high ceilings. A plaque over the porch read: 'Plassey Inspection Bungalow, PWD, 1907'. The bungalow was meant for supervisory level Public Works Department staff when they toured the district and, with three small guest rooms, was as austere as an army mess. The beds, fortunately, had mattresses, Kapil noted. There was a dining hall with old wicker recliners and a dusty glass display case in the corner.

A week later, an army truck brought seven tanned, lean-bodied, exceedingly fit men carrying holdalls into the camp. All of them were in civvies, sports shoes, trousers and short-sleeve shirts. They sported crew cuts and Omega Seamasters – the navy's standard-issue diving watch. All but two of them were clean-shaven. They were the cream of the enlisted cadre of the navy's diving branch, trained in India from 1960 onwards by the first officers and men returning from the UK.

Some of them were in the checklist Captain Roy had drawn up in New Delhi. The group in-charge was Gurnail Singh, chief petty officer and Clearance diver (CD)-1, a proficient diver trained by the Royal Navy at Vernon, strict and serious in disposition. Then there was Petty Officer Pandurang Dhole, of medium height and build, efficient and very quiet. Quiet, as the joke went, because of the tobacco he stuffed into his cheek. Finally, there was Madhusudhan Gupta, leading seaman CD-3 and the navy's most experienced enlisted diver, who hadn't made it to the next rank of petty officer because of his ongoing struggle with clearing the Educational Test-1, a simple mathematics and general knowledge test.

There was Leading Seaman Karan Singh, CD-2, a tall and beefy, quick-tempered diver from Jodhpur with a thick beard and handlebar moustaches; a man who bristled at naval regulations that forbade 'moustache without beard'. Leading Seaman CD-2 P.K. Bhattacharjee was an introverted diver from Assam. Leading Seaman Eranullil Joseph Princhan and Leading Seaman Chiman

Singh, both CD-2s and twenty-three years old, were the youngest in the group.

The seven divers represented a breathtaking geographical diversity in terms of their background – the fields of Punjab, deserts of Rajasthan, Haryana's rural idyll, Kerala's backwaters, the arid Deccan, the plains of Bengal and Assam's Brahmaputra valley. They had joined the navy as 'boy entries', just out of school, and had volunteered to join the diving branch.

A week back, the men had been asked to report at the INS Hooghly with no clue about their task. That morning, they were driven to an army unit on National Highway 12 for lunch, where their next destination would be disclosed. Now, they had finally arrived and their eyes widened as Das and Kapil briefed them about their mission.

For the first week, the navy team camped in the PWD guest house. The navy crew walked past the fields and into the flat areas near the riverbank, identifying the exact spot where the camp would be set up. They settled upon Tejnagar, a 300-acre farm, one of twenty such farms where sugarcane was cultivated. It was 100-acre, rectangular brown strip that ran parallel to the river.

DNI had codenamed the camp 'Camp 2 Plassey' or C2P. Roy appointed Kapil officer-in-charge of the clandestine unit since he was a week senior in the course to Lt Das. The Eastern Command had 'logistically attached' the camp to the 2 Sikh LI battalion. This meant they were entirely dependent on the battalion for food, transport, communications and transport.

A week later, two military vehicles rattled into view. A Sikh LI junior commissioned officer (JCO) led a two-vehicle convoy into the camp. The vehicles, an old Shaktiman and a Nissan Carrier 4W73 utility vehicle, were those which the military referred to only by their weight classification – 3-tonne and 1-tonne. On board were a dozen Sikh LI personnel and eight Ordnance Factory Board-made olive-green waterproof canvas tents, and aluminium dekchis (flat-bottomed cooking pots the size of little lifeboats which were used to cook the staple army diet of rice, lentils and curry). The JCO also brought in two soldiers who would be with the navy unit for the duration of their stay. The soldiers were complete contrasts – Havildar Mane, a short, stocky, clean-shaven non-commissioned officer and an expert in unarmed combat a scanty-bearded, and spindly Sepoy Maninder Singh, the camp cook.

The Sikh LI soldiers, meanwhile, went about hammering staves into the ground, erecting the tents in a neat row and digging shallow snake trenches around them. The navy personnel, with absolutely no knowledge of tentage, could only watch in amazement as their tiny encampment rose barely 100 metres from the riverbank.

The tents were lined with plastic sheets to counter ground dampness. The Sikh LI unit left a few hours later, leaving behind two vehicles which they parked in front of the camp. Kapil and Das chose to live in the tents not only because of the unique camaraderie of the diving branch – officers and men shared their work environment– but also because of the fact that the camp's multi-national composition meant they would have to keep a close watch on things.

C2P had nine tents – Kapil and Das shared one, the enlisted men shared two, four tents were set aside for camp recruits, one for camp stores and the ninth, the langar tent, was where Maninder Singh slept with the food supplies. A week later, an army vehicle brought in another interesting group: the *Mangro* escapees who had been flown in from Delhi.

C2P, with a tenth of the navy's diving specialists, and Pakistani submariners, was already India's most unusual military unit. Now they needed the raw material which would complete the picture.

Less than 100 kilometres away from C2P, the Pakistan Army was on the verge of winning a victory against its own people. On

April 11, Tikka Khan had handed over charge as eastern army commander and chief martial law administrator to Lt General Amir Abdullah Khan Niazi. 'Tiger' Niazi, as he was called, had issued a new operational directive to be implemented by 15 May 1971 in five phases. Operation Searchlight was never formally called off, but by the end of April, it had achieved its objectives – Khan's men had crushed the armed Bengali insurrection. The Pakistan Army's reign of terror, however, continued unabated.

At C2P, the navy commando training team then broke up into smaller recruitment units headed by lieutenants Das and Kapil, with each team including at least one *Mangro* crewmember. The teams fanned out into refugee camps, looking for volunteers. The criteria for selection included able-bodied youth who displayed motivation and physical stamina to become strong swimmers, and who had the aptitude and educational background for and dedication to the cause. They wanted educated youth because of the specialized skill sets they would have to imbibe. They also needed to be politically aware and amenable to being trained as soldiers.

East Pakistan was a diverse region, roughly divided into four divisions – Khulna, Rajshahi, Dacca and Chittagong – by the giant rivers Padma, Jamuna and Meghna that bisected it. These regions were not only geographically distinct, but their inhabitants had varied dialects and even physical features. Roy was well aware of this. His blueprint recommended selecting a broad mix of volunteers who hailed from potential operational areas of East Pakistani riverine terrain. This was to ensure that they were familiar with the terrain and could blend in as locals. This approach had multiple advantages. It allowed Naval intelligence to develop a database of terrain, currents and other factors critical to riverine warfare and also helped maintain a cover for the volunteers.

The recruitment of these guerrillas was always done with the approval of the provisional government of Bangla Desh. Detailed lists of volunteers were copied to them and movement orders issued by General Osmani's headquarters in Calcutta. This made it substantially different from clandestine activities the world over. As far as India was concerned, training and equipping of the Mukti Bahini and the naval commandos was part of the military assistance it was providing a friendly government.

A few days later, a three-tonner slowly lurched past the muddy sugarcane fields like a ship in a storm. It was waved past by the sentries on guard duty at Camp C2P. The driver got off, walked around the rear and flung the panel open. There was a murmur in the human cargo in the rear, from where around sixty slightly bewildered volunteers stirred and hesitantly clambered out. Most of them wore lungis and vests and didn't even carry a change of clothes.

Among the recruits was Humayun Kabir, a lean coffee-complexioned eighteen-year-old former police constable. He had joined the East Pakistan police in 1970 after completing his training and was posted in the Rajarbag police line during the Operation Searchlight crackdown. His father Sheikh Abdul Mazid brought him back to Khulna, for he did not want his son to be used to kill his own people. Kabir joined the naval commandos, while his older brother, Mohammad Jahangir Alam joined the Mukti Bahini land forces.

Kapil stood in his shorts and T-shirt outside his tent, watching his first batch of trainees with growing astonishment. The recruits seemed to be in the age group he had wanted, but most were scrawny and xylophone-ribbed, the result of days of starvation and fighting for rations in the food queues of the youth camp.[10] *They can barely lift a dive set, leave alone swim five miles underwater,* he thought to himself.

---

10 Camps set up by the Bangla Desh government in exile along the border with East Pakistan to recruit youth of fighting age

The recruits had witnessed horrific atrocities in East Pakistan; their shoulders were stooped as if from the weight of those terrible memories. Yet, there was something else the young camp officer-in-charge saw right away in the eyes of his potential recruits – they burned like coals. They wanted revenge. That was a good start.

The trainees spent the first few days at camp eating and sleeping. Maninder Singh watched them gobble up large quantities of rice, sometimes not even waiting for it to be cooked fully. Food and rest were two luxuries they had not seen in several weeks. Then the training began. The naval instructors put their recruits through the same drill rookie divers would be put through at the naval diving school in Cochin. Trainees were handed their uniform – the blue or black Defence Ministry-issue swimming trunks, secured with a white drawstring. Officers, men and recruits, everyone wore it.

The camp's first dropout surprised everyone. Less than a fortnight into training, Gurnail Singh left the camp for good, handing the baton over to Petty Officer Dhole. It wasn't entirely his choice. The navy, already feeling the pinch of a depleted strength of clearance divers, had recalled him.

At the crack of dawn, the recruits were woken up and sent on endurance runs of five to six kilometres through the sugarcane fields. Kapil and Das, meanwhile, focused on completing the equipping of the camp and finalizing the blueprint for the advanced training programme. Two critical items they had to procure were swim fins and diving utility knives. US Navy and British frogmen in the Second World War used Churchill Fins – de Corlieu's fins copied and patented by an American yachtsman, Owen Churchill, in 1943, designed to resemble a dolphin's tail. The invention allowed frogmen to move at twice the speed of a fast crawl stroke swimmer.

Help came through a fortuitous turn of events. Lieutenant Adhir Chandra Bhattacharjee, among the navy's first deep-sea divers, had hung up his diving boots in 1971 and formed the country's first commercial diving company – Abee Engineering Corporation – and had begun supplying diving fins and floating divers' knives for the navy. The 'Abee' fins were copies of the famous Churchill fins; the knives resembled the standard-issue Royal Navy knife – nine inches long with a straight four-inch stainless steel blade with two edges, one sharp and the other serrated. The rubber-handled knife came in a rubber sheath, which could be strapped to the diver's ankle or thigh.

C2P trucks drove the officers between the Eastern Army Command Headquarters in Fort William and the ordnance depots, to bring in the weapons and supplies for the camp. Even as the recruits hit the water for their first swimming lessons, one tent in C2P had begun stockpiling carbines, grenades and plastic explosives.

When the training of the first batch of 100 recruits began in early May, the eight-man *Mangro* crew were invaluable as interpreters between the raw Bengali recruits and their naval trainers. The navy aimed to transform their recruits into underwater weapon delivery units – assault swimmers who could swim up to six hours at a stretch, carrying a three- to four-kg limpet mine under all operational conditions – blinding rain, at night, and in zero visibility conditions.

The residents of C2P woke at 5 a.m. each day. A fall-in-line whistle was blown at 5.30 a.m. The recruits donned their swim trunks and stood outside their tents in rows to sing Bangla Desh's national anthem, Tagore's *Amar Shonar Bangla* ('My Golden Bengal'), and saluted their national flag– a green flag with an orange map of the country inside a red circle – hoisted by a naval instructor.

Training began at 6 a.m. with a fall-in, followed by standard PT – push ups and pull ups and barefoot runs across the sugarcane fields.

After an hour's break for bath and breakfast came a short spell of theoretical training about the use of explosives, the role of a waterborne saboteur, recognizing the type of ship from its silhouette and then identifying its vulnerabilities from the waterline – the engine room, the stern gland, the propeller shaft, and, in warships, the magazine area under the turret. The Indian Navy trainers poured out all they knew about the dark arts of sabotage and clandestine warfare. Chowdhury and his seven *Mangro* comrades, their names suffixed with the Bengali honorific 'dadu' (older brother), stood by and translated for the recruits.

Theoretical training was followed by the most important item of the day – endurance swimming. Trainees entered the water for hour-long surface swims, replicating those by naval divers who leapt off Ernakulam bridge and swam the three-kilometre distance to the boat pool at the INS Venduruthy in Cochin. Swimming class ended at lunch when the exhausted trainees emerged from the Bhagirathi and jogged to the mess tent for a ninety-minute break. Post lunch, they broke up into small groups for instruction in small arms and explosives training conducted by army instructors from the Brigade.

A low-lying patch of sugarcane field behind the camp became the improvised firing range. Here, the naval commandos trained to shoot at man-sized Figure 11 targets using the British-designed Sterling sub-machine gun. The compact black Sterling was less than two-feet long, and had a curved, banana-shaped magazine which held thirty-four 9 mm bullets. It was the successor to the World War II Sten, millions of which had been distributed across occupied Europe by Britain's Special Operations Executive (SOE). They were now being manufactured under license at the government-owned Small Arms Factory in Kanpur as the 9 mm 1A1 carbine, and earmarked for distribution among the naval commandos. Smaller groups of around a dozen trainees were taught to use hand grenades and explosives.

Two hundred and thirteen years after Clive's victory, Plassey resounded with the boom of explosives and the crack of carbines once again.

Havildar Mane, dressed in his white vest, khaki shorts and brownish-orange army-issue canvas shoes, conducted the close-quarter combat class. He taught recruits the art of unarmed close-quarter combat – Jujutsu (to disarm an opponent with the minimum use of force), disarming sentries and how to save oneself from a bayonet charge.

Physical training ended at 4.30 p.m. A forty-five–minute tea break was followed by another hour of endurance swimming. After sunset, when the recruits were bone-tired and gasping for breath, they entered the water again, for the most challenging assignment of the day – night endurance swimming – traversing long distances in near-zero visibility.

The X-men – as the trainers Chiman Singh, Karan Singh, Princhan, etc., were called – rotated the training modules among themselves. P.K. Bhattacharjee would handle the small arms and grenade-throwing class for a week; Chiman Singh would be in charge of swimming training; M.S. Gupta would look after camp administration duties; and Dhole, the explosives training.

Towards the end of May 1971, the commander of the Bangla Desh Army made his first visit to C2P. Colonel M.A.G. Osmani, visited the camp along with his aide, Group Captain A.W. Khondkar. They were accompanied by the Indian liaison officer, Brigadier U.K. Gupta.

Colonel Osmani's Mukti Bahini forces were now holding a fast-contracting swathe of territory. Around 500 square miles in small pockets in Dinjapur, Rangapur and Sylhet districts. But there was hope still. 'Everybody's efforts matter to our struggle,' he said in Bengali to his recruits who sat cross-legged and listened to him in awe. 'But your efforts are special … because you are in the navy.'

C2P then proceeded to the next stage of training for the recruits. The advanced training comprised map reading, infiltration, exfiltration, survival techniques, conduct in hostile territory, and ship and target recognition.

Capture and death were the natural hazards of their mission. The trainers taught their understudies how to escape in enemy territory and evade capture. The areas they could hide in, how to commandeer a boat or canoe to escape, and to mentally note all the geographical features of the place they were in. 'Never panic', they said, 'always think. When the mind starts working, panic disappears.' These were drilled into the naval personnel by their Royal Navy trainers.

DNI's launch window for the first attacks was approaching. Training was cut down from the required five weeks to just three weeks of very intensive swimming training.

In offices and workshops across the Indian subcontinent, hectic efforts were underway to perfect the weapons these recruits would carry into battle. With Captain Roy's briefing of the criticality of the limpet mines, Admiral Nanda had issued confidential directives to the Director of Naval Armaments to liaise directly with the local heads of the Armaments Research and Development Establishment (ARDE) and the senior inspector of naval armaments (SINA), Calcutta. Development of the indigenous limpet mine was seen as critical to the entire operation. Without fully-functional and mass-produced limpet mines, the entire operation would fail.

Design work began at the NAIO, which maintained the navy's store of ammunition, sea mines, torpedoes and missiles. The NAIO worked in tandem with the Pune-based laboratory of the Defence Research and Development Organisation (DRDO) and the ARDE, and reverse-engineered the British Mark-III limpet mines provided to them by the navy.

The design for the Indian limpet mine had to be kept extremely simple, for it was to be operated by volunteers with just four weeks of military training. It had to be rugged in order to withstand the rigours of concealed transport into their areas of operation. The mines would also have to be used together and detonated sequentially, which meant extra reliability – one blast should not trigger off the others. Its weight could not exceed three kilograms so that a swimmer could comfortably carry it. The developers, in consultation with the users, decided to skip fitting complicated anti-lifting devices or booby-traps which set the mine off in case the enemy tried to remove them.

TNT or Trinitrotoluene was the limpet's main high-energy explosive charge. To trigger off the firing chain, a spring-loaded striker would fire a percussion cap, which would set off the detonator to produce a concussion, which would then trigger off the booster – a charge explosive or CE pellet inbuilt into the limpet – which would trigger off the TNT.

When detonated, the TNT would change from solid to gaseous almost instantaneously, expanding to 6,940 metres per second, releasing heat and pressure in all directions, producing what was called a 'shattering effect' on the target. The Mark III could punch a hole in a 60 mm (2.3-inch) steel plate.

Pouring the molten TNT into the steel shells of the limpet and fitting the detonators and charge explosive was easy. The trouble lay in perfecting the timer – a delay mechanism which would enable the diver to swim to safety after planting the magnetized charge. The Mark III had a regulator, like the one in a ceiling fan, which allowed for a time delay to be set on it from a half-hour to twenty-four hours. Once the mine was planted on the target, the diver yanked off a small ring to activate the timer. The Indian limpet mine needed to have something similar, but without the imported components in order to ensure deniability of the operation in case the ordnance was captured.

Samples of the Indian-designed limpet mine were manufactured and tried out under the supervision of Lt Sameer Das. The prototypes weighed about three kilograms and included the firing mechanism – timer clocks, for which two NAIO officers had offered competing designs.

Commander Thumbavanam Rajagopala Iyer Srinivasan who worked in the DRDO's ARDE laboratory offered a conventional clock mechanism design that could trigger the explosion with a clock-controlled time delay, ranging from a few days to a few hours, to even months. Commander Jagjit Singh Pantle from SINA in Calcutta offered a far simpler solution: a limpet mine with a soluble plug that would dissolve within half an hour of coming in contact with seawater. With the contact, a circuit would be completed and the explosive triggered off.

The team decided to try out the clock mechanism. During extensive tests supervised by Lt Das in a water tank in the INS Hooghly, the mine's sensitive spring mechanism malfunctioned due to the vibrations set off by sympathetic explosions from other mines. The clock timer design was discarded. Commander Pantle's soluble plug design was taken up. The soluble plug was made of compacted salt and based on the firing mechanism of a depth charge. When a depth charge was tossed in the water, the soluble plug dissolved, completing a firing circuit and exploding the charge, which would cripple the submarine.

Removing the bulky clock left a cavity which could be stuffed with an additional 1.5 kgs of explosive. All that the saboteur had to do was stick the limpet on the target and swim away, for the soluble plug would dissolve thirty minutes after it made contact with the water. And this time lapse was also the design's critical flaw. A waterborne saboteur would need at least an hour to swim to his target, place the limpet on it and swim away. A thirty-minute soluble plug could endanger his life. There was no time to develop another time-delay fuse. After several more tests, the firing mechanism on the limpet mine was perfected. The designers added a dome-shaped polystyrene (thermocol) cover on the mine, which reduced its underwater weight from three kgs to just one kilogram. There was a reason why they needed to reduce its weight. The Mark-III was carried by frogmen who swam under the water. The Indian limpet mine was borne by swimmers who swam on the surface and who had to carry the lightest load possible.

Camp C2P, meanwhile, was wrestling with more mundane issues. Kapil noted that the army unit had passed on hand-me-downs. The vehicles were Class V, which basically meant they had reached the end of their service lives and were waiting to be scrapped. As for the tents, at night, the ripped and frayed tents turned into night observatories to watch the starlit sky. Things could get worse in the rains. And so he drove down to see the 2 Sikh LI CO to relay their requirements to the brigade headquarters. Lt Colonel A.B.C. D'Mello explained that this was the best they could provide in their existing circumstances as they needed tents and road transport too, due to their own increased needs. 'We're not on holiday here, sir!' the exasperated young officer told the CO.

Then he sought an appointment with the brigade commander, Lt Colonel D'Mello's superior. A few days later, Kapil was outside a door in Krishnanagar which read 'Brigadier J.S. Gharaya'. Brigadier Joginder Singh Gharaya had a fearsome reputation. It was hard to tell who feared him more – the enemy or his troops. He had been awarded a Kirti Chakra, the nation's second-highest peacetime gallantry award, for leading his company to charge a razakar (volunteer) force during the 'police action' against the Nizam of Hyderabad's forces in 1948.

Gharaya commanded the 42nd Brigade, one of three brigades of the 9th Infantry Division brought in to supervise general elections in West Bengal. They had stayed on after the tensions with Pakistan began. With the enemy less than fifty kilometres away, he was focused on getting his units into combat, and disregarded the protestations of the army-captain–ranked navy officer who stood before him in civvies. 'That's all we can spare. Take it or leave it,' he snapped at Kapil.

Before he was dismissed, Kapil requested for permission to use Gharaya's radio to send a message to NHQ. 'Give him what he wants,' the brigadier instructed a staff officer before going back to his war plans.

'Training considered difficult due to lack of support from the army', the lieutenant punched out in his High Frequency (HF) transmission from the Brigade HQ to NHQ, before returning to C2P. The rest of the day passed off uneventfully.

The following day, C2P erupted in a flurry of activity. Lt Colonel D'Mello, led by hundreds of Sikh LI personnel, descended on the camp with a new three-tonne truck and brand-new tents. The older tents and vehicles were replaced with much fervour and an engineer corps bulldozer noisily levelled a clearing near the camp.

'Your chief is visiting tomorrow,' Lt Colonel D'Souza informed Kapil grimly, 'with my GOC-in-C.' Nothing moves the wheels of military bureaucracy more than a visit by the brass. So now C2P was getting red-carpet treatment.

Early next morning, Brigadier Gharaya and his staff drove into C2P. Kapil supressed a smirk as he saluted him. There was no conversation. They lined up near the clearing painted 'H' and looked skywards.

A green Army Aviation Corps Alouette clattered into view and dropped out of the sky into the white circle, scattering dust. When the blades stopped rotating, the pilot stepped out, slid the door open and saluted. Admiral Charles Nanda stepped out, baton in hand, to return the salute. With him was Lt General Jagjit Singh Aurora – a tall, wiry man with a prominent hook nose and a moustache waxed up like little sickles – commander of the Indian Army in the east. Captain Roy, the King Cobra, architect of the covert campaign, followed behind, at a respectful distance.

Charles Nanda had come to supervise his smallest naval command. Lieutenants Kapil and Das had lined up with their men, all of them in swimming trunks and T-shirts. Kapil then escorted the brass hats around the camp. Nanda sailed about like a white sailing ship in an olive-green sea of army personnel. Captain Roy bore good news for Kapil. 'From now on,' he said, pointing towards Lt General Aurora, 'this camp will be under him.' An officer's rank mattered a great deal in the deeply hierarchical armed forces. Roy informed Kapil he was placing a senior naval officer in Fort William, Calcutta, to supervise NCO(X). That naval officer would report directly to Lt General Aurora's chief of staff, Major General Jacob.

The Emperor, meanwhile, was impressed by what he saw. He had a lot on his mind then. He was locked in a bitter tussle with his friend and junior colleague, Vice Admiral Kohli in the Western Naval Command, who had opposed his plan to strike at Karachi. Kohli had cited naval history – the Royal Navy's loss of the *Prince of Wales* and the *Repulse* to shore-based aircraft in 1942 – to warn against attacking the Pakistani port city. Nanda had threatened to get himself a new C-in-C. But here, on the Bengal floodplain, Nanda saw his eastern plan humming quietly and efficiently, answerable only to him and not known to many others including, Kohli.

Nanda leaned towards the young officer whose one-line SOS had necessitated this trip. A smile creasing his face, he whispered in Punjabi, 'Theek kitta' (you did the right thing). And with that, the Emperor disappeared in a roar of rotorblades. A new and exciting phase had begun in C2P's existence.

4

NO MAN LIKE SOMAN

The short, stocky, clean-shaven individual who identified himself only as 'Mr Bhaskar Soman' of the Border Security Force, hopped out of the military-green Willys Jeep and hurried down the corridor in Fort William – headquarters of the Indian Army's eastern command since 1963. Soman wore a short-sleeved shirt tucked into his trousers and his army-issue green canvas jungle shoes squeaked as he walked down the corridor. He carried a black faux leather attaché case with him and wiped the sweat from the muggy Calcutta weather off his brow as he headed towards an unmarked 250-square-foot room at the far end of the passage near the map room. The army sentry in olive-green fatigues posted outside – the only sign that this was no ordinary room – snapped his rifle back in recognition. Soman nodded cursorily at him and entered, gingerly putting the attaché case on his table at the far end of the room.

The briefcase held his insurance – a 9mm Sterling carbine with two loaded magazines and two Ordnance Factory-made HE-36 hand grenades. The weapons had been wrapped in improvised noise dampeners – old vests. He reached for the only thing remaining in the bag – a green-jacketed file, stamped 'Top Secret'. The file, with a hand-scrawled legend, 'Naval Commando Operations (X)' – (NCO[X]) in short – was far more explosive than the ordnance he carried. It was the plan for an operation of the kind not seen since the underwater exploits of the Decima Flottiglia MAS in the Second World War. It contained codenames, places, personnel, equipment and targets for Operation Jackpot's naval missions. Soman was the sole custodian of this file, which he slid into a large iron safe that sat to his left.

Curiously, for someone walking around the precincts of a sensitive army command, Soman didn't carry a shred of identification on him. The labels on his clothes and shoes had been snipped away. He had no identity card, no wallet, no identity papers, for an important reason – he was not Bhaskar Soman. He was Commander Mohan Narayan Rao 'Sammy' Samant, a serving Indian Navy officer. The man on the ground who oversaw all covert naval operations in the east. Very few officials in Fort William knew him by his official designation – 'Staff Officer-1 Naval Operations (X)'.

Samant had his own staff officer – Lt Commander C.S. Menon, a specialist navigation officer like him, who sat at a nearby table. A curtained door behind him led to a smaller room where his communicator, Leading Telegraphist S. Biswas, sat typing out the confidential stream of communication to NHQ. Samant had just returned from his first tour of his new charge – Camp C2P. An army-like camp, he noted. His father would have been proud.

Samant was the eldest of five children of a viceroy's commissioned officer, Narayan Ramchandra Samant. Subedar Major Samant's family hailed from Parule village in Sindhudurg district, along the Konkan coast in Bombay State, but he had left home to join the army. Samant junior was born in his grandmother's home in Vasai, north of Bombay, and had moved along to his father's postings across military stations in Peshawar, Chaklala and Meerut before Subedar Major Samant was shipped off to North Africa in 1940.

There, he fought with the British Army until his whole garrison was captured by German Field Marshal Erwin Rommel's Afrika Korps and transported to POW camps, first in Italy and then Germany. Samant senior returned from the war in 1945 and was surprised when his son, studying in an intermediate Science course in Wilson College, Bombay, cleared the federal public services examination held in March 1948 and opted to join the Royal Indian Navy. Samant was sent to the Royal Navy College, Dartmouth, where he spent four years training as an officer. After a fifth year as a midshipman, Sub Lieutenant Samant returned home in 1953. He was among the last batch of Indian executive officers commissioned in the UK, all steeped in the Royal Navy ethos; wry, straight-faced humour; and expressions like 'get on with it chop-chop'.

Over a decade later, Samant epitomized the Indian Navy's tack towards the Soviet Union when he returned from Russia as commissioning CO of the third Foxtrot-class submarine, the *INS Karanj* in 1969. He learnt Russian, could toast *Za vashe zdarovje* before gulping down vodka shots with his instructors, and was proficient in the workings of this terrifying new engine of war which he sailed around the coast of Africa to Visakhapatnam, a sleepy civilian port on the east coast that was being transformed into a major naval base. Soviet specialists had helped set up a dockyard, submarine base and training facilities for India's new fleet of Russian warships and submarines.

The call to meet DNI Captain Roy came in April 1971. Samant was posted in the Eastern Naval Command in Visakhapatnam and had finished drafting the Command War Orders – classified directives which told every officer of the command, from operations to support systems, what to do in case of an outbreak of war.

Captain Mohan Singh Grewal, chief staff officer of the Eastern Command had slipped him the terse signal: 'Request Direct Commander Samant to report to NHQ.' Something was afoot, but exactly what, Samant didn't have a clue. He was in New Delhi the next day, striding through the labyrinthine corridors of South Block in crisp naval whites, the golden dolphins of the submarine service gleaming on the breast pin above his left pocket.

Captain Roy warmly welcomed Samant into his room. The two had briefly been shipmates on the *INS Vikrant* during the liberation of Goa in 1961. Samant, a young navigator–lieutenant on loan from the Tactical School, Cochin, directing aircraft off the carrier, and Roy, the dashing King Cobra, whose Alizés flew patrols around the fleet, looking for enemy submarines.

Roy's office in Delhi was sparsely furnished, but his desk had five telephones of varying colours, testifying to his importance. A civilian, whom Roy did not introduce and who Samant later discovered was a senior RAW officer, sat in the room, watching him intently.

Over the course of an hour, the DNI explained how the covert naval warfare unit comprising divers had started training East Bengali college students. He wanted a pointsman within the Eastern Army Command to lead the operation. Roy then escorted Samant to the floor above to meet the Indian Army's director military operations (DMO), Major General Inderjit Singh Gill. The DMO gave Samant the big picture – the army's training of the Mukti Bahini. It was, as Samant recalled, similar to the British training of Burmese and Thai ethnic groups to resist the Imperial Japanese Army during the Second World War.

The next stop was at Admiral Nanda's corner office, on the same floor. It was a brief meeting. 'So Samant, are you on board?' the gruff-voiced Nanda asked. The submariner accepted without hesitation. By then, he figured, he was already a man who knew too much. Refusal could mean a long period of surveillance to ensure he didn't breathe a word to anyone.

Roy and Nanda were pleased. As the trio stepped out of the CNS's office, there was a flutter in the corridor – the kind that heralded the arrival of someone powerful. Samant stiffened. Mrs Gandhi walked past, accompanied by her aides. She was clad in a cotton saree and smiled to acknowledge the navy chief's salute as she walked to the PMO at the northern end of the 300-metre long building. It was Samant's first glimpse of the PM. Her appearance added to the mystique of the subcontinent's most important office building.

As Samant headed to his next port of call, Fort William, Roy slipped him a farewell gift – a chunky one-time cipher pad, a combination of numbers and alphabets which could be deciphered only by an identical set kept in Roy's office. Pages would be torn out and destroyed once a message had been sent. He hadn't asked Roy how long the operation would last – in the forces, orders were followed unquestioningly. But the pad's thickness held a clue. It had a hundred pages – double the usual ones. This was going to be a long deployment.

Samant landed in Calcutta the next day and headed to Fort William. The fort, rebuilt in a new location after the battle of Plassey and completed two decades later was, until 1911, the seat of British India's military power. It was an irregular octagon with five sides towards land and three facing the Hooghly river. The citadel had, in the words of 19th-century British bureaucrat and historian Henry Cotton, 'stood no siege, fired no gun against an enemy from its ramparts' and had yet to be 'baptised by fire'. In 1971, Fort William was the strategic military nerve centre for the coming war in the East. The command insignia – a rising sun with yellow and black rays – and its motto, 'Defenders of the Dawn', spoke for the army's largest and most complex operational formation which guarded a quarter of a million square kilometres from the Himalayas, and encompassed the Brahmaputra valley and the steaming jungles of the north-east, and bordered six countries, two of whom India had fought three wars with.

Samant arrived in the fort sometime after 15 May, when the Eastern Command had taken over all logistical support and training of the Mukti Bahini from the Border Security Force (BSF) under Operation Jackpot. The operation encompassed all support to the East Pakistani guerrillas, including the tiny naval element in Plassey. He was asked to avoid the officers' mess, and his accommodation was on the first floor of the ramparts, a short distance away from Command HQ. Samant and his office staff were always in civvies under the cover of being central government officers aiding the Bengali refugees streaming into India. His assumed name was a nod to a former navy chief, Vice Admiral Bhaskar Soman, whom Micky Roy had once pranked.

The brass sat on the stone floor above Samant. The commander-in-chief, Eastern Command, Lt General Jagjit Singh Aurora's office was at the end of a long corridor. Lt General Aurora was a seasoned soldier. Commissioned into the army from the Indian Military Academy in 1938, the Punjab Regiment officer had seen action in nearly every war since – in Burma during the Second World War, Pakistan in 1947–48, the Sino–Indian War in 1962 and the 1965 Indo–Pakistan War.

Aurora's chief of staff, Major General Jacob Farj Rafael 'Jakes' Jacob, sat in the office adjacent to him. Jacob was of medium height, barrel-chested, with twinkling, inquisitive eyes, a thin-lipped smile that wrapped around his face, and hair neatly parted to one side from just above his left ear. He was born in Calcutta into a prosperous business family of Baghdadi Jews who had settled over two centuries ago in the new British capital. Commissioned into the Indian Army in 1942 into the Regiment of Artillery, he was wounded in action against the Japanese in South East Asia during the Arakan campaign in 1943 and was, by 1971, one of the army's rising stars. A bachelor, erudite and extremely well-read, he was also a hard taskmaster with a thunderous, expletive-laden temper, a stark contrast to his staid superior, Lt General Aurora.

One of Samant's tasks was to bifurcate NCO(X) into a special unit that would be directly under NHQ and DNI. The short chain of command would also completely bypass Vice Admiral Krishnan's Eastern Naval Command. Within Fort William, however, Samant had many superiors. He reported to the C-in-C through Major General Jacob but Major General Onkar Singh Kalkat – director of Operations 'X', which controlled all Mukti Bahini training and equipping – was also his boss. These lines of command were, however, never clearly defined and varied according to the situation. His immediate charge, however, was C2P, where the training of the naval commandos had just begun.

Lt Kapil recognized the grim-faced Cdr Samant on his first visit to C2P. The senior officer's reputation as someone who despised small talk and who could be curt to the point of being rude had preceded him. Kapil had heard about the commander from his friend Lt Franklin who had been Samant's assistant torpedo officer on the *INS Karanj*.

Samant had brought with him C2P's new officer-in-charge – Lt Cdr George Martis. Martis stood at five feet ten inches, was well built and square jawed. Called the 'diving cowboy' not only for his diving skills but his quick wit as well, he was a legend within the navy's small diving fraternity. He sometimes exhibited a cavalier attitude and a knack of getting embroiled in 'adventures'. George was the third of eight children born to an education officer Mathias Martis and his wife Alice. George was once mortally afraid of water. As a five-year-old, he had nearly drowned in Kadri Lake near his native town, Mangalore. He joined the navy as a 'boy entry' or young sailor, aged fourteen, rising through the ranks to become an officer, slowly conquering his fear of water by becoming a proficient swimmer and later, a deep-sea diver. In 1966, as part of a ship-borne naval team, Martis had escorted Mihir Sen the first Indian to swim the forty-mile–long Palk Straits between Ceylon (Sri Lanka now) and Dhanushkodi.

Now, in the searing heat of May 1971, Martis noticed something alarming. C2P's first batch of commando trainees tired easily and faltered during the long-distance swimming classes. Their dal-rice rations were clearly insufficient to build stamina. This could have adverse implications when training shifted into high gear. An SOS was flashed to Samant in Fort William. The naval officer had by then established a rapport with C.P. Ramachandran, the MoD's additional financial advisor posted in the Eastern Command. As the MoD representative in the command, Ramachandran signed off on all the secret funds for the operation which was deemed a high government priority. He sanctioned the funds for the increased rations without question.

At C2P, Maninder Singh's langar tent soon bulged with extra rations – eggs, lemons and fruit. Under the new scales, each trainee was authorized two eggs, 120 grams or half a cup of fresh milk, twenty-five grams or a tablespoon full of lime juice and eighty grams of fresh fruit. The extra rations worked. Recruits were soon effortlessly doing their ten-kilometre training runs.

Conflicts rarely arose within Fort William despite the multiple chains of command, even though Samant quickly got the feeling that he was seen as running an inconsequential operation. Jacob's staff officers felt the naval operation was simply too small to make a difference. Yet, the army didn't see what Samant and his bosses in Delhi saw. As the Mukti Bahini struck at the bridges, making road transport difficult, the Pakistan Army increased their reliance on the waterways. They had rapidly begun acquiring an impressive fleet of shallow-hulled merchant vessels to keep men and material moving between Chittagong, Dacca and Khulna. They had twenty-eight Chinese-supplied vessels, each capable of carrying 1,000 tons of cargo, nine US-supplied mini-bulkers with a capacity of 2,500 tons, and seventeen coasters that could carry cargo of between 600 to 1,000 tons each. These coastal vessels loaded and unloaded cargo from large merchant ships at Chittagong and Chalna/Mongla and traversed the waterways which radiated inland towards the capital Dacca and industrial hub Khulna.[11]

Samant noted that most of these important waterways were located further away from the West Bengal border and closer to Tripura, a small state in north-eastern India which jutted, thumb-like, into East Pakistan's eastern wing. The state, which shared an 856-km border with Pakistan's eastern province, was also a gateway through which hundreds of thousands of refugees and deserting soldiers had crossed over into India. The state capital, Agartala, was where Operation Jackpot had located 'Delta Sector' under a brigadier. And so, one day in June, Mr Soman boarded an IAF Fairchild Packet (an IAF transport aircraft) at Dum Dum airport to meet the brigadier. The courier flight, as it was called, would take a circuitous six-hour journey around East Pakistan to land in Agartala.

Delta Sector was commanded by Brigadier Shabeg Singh, a short, slim and balding Sikh officer with a close-cropped beard. The brigadier, commissioned into the Garhwal Rifles during the Second World War, had gone on to command the 3rd Battalion of the 11th Gorkha Regiment. He now operated from a clump of single-storeyed World War II-era barracks in Lichu Bagan, a dense orchard on military land five kilometres north-west of Agartala airport. The barracks were surrounded by a tent city inhabited by the Mukti Bahini and their Indian Army trainers.

---

11 Vice Admiral M.K. Roy, *War in the Indian Ocean* (New Delhi: Lancer Publishers), 1995

Samant was escorted to his living quarters – a tent outside the brigadier's office. From then on, a curious waiting game began. Shabeg declined to meet him on the first day. He was busy, his staff informed Samant, who could tell that they were mortally afraid of Shabeg. The waiting continued for a second day, even as the brigadier – a Spartan figure in civilian rig – went about his duties. In the austere camp where nearly everyone was in plainclothes, the senior officer asserted his rank by maintaining distance – he ate meals away from the men in the mess tent and seemed unapproachable. The brigadier was unfailingly courteous, politely acknowledging Samant's presence, but the strange waiting game continued. There was no sign of a meeting. On the third day, Samant's patience snapped. 'I'm clearly wasting my time here,' he respectfully informed the brigadier's staff officer. 'I need to get back to General Jacob.'

That hint rapidly travelled up the chain of command. The next morning, Samant was ushered into Brigadier Shabeg's office. It was a primitive set-up – just a table and a few chairs. The brigadier, dressed in simple civilian clothes, was courtesy personified. The meeting lasted an hour and Shabeg informed Samant that he had arranged a two-day tour of the India–Pakistan border, which was just five kilometres away from the camp. Over the next two days, Brigadier Shabeg drove the naval officer around the border outposts in his jeep, explaining the lay of the land and the ingress points through which the Mukti Bahini were launched into East Pakistan. The guerrillas were being used not only for covert raids, the brigadier said, but also to gather intelligence regarding the strength of the Pakistani forces – information Shabeg said would come in handy when the Indian Army finally moved in. He seemed very hands-on, a soldier who seemed very good at what he did.

In the tour through the slushy border, Samant explained the purpose of his visit – to create a navy-run launch pad in Delta Sector, over which the army would have only administrative control. The navy would do everything else – brief and debrief the commandos and decide their targets. And that was also when Samant figured out the reason for the brigadier's initial aloofness. Shabeg wanted complete operational control over all the guerrillas in his sector. He resented the prospect of a force operating independent of his setup. But since he knew that Samant was under direct orders from the brass in Fort William, he could only hint at this discomfort.

On the courier flight back to Calcutta, Samant reflected on his task ahead. A major part of his work would involve gathering intelligence on the Pakistani Navy's strategy in Bangla Desh. Samant felt no animosity towards the Pakistanis, though a nasal voice did ring in his head, suggesting otherwise. 'Sammy, you Indian rogue, I know you hate Pakistanis,' jibed his cabin mate Zamir Ahmed at the Royal Naval College, Greenwich. Zamir Ahmed the only Pakistani trainee in Samant's batch in Dartmouth, was five feet nine inches tall, slim, clean-shaven and walked with a pronounced stoop. He was the son of Nazir Ahmad Qureshi, a prominent Muslim businessman and blue-blooded family from New Delhi who had migrated to Karachi after Partition. Zamir had dropped his family name Qureshi when he came to Dartmouth in August 1949, never to use it again. He was introverted, deeply religious, recoiled at the presence of women and insisted on knowing the composition of the tallow used to cook his favourite Chinese fried rice. Zamir was commissioned into the Royal Pakistan Navy the same date that Samant was into the Indian Navy – 1 January 1952. Both countries had only lightly tweaked their Royal Indian Navy uniforms – the Indians had replaced the British crown on their cap crests and the buttons with the Ashokan lions; the Pakistanis had swapped it with the crescent and the star.

There was tremendous bonhomie among the two navies at Dartmouth – they had a joint hockey team, captained by Karamat Rahman Niazi, a strappingly handsome Pathan officer. Niazi (no relation to the general) went on to induct the *PNS Ghazi*. During the 1965 war, he had patrolled in the *Ghazi* off Bombay, looking in vain for the Indian Navy's flagship *INS Vikrant* and claimed to have torpedoed the frigate *INS Brahmaputra*. In 1971, it was Samant who was on the prowl, looking for intelligence on his erstwhile comrades across the border.

Events sometimes took an interesting turn. In June, during a visit to Hasnabad, a riverine border town nearly eighty kilometres west of Calcutta, he met Lieutenant M.A. Beg, a thirty-year-old former Pakistan Navy officer now fighting with the Mukti Bahini. Lt Beg had joined the Pakistan Army in 1963, and after training in the Special Service Unit, was transferred to the Pakistan Navy. He then underwent frogman and midget submarine training, including chariot operations in Italy. Lt Beg was part of a Pakistan naval special unit that had been earmarked for attacking Bombay, a revelation which confirmed DNI's intelligence warnings. Beg also gave Samant a list of eight former Bengali SSU personnel who had escaped into India. Samant now planned to locate them to lead naval commando strike teams into East Pakistan. His personal cipher pad was rapidly thinning out as he despatched a steady stream of coded messages to his boss DNI Roy in Delhi from the wireless office in INS Hooghly.

Samant occasionally called his wife Nirmala in Vizag and played the doting father, asking after his daughters Ujwala, 12, and Natasha, 4, and enquiring after their studies, and particularly Ujwala's maths grades.

What was he doing in Calcutta, his wife asked him.

'I'm working for the Bengali refugees,' he would tell Nirmala. The prospect of a specialist submariner engaged in relief work did puzzle the homemaker, but she never probed further.

It was May 1971, and the human flood from Bangla Desh continued unabated. Over three million refugees poured in to occupy open spaces in West Bengal, its villages, towns and cities. Hundreds of tents lined the roadsides, even the ones leading to camp C2P in Plassey. In the heart of Calcutta, the camps were filthy, the sight of dead bodies was common, and there was the overpowering stench of human excrement. Aid workers thrust packets of dried milk and biscuits and clothes into forests of human hands.

That month, both India and Pakistan had begun arming and training civilians on both sides of the border. The Pakistan Army was training and raising a force of civilian collaborators to tighten its grip on the rebellious province. On 28 May, Governor General Tikka Khan promulgated the East Pakistan Razakar Ordinance, which sanctioned the raising of razakars to augment the army. Around 50,000 volunteers – drawn mostly from the Urdu-speaking pro-Pakistani Bihari Muslims, Bengalis, and the Islamist Jamaat-i-Islami political party – were trained and equipped by the Pakistan Army.

In one camp in Juliet Sector in the north-eastern Indian state of Meghalaya, Lieutenant 'Delta', an officer from an infantry battalion, was training the first batch of Bengali refugees to lob grenades, lay ambushes and fire weapons used by the Pakistan Army – .303 bolt action rifles, German G3 rifles and Chinese Type 56 self-loading rifles. The lieutenant had earlier been posted at Sikkim's Doka La plateau as the army kept watch over a possible incursion route if the PLA decided to roll down from the Tibetan plateau down through the Chumbi Valley to aid East Pakistan. That month, he and dozens of army officers qualified as instructors in small arms and commando courses were vacuumed up by the Indian Army as training officers. In the camp, Mukti Bahini volunteers aged between seventeen and forty years were divided into five groups of ten each, and lived in thatch- and tin-roof dwellings. The lieutenant would, over the next three months, turn nearly 250 Bengali civilians into guerrillas and inculcate in them confidence and a fighting spirit.

Hundreds of miles away, Palashi's villagers had by now got used to the sight of bare-bodied Bengali youth running and swimming near the sugarcane fields, the occasional boom of explosives, and the rattle of sub-machine guns. The camp, they reasoned, was no different from the dozens of Mukti Bahini camps along the border, about which word had started to spread. But just who was training them was never clear. From a distance, the trainers were indistinguishable from their trainees.

Inside C2P, however, things were different. The X-men had quickly become legends, the three officers Martis, Das and Kapil supervising and stepping in only when things got out of hand. The physically imposing Karan Singh whose drill-sergeant–like voice barking out commands rang in the ears of his trainees long after the day's end. The short and ripped close-combat trainer Havildar Mane – affectionately called 'Nanabuz' by his recruits – who could never be thrown off his feet. Lt Samir Das, who effortlessly explained diving terminology to them in Bengali, was the star footballer during games sessions.

The camp pushed the college student trainees to their physical limits and, when they were finally proficient long distance swimmers after several weeks, the X-men finally introduced them to the last lesson – camouflaged swimming – the art of stealthily navigating to their targets in the water without exposing themselves. Trainees slipped on their fins and tied two bricks to their stomachs with a cloth towel to simulate the weight of a limpet mine. They had to swim to their targets downstream and backwards, propelled only by their fins. It was the stealthiest way to manoeuvre a three-kg limpet mine on their stomach to the target.

That month, the limpet mines began arriving at the camp. The first ones were dummies – inert rounds minus explosives, but as heavy, to give recruits a feel of the real weapon and its components. Training was rigorous and tempers were frayed. Arguments sometimes exploded into fisticuffs. Kapil separated one such bout between two trainees who seemed intent on killing each other. 'It's good to fight, but remember, your enemy is someone else, you've got to learn to fight them.'

On another occasion, Kapil noticed a Mukti Bahini trainee fumbling with the practice mines and took him aside to ask why. Atharuddin Talukdar confessed he suffered from acute long-sightedness. The Dacca University student had lost his glasses in the melee of fleeing Bangla Desh. He had hidden this fact from his recruiters and from C2P authorities when he reported at the camp in late June. Kapil sent him off to Krishnanagar to get a prescription and a new pair of glasses. On his return, Talukdar was an unusual sight in C2P. His thick, black-framed spectacles made him stand apart.

Recruits could leave the camp only in unusual circumstances like Talukdar's. Two 'welfare officers' set up tent inside the camp as soon as C2P had begun training. These were Bengali-speaking operatives from the State Intelligence Bureau, the IB's local unit, tasked with keeping a tab on the training and to ensure no spies infiltrated the camp.

NCO(X)'s strategists had envisioned the naval commando war as a 'build to last' campaign like the Vietnam War. If the early batches of commandos were either killed or captured, as they feared, more would have to take their place. The operation thus needed a steady assembly line of recruits. Nanda, in all his visits to the camp, asked his officers to 'think big' and authorized an expansion of recruits. These were the same sentiments he expressed when the defence ministry frowned upon the construction of the lavish WNC mess for officers in Bombay – Kapil's den – in the late 1960s. 'We will build it only once; let's do a good job of it,' he reportedly said.

Kapil and Das had established an efficient recruitment system. Light-weight units would visit refugee camps to select youth based on rigorous criteria – aptitude, swimming skills, educational background and dedication to the cause. This process became the camp's recruitment blueprint. After doing the initial groundwork, both the officers concentrated on training and work-up, while senior CD sailors were sent for recruitments under a specialist recruiter whom Samant brought into the operation in June. Surgeon Lt Commander A. Abraham, a medical officer and submarine specialist screened volunteers for the navy's submarine arm. Operating out of Samant's office for a month in Fort William, he visited youth camps in various sectors to select and screen volunteers for the operation. The surgeon toured the border camps to personally select 150 naval commando volunteers.

Meanwhile, the soluble plug in the limpet mine was proving to be a four-inch–long problem that evaded a solution. Thirty minutes was way too short a time for mission success – a diver could be in the water for nearly an hour. And then, one night, over drinks at the camp, one of the exasperated X-men shouted, 'Why not slip a condom on the damn thing?'

Yes, why not? There was laughter.

But then, a few days later, they actually did it. A condom was procured from a local medical shop, wrapped around the soluble plug and lowered into the water. It sat there undisturbed. It had worked – a solution so simple, they wondered why the answer had evaded them for so long.

A standard operating procedure was drawn up. An assault swimmer would roll the condom over the soluble plug before he swam to the target vessel. Once he reached the shipside, he would peel the condom away and stick the limpet mine on the side of the target. He now had thirty minutes to swim to safety.

In Fort William, Samant raised an eyebrow over Lt Cdr Martis's indent for a large supply of condoms until a guffawing Martis assured him: 'Sir, it's not for what you are thinking!'

The X-men were far from home and incommunicado. Their absence was not unusual because naval families were used to their kin sailing for weeks and months on overseas deployments.

Letters were written home, but personnel were specifically asked not to reveal where they were based. The mail was despatched to the 2 Sikh LI camp, from where they passed through military censors before reaching the family. They could not reveal, for instance, that the camp had no electricity or running water. Shaves and haircuts were unheard of luxuries. The men marked their time by the length of their hair. The clouds of mosquitos that descended on the camp could be kept at bay only by applying a foul-smelling military-issue ointment that came in thumb-sized bottles.

C2P thus functioned as an island of military intrigue amidst nature. Nightfall only accentuated the camp's solitude. The deathly stillness was only interrupted by stridulating crickets, the bark of village dogs and the distant gurgle of the Bhagirathi.

There were no radios, no newspapers and no entertainment. The exhausted trainees fell asleep almost as soon as they hit the floor of their tent, some using their plates as pillows. A few sat up at night talking amongst themselves and occasionally sang Bengali folk songs.

A few tents away, the X-men sat down together on evenings for their dose of military-issue rum. The tent was lit by a hissing kerosene lamp, the night-sky stretched above them like a diamond-strewn black carpet,

'Saab,' Maninder Singh said as he sat cross-legged on the sheet on the ground, cupping his hands around his glass – basically meant for tea – of rum.

'Mujhe naik banwa do…' (Please give me the rank of a naik.)

'Kya karega naik ban ke?' (What'll you do with that title?) Martis asked.

'Roti chadd jayegi!' (I won't have to make rotis)

In Bombay, Franklin, Bhende and Aku weren't going to let their friend's inexplicable disappearance come in the way of cabin 411's revelry. Aku, now torpedo and anti-submarine officer of the R-class destroyer *INS Rana*, was the DJ – he once played Leapy Lee's '*Little Arrows*' on a loop all night, driving Kapil's friend Lt Shrikant Bhende up the wall.

Across the border, meanwhile, the Pakistan Army's sinister plan for what it called a renegade province, was rapidly unfolding. On 13 June, a 9,000-word story in the UK's *Sunday Times* electrified the world. The two-page story had a one word headline: GENOCIDE. It was written by a Pakistani journalist, Anthony Mascarenhas, who had returned from a ten-day tour of East Pakistan as a journalist embedded with the army that April. What Mascarenhas saw during his travels through East Pakistan shook him to the core. It was clearly a story he could never publish either in the *Morning News* in Karachi, where he worked as assistant editor, or in any other paper in Pakistan. He returned to West Pakistan and sent his wife and five children to London, before himself slipping out to the UK via Afghanistan, never to return. In London, he met Harold Evans of the *Sunday Times* and handed him the manuscript.

In his despatch, Mascarenhas, born into a Goan Catholic family in Belgaum, Karnataka, and who had moved to Karachi, spelt out the method in the madness unfolding in East Pakistan. There were no contradictions in the government's East Bengal policy, Mascarenhas noted: 'East Bengal is being colonised by the Pakistan Army ... This is genocide being conducted with amazing casualness.' He wrote of army men drawing up kill lists, gunning down East Bengalis, the corpses littering the countryside, and the silent shuttered villages where the army rampaged about on 'kill and burn' missions.

As a major-general explained to the reporter, the Pakistan Army aimed at doing a thorough job since it could not be expected to return every four or five years for another round of cleansing. The three elements of the genocide were explained to him (in the Eastern Command HQ in Dacca) as follows: 'Bengalis have proved themselves "unreliable" and must be ruled by the West Pakistanis. The Bengalis would have to be re-educated along proper Islamic lines. This Islamization was intended to eliminate secessionist tendencies and provide a strong religious bond with West Pakistan. When the Hindus have been eliminated by death and flight, their property will be utilized as a golden carrot to win over the underprivileged Muslim middle class. This will provide the base for erecting an administrative and political structure in the future.'

This was an article that changed history, and as Indira Gandhi was to tell Harold Evans over lunch a year later, 'Your article in the *Sunday Times* made me do that. That's why I sent in the army, because I'd read the story of the massacre.'[12]

Tales of brutality, detentions, abductions of Bengali women to be used as sex slaves and mass rape were regularly reported in intelligence briefs and through personal accounts of people pouring in from across the border and hence known to Samant and the navy team in West Bengal. The sheer scale of the pogrom as described by Mascarenhas did worry them.

---

12 Sir Harold Evans, 'The decline of the printed newspaper is a great loss for English', *Open* magazine; 16 June 2017

Three days after this single-most–damning media report of the crisis, Commander Samant was making his own assessment of his naval commandos.

On 17 June, Commander Samant drafted a situation report on C2P to navy chief Admiral Nanda. The first batch of sixty-seven Mukti Fauj volunteers were in training in unarmed combat, infiltration and survival techniques, in addition to advanced swimming techniques. Members of the batch had been teamed off in Task Element organizations – the grouping under which they would be operationally deployed.

The first group had already completed the land-fighting aspects of training in Agartala, and their basic training at the camp would be completed by 19 June. A second batch of thirty volunteers, selected from Hasnabad camp on 14 June, would report to C2P by 17 June.

Procedural bottlenecks in the supply of explosives and small arms had been resolved and the stores would now be delivered by 19 June. Preliminary planning for the operations had already commenced, he said. Lt General Aurora had directed that NCO(X) concentrate on the ports of Chittagong, Chandpur, Khulna/Mongla and Narayanganj during Phase I. 'Arrangements are also being made to establish a chain of safe havens for infiltration,' Samant wrote.

The phone calls home to Vizag became infrequent as he remained immersed in work. 'How is your work with Vaini?' Nirmala Samant casually asked during one of Samant's rare calls home. She was punning on the Mukti Bahini with the Marathi word for sister-in-law.

Samant shrugged and laughed as he guessed what had likely happened. During one of his border recces with the army, he had bumped into an army engineer based near his home in Vizag. In the brief, furtive meeting, the army officer must have guessed why Samant was in a vest and lungi.

In Bangla Desh, meanwhile, Pakistani heliborne troops, backed by artillery, began their offensive against the last rebel-held strongholds in the Belonia Bulge, a finger of territory eleven kilometres wide and twenty kilometres in length that jutted into south-western Tripura. The battle ended on 20 June with the retreat of rebel forces into Tripura. 'We were holding no territory of our own, except for a few square miles along the Indian border in Comilla and Sylhet sectors. A long-drawn, protracted guerrilla war had taken birth,' Mukti Bahini officer Major M. Rafiqul Islam noted.[13]

With C2P humming like a well-oiled machine, none of the trainers could be spared from their training duties. So, one day, Kapil and Das took the camp's three-tonner for the 100-kilometre drive south to the army's Kanchrapara ammunition depot in Barrackpore district. This was where they were to pick up the camp's fresh supply of training ordnance – nearly three tonnes of plastic explosives, detonators, TNT blocks and detonating cords. During their return through pouring rain, the truck – filled with nearly three tonnes of high explosives, lost control and skidded over a flooded causeway before screeching to a halt. The divers thanked their stars at the narrow escape as they drove to the camp.

One day, in the stifling heat of June, a hush descended over C2P. The naval commando trainees had paused their cross-country runs and swims. All the camp officials crowded on the riverbank south of the camp, their eyes fixed on an eight-feet–high steel plate anchored in the sand. Lt Cdr Martis sloshed through waist-high water, carrying a hemispherical limpet mine in his hand. The three-tonner had ferried in the six-feet–wide, eight-feet–high steel plate which mimicked a ship's hull – from Calcutta. Trainees had dug it into the shallows near the river and ringed it with sandbags. The camp

---

13 Major M. Rafiqul Islam, *A Tale of Millions* (Dacca: Adeylebros & Co.), 1974

commander was now going to personally test the ARDE-developed prototype that used Commander Pantle's soluble plug. Martis waded into the water and placed the limpet mine underwater with both hands. The magnets latched onto the plate with a clunk. The team then walked back from the plate towards the shore. Fifteen minutes later, a spout of water blossomed out of the water and a dull explosion resounded through the camp. The underwater shockwave caught Martis by surprise, nearly knocking him off his feet. He gritted his teeth and composed himself. The men were watching. He was more interested in the plate, which still stood erect on the riverbed, seemingly intact. The plate was brought ashore for an inspection. The obverse side had opened up like a steel flower. The limpet had punched right through. 'This is how it works, boys!' Martis was ecstatic. The explosion, was proof of concept. Limpet Mine Mark 1, designed, built and tested by the navy in record time. The mine went into mass production at the Ordnance Factory in Khamaria near Jabalpur in Madhya Pradesh. 650 mines would eventually be made until December.

In NHQ Delhi, Nanda and his staff worked feverishly to prepare for the coming conflict, dividing their curious mix of British- and Soviet-built warships between the eastern and western theatres. NHQ had binned its British-era Indian staff manual and decided on aggressive deployments for its forces.

The western fleet would deliver Nanda's left hook – the attack on Karachi. The Eastern Naval Command's broad plans were to strangle the Pakistan Army's sea supply lanes from West Pakistan to the Eastern sea ports of Chalna–Mongla and Chittagong

C2P was not the navy's only closely guarded secret in mid-1971. Another one was the news of the rupture in one of the *Vikrant*'s four steam boilers. This meant that the carrier could not do top-speed, for the boiler could burst. A replacement, which would take the carrier out for several months, was not an option. War was coming. The navy thus decided to weld a metal strip on to the boiler and halved the carrier's top speed to just fourteen knots. As a naval assessment noted with considerable worry, this was also the top speed of a Daphné-class submarine like the *Mangro*. So, by June 1971, Admiral Nanda had decided to deploy the *Vikrant* to the Bay of Bengal, where the possibility of Pakistan deploying its shorter-ranged Daphnés was low. The carrier would be escorted by the Foxtrot-class submarine *INS Khanderi*, Petya-class corvettes – the *Kavaratti* and *Kamorta* – and a vintage 'R'-class destroyer, the *INS Ranjit* for a right hook in the east. These were eventually placed under the newly created Eastern Naval Fleet created on 1 November that year.

In July, major global realignments caused serious worry in New Delhi. On 15 July, President Nixon stunned the world with his announcement of a visit to China by February 1972. The announcement was the culmination of several months of what was called ping-pong ball diplomacy – the invitation for a US table tennis team to visit China. It had been preceded by covert diplomacy undertaken by Nixon's Machiavellian Secretary of State and National Security Advisor Henry Kissinger. Pakistan, particularly its military dictator General Yahya Khan, had played a significant part in this realignment. Kissinger had embarked on a visit to the subcontinent during which he met Prime Minister Indira Gandhi in New Delhi on 7 July and told her that the US would not support India if it went to war over Bangla Desh.[14] Flying across the border to Islamabad the next day, the Secretary of State had feigned a stomach illness which

14 Katharine Frank, *Indira: The Life of Indira Nehru Gandhi* (New Delhi: HarperCollins Publishers), 2001

would need him to recuperate at a nearby hill station. A mock convoy with a Secret Service agent pretending to be the Secretary of State was even driven to Nathiagali, even as Kissinger boarded a PIA Boeing 707 aircraft from Islamabad's Chaklala air force base to China, where he met Chinese premier Zhou En Lai to discuss the Nixon summit. It was the first official contact between China and the US in over two decades and explained the Nixon administration's prominent Pakistan tilt during the crisis. The US not only wanted to reduce the threat from a nuclear-armed adversary, it wanted to use the Sino-Soviet split to open a new Cold War front against the Soviet Union. Kissinger even offered to withdraw US troops from Taiwan, which China called a 'renegade province', in exchange for Chinese assistance in ending the war in Vietnam.

During the series of meetings over two days, Zhou blamed India for the situation in East Pakistan because it was supporting Bangla Desh and had allowed a 'headquarters' for the movement to be set up on Indian territory.

Kissinger assured Zhou that the US was bringing all the influence it could bear on India to try and prevent a war. Zhou said it was a good thing, but the US was 10,000 miles away. China, however, was much closer. Zhou recalled the Chinese defeating India in 1962 and hinted rather broadly that the same thing could happen again. The Chinese premier said that Pakistan was militarily weaker but its morale and fighting capacity were greater than India's.

Zhou's final words in the meeting were a request to Kissinger to convey to Yahya Khan that in case India committed aggression, China would support Pakistan.[15]

---

15 William Burr, ed, National Security Archive Electronic Briefing Book No. 66 (September 1970–July 1971), 27 February 2002

The Vietnam War that the Nixon–Kissinger duo were so keen to end also had a naval guerrilla element. The North Vietnamese Army (NVA) had established naval sapper units, comprising military demolitions engineers, tasked with attacking shipping and infrastructure near the waterways of south Vietnam. A naval sapper group was activated in North Vietnam to train water (naval) sappers and by October 1968 it had trained between twelve and fifteen five-man companies, nine of which had infiltrated into the Republic of Vietnam. The first significant appearance of swimmer-placed mines was in May 1966 in the Nha Be Harbour. On 26 May 1966, swimmers mined three ships, one of which was holed and subsequently beached. On 15 August 1966, mines were placed under two bridges near Dong Tam in Dinh Tuong Province.[16]

In the subcontinent, the uninterrupted flow of refugees into India was making a powerful case for India going to war with Pakistan. By 31 July, 7.2 million Bangla Deshi refugees had entered India – a number that would go up to 9.8 million by December. Eighty-two per cent of them were Hindus, 17 per cent Muslim, and less than 1 per cent Buddhists and Christians. The government was forced to divert its already meagre resources to feed them. To maintain eight million refugees in camps for six months, at the rate of Rs 3 per day, per person, would cost Rs 4,320 million, or about US $576 million. A World Bank report estimated that this could rise to $700 million during the fiscal year 1971–72. The influx threatened the demographics of states like Assam and especially Tripura, where they made up over two-thirds of the population.[17]

---

16 United States Mission in Vietnam, Saigon, 'The Impact of the Sapper on the Viet-Nam War: Background Paper', October 1969

17 S.N. Prasad and U.P. Thapliyal, *The India–Pakistan War of 1971 A History* (New Delhi: Natraj Publishers), 2014

'The butchery of unarmed people had so far taken a million lives … another nine million had to flee the country to save their lives … The flight of this mass of humanity can only be comprehended by imagining the total evacuation of the city of New York,' a release from the Bangla Desh mission in Washington, DC, grimly noted.

Amidst these swirling global developments in late July, a naval officer in plainclothes reported for duty at Samant's office in Fort William. It was Lt Cdr 'Aku' Roy, Kapil's mercurial pilot pal from 310 Squadron, pulled away from his wild ways in Bombay and flown to Calcutta by Captain Roy.

Aku, the half Bengali-half Estonian, looked like a Pathan. He spoke the local language, was an excellent swimmer and had maritime roots – his maternal grandfather had been a merchant navy captain.

Perhaps these were the qualities the naval intelligence chief Captain Roy ticked off as he recruited him for the covert mission. What the senior Roy had missed, however, was the young pilot's reluctance to do anything other than fly. Samant sensed this as he briefed Roy about his mission. Aku's friends from the 310 Squadron would have understood why. Their pilot buddy was a dyed-in-the-wool aviator who cared for nothing more than flying. He opted for the branch straight after graduating from the seventeenth course of the NDA, trained as a pilot with the IAF, and was assigned to the Indian Naval Air Squadron 310 in 1964. There, he swiftly qualified for 'catapult assisted take off and arrested landing'. Over the years, he had developed a deep bond with the Alizé and, as Samant discovered, Roy already had a Nao Sena Medal under his belt in 1969 for displaying 'professional skill, courage and presence of mind' while executing a near-perfect ditching in the choppy Bay of Bengal and evacuating two fellow crewmen after his throttle failed during an ASW exercise off the *Vikrant*.

The Alizé was no fast jet. Its modest patrol speed (just over 300 kmph) enabled the aircraft to prowl over the sea, sniffing for submarines. Against a fast-moving Sabre or Starfighter, the turboprop was a sitting duck. But Aku had figured out what he would do if he ever came across a Pakistani jet. He would fly even slower. 'Fly low, drop my speed, lower my undercarriage,' as he explained to his squadron mate Lt S. Gopalakrishnan.

In Calcutta, Aku was soon on another slow-moving military aircraft. Not the one he would have wanted to be in, though. It was the IAF courier flight to Agartala. He was accompanied by Cdr Samant. The submariner and the submarine hunter were poles apart, physically and temperamentally. Aku was a child of two worlds. As he told Samant, his father, Major General Amar Nath Roy was studying medicine in pre-War London's St Bartholomew hospital when he had met the pretty Irana Juliana Kastni. Irana, a native of Estonia's Baltic seaside town Kasmu, had been sent to London by her sea captain father to study English. The couple had met, fallen in love and got married, a union stridently opposed by Roy Senior's deeply conservative Bengali family in Allahabad. The family warmed up after Irana learnt their language and draped a Bengali saree. Resistance ended when Niila, Ashok, and their siblings – Alok and Indira – were born.

In Agartala, Samant escorted NCO(X)'s new pointsman to Brigadier Shahbeg Singh's camp. As decided earlier, much to the brigadier's chagrin, Aku would control all the operational aspects of the naval commandos.

The operation had to achieve complete surprise. Roy and Samant accorded highest priority to operational secrecy. The location of camps, nature of training and the personnel were cloaked in secrecy. Samant ensured none of his team either wore a uniform or contacted local navy units. C2P was referred to as 'Camp Watermanship' in NCO(X)'s coded communications. Its location was never mentioned. Lungi and vests were standard uniform for trainers and civilians. For conducting business outside the camp, officials changed into shorts and T-shirts. The operative words in NCO(X) were need-to-know. In Delhi, Admiral Nanda had decided that even Captain Oscar Stanley Dawson, his sharp director of naval operations, needn't know. Few officers even in the Naval Intelligence Directorate knew of the operation. Even inside the operation, the information was so siloed that even bosom buddies Kapil and Aku didn't know they were at two ends of the same operation, in tents just 300 kilometres apart.

In Calcutta, meanwhile, Major General Jacob was directly overseeing Operation Steeplechase. Launched on 1 July, it aimed at suppressing the rural Naxalites who threatened rule of law in the state. West Bengal was under President's Rule and hence directly administered by the Centre through Governor Anthony Lancelot Dias. In one of the army's largest counter-insurgency deployments, the 9th Infantry Division, the 4th Mountain Division and the 50th Parachute Brigade joined the paramilitary and police in cordon-and-search operations through the Bengal countryside.

The Pakistan Army continued its fight against the Mukti Bahini. The 25,000 soldiers airlifted into its eastern province were now turning the tide. The morale of the Bengali guerrillas was at its lowest and they were fighting with their backs to the border with India, where Tiger Niazi's ferocious assault had pushed them. The dream of an independent Bangla Desh, it would seem, was being ground under jackboots.

'In June–July, the Mukti Bahini operated in border areas where Indian troops could support them morally and materially,' wrote Niazi's media advisor Siddiq Salik. 'The rebels, during this phase, behaved very timidly and retreated quickly to their sanctuaries at the slightest sign of detection or counter-action. The main achievements included blowing up of minor culverts, mining abandoned railway tracks, lobbing a grenade or harassing an insignificant political adversary.'[18] Salik called it Phase 1 of the Mukti Bahini operations.

As Major Rafiqul Islam noted ruefully, 'No attempt was made on the enemy leadership. Even top Bengali collaborators were comfortably carrying on their daily activities. A few odd, hasty and unplanned attempts were made on the lives of such people. But those failed and some of the guerrillas were apprehended and killed by the Pakistanis. Enemy logistics areas, HQs, officers' messes, dumps, stores and important sources of power and fuel, ports, railway – all remained untouched. Very few small bridges were damaged by guerrilla action. In June, July and August, guerrillas inflicted perhaps a little more than routine casualty. Foreign radios were broadcasting negative news commentary, portraying the return of normalcy in Bangla Desh. In the diplomatic circles, Bangla Desh became almost a dead issue. We failed to create the desired impact. The rate of attrition had slowed down and the morale of our boys was at the lowest. The Pakistan Army, on the other hand, was in quite a comfortable position – much better than it was up to the middle of June. In the early stage, our regulars had inflicted heavy casualties on the Pakistan Army. Even the most sober estimate after verification from various sources would put the figure between 5,000 and 6,000 dead and 8,000 to 10,000 enemy soldiers injured; at least one-third of whom were physically disabled and unfit for military service.'[19]

Even as the Mukti Bahini agonized over the flailing guerrilla campaign on land, the naval commandos were being convinced

---

18 Siddiq Salik, *Witness to Surrender* (New Delhi: Lancer Publishers), 1977

19 Major M. Rafiqul Islam, *A Tale of Millions* (Dacca: Adeylebros & Co), 1974

about the importance of a new medium using which they would make a difference.

'Work with and respect the current of the river. It will be your greatest ally,' the X-men told their young understudies. This meant swimmers had to go with the flow of the river and literally blend into it. Suspicious directional movement or changes in speed, either while approaching the target or escaping from it, would give them away.

Training began for infiltration, escape and evasion. These skills were usually imparted to special forces who infiltrated enemy territory and were meant to evade detection as they made their way to the target and escaped after carrying out an attack. This was eased by the fact that the operation was being carried out by local Bengali youth. If captured, they had a better chance of convincing the enemy that they were indeed local residents. During operations, they were directed to be dressed in local attire so that, if spotted, they could immediately discard their equipment, weapons and explosives in the water. Upon capture, they were to assume the identity of unwitting locals.

Army instructors who specialized in map reading were brought in to train commandos to recognize vantage points, topographical features, and read available survey maps to identify access and escape routes to and from target areas.

The navy worked out the infiltration plans. They would hand commandos over to the Mukti Bahini sector commanders at border launch points. Thereafter, the Bangla Deshi underground network would take over, providing suitable guides and plugging commandos into the network of safe houses across the border. The guides would escort the commandos in groups of twenty to their targets. Trainees were advised to travel by night and rest by day. Teams were not to exceed four to five members while travelling on land, to avoid raising suspicion.

Samant was once on a routine visit to C2P and was staying in the PWD inspection bungalow. The dusty, glass-enclosed display case on a table in the hall caught his eye. The case was around four-feet-by-four-feet, covered in wood-framed glass and government-issue varnish with 'PWD' stencilled on it. It appeared to be a miniature display of some sort. Samant re-aligned the four scattered squares. A half-hour later, he dusted himself to regard his work with child-like satisfaction – he had uncovered a finely rendered table-top miniature battlefield of Plassey as it was on 23 June 1757. Rows of little chalk-white boxes with green flags depicted Siraj-ud-Daulah's camp near the Bhagirathi's oxbow-like bend. The little green puffs near the bottom depicted the mango orchard – Clive's encampment towards where the Nawab's men had made their final charge. The miniature, by an unknown artist, was to re-emphasise the significance of the location. It only strengthened Samant's paranoia about leaks in the operation. 'I hope there are no Mir Jafars here among you,' he said as he addressed the naval commandos a short while later.

Between 11 and 17 July, significant developments were unfolding in the headquarters of the Bangla Desh government in exile on Calcutta's, 8, Theatre Road. Battered by the Pakistan Army and its newly-raised razakars, the government of Bangla Desh in exile eschewed its conventional military campaign. In the week-long conference, it formally switched to guerrilla warfare, the weaker side's preferred way of warfighting throughout history. Bangla Desh was divided into eleven sectors, each with its own Mukti Bahini sector commander and guerrillas who specialized in hit and run attacks. The guerrillas were under the overall command of the Indian Army's Brigadier Anand Sarup. All Bangla Desh sectors were placed under the commander-in-chief of the Bangla Desh forces, Colonel M.A.G. Osmani. The conventional force, the Liberation Army or Mukti Fauj's existing battalions were divided into brigade groups, each headed by three key East Bengal officers who had mutinied – 'K

Force' under Major Khaled Mosharraf, 'S Force' under Major Kazi
Mohammed Shafiullah and 'Z Force' under Major Ziaur Rahman.

The Indian Army sector commanders coordinated one or more
Bangla Desh force sectors. They continued to report directly to
Major General Jacob and thus formed a vital link between Bangla
Desh Forces HQ and the army's Eastern Command. Operational
policies were drawn up by the Eastern Command and the Bangla
Desh Force HQ, and implemented by the Indian and Bangla Desh
sector HQs.

One sector stood out amongst these, geographically, strategically
and operationally. Sector X was called the 'C-in-C's Special Force.'
It encompassed all the waterbodies of East Pakistan – the Padma,
the Jamuna and the Meghna, the nearly 700 tributaries and the sea
coast. Its operations were directly under Colonel Osmani. The men
who would operate in this sector were being trained to deliver a
covert blow unlike any seen since the Second World War.

These men were being trained to carry out operations in the
dark and being familiarized with the structure and layout of ships,
barges, pontoons and likely targets. They were taught about the
most vulnerable, accessible and effective spots for attaching limpet
mines. The best place to attach the mine was six feet below the
waterline. They had to focus on areas on mid-ship holds, the engine
room, forward holds, and areas in the vicinity of the propellers, near
the propeller shaft and stern glands. The chosen targets, they were
continually reminded, were cargo vessels and those that served the
Pakistani military and transported men and material. They were
also taught to identify other targets of opportunity, like pylons and
bridges. Once they had identified target areas, the next step in target
profiling was to identify the launch points for attack runs. These
had to be upstream, between two and five kilometres or closer,
depending on the security cordon around the target. Commandos
were advised to take advantage of river currents while staging attacks
and escapes. It was important that they lived to fight another day.

5
SECTOR X

Bangla Desh, Bangla Desh
Where so many people are dying fast
And it sure looks like a mess
I've never seen such distress
Now won't you lend your hand
Try to understand
Relieve the people of Bangla Desh[20]

George Harrison, 'the quiet Beatle' was making a splash, playing live before 20,000 cheering Americans at New York City's Madison Square Garden on 1 August 1971. He was accompanied by Indian sitar star Pandit Ravi Shankar. And Ringo Starr. And Bob Dylan. And Eric Clapton. And Billy Preston. This astonishing line-up played at two sold-out benefit shows that day, and raised global awareness about the province's refugees and cyclone-affected people. The 'Concert for Bangla Desh' was the brainchild of Harrison's close friend Ravi Shankar, whose forefathers were natives of Jessore.

---

20 Later released as 'The Concert for Bangla Desh Live' album by George Harrison and Pandit Ravi Shankar

The name for this first-of- its-kind fundraiser should have indicated to Pakistan's military rulers that the writing was on the wall. Bangla Desh was now a country at least in the popular global imagination. It certainly was in all the communications that flowed out of Samant's office. For the Pakistani Army on the rampage in the eastern province, Bangla Desh was a grisly code name – 'for death without trial, without detailed investigations and without any written order by any authorised authority. A Bengali who was alleged to be a Mukti Bahini or an Awami Leaguer was sent to Bangla Desh.'[21]

Just the previous day, on 31 July, Pakistan's president, General Yahya Khan, warned India that 'total war' was very near. And on 3 August, he told PTV in an interview that Sheikh Mujibur Rahman, then in solitary confinement in Lyallpur prison, was arrested for 'political betrayal' and would be brought under trial. Sheikh Mujib, the president said, had inspired armed struggle. The implication was clear and ominous – the punishment for fomenting armed insurrection was death. Death was something Sheikh Mujib's people were fleeing from by the millions.

In August, the flow of refugees into India had turned into a torrent indistinguishable from the monsoon rain. 'Over the rivers and down the highways and along countless jungle paths, the population of East Pakistan continues to infiltrate into India,' TIME magazine's 2 August 1971 cover story 'The Ravaging of Golden Bengal' noted.

In Fort William, Major General B.N. 'Jimmy' Sarkar relieved Major General O.S. Kalkat as director, operations (X). Sarkar was an armoured corps officer, and, like Captain Roy, he hailed from a

---

21 Deposition by Lt Col Mansoorul Haq in 1974, GSO-I, 9 Division, Witness No 260; declassified by the Pakistan Government in the year 2000; https://web.archive.org/web/20120304011310/http://www.pppusa.org/Acrobat/Hamoodur%20Rahman%20Commission%20Report.pdf

zamindar family in East Pakistan. He cut an impressive figure – tall, hair slicked back over his broad face, and an aquiline nose which sat over a coiffed moustache. He was a teetotaller and a widower, not socially gregarious, a hard task master with an eye for detail and a phenomenal capacity for hard work. If he hadn't been a general, Samant figured, he would surely have been a distinguished college professor.

NCO(X)'s covert war was planned at the NHQ with the navy chief Admiral Nanda and Captain Roy giving directives. Samant was responsible for translating these directives into action, taking ground realities into consideration. For him, NHQ directives were paramount as he juggled wishes and inputs from other authorities in the loop – HQ Eastern Command, Eastern Naval Command and the Bangla Desh government in exile.

C2P was the site for the logistics and training unit. Samant's arrival turned it into an operations unit. Operational secrecy dictated that recruits be kept in the camp for as long as possible before being sent to the launch points along the border. The launch pad was a quarantine where they had to be kept in still greater secrecy before being sent across. Samant was assisted by the Jackpot directorate, whose intelligence chief, Colonel Vora, was exclusively focused on East Pakistan and in close contact with the Mukti Bahini.

Samant's camp, meanwhile, was wrestling with issues of its own. On 3 August, Lt Samir Das dashed off a frantic letter to Brigadier Gharaya.

'The flood situation in the locality has deteriorated menacingly, following a sudden increase in the level of the Bhagirathi and subsequent breaches in the bund at a number of places. A vast area around Plassey is already under about six feet of flood water. The camp inmates have been busily engaged round the clock in repairing the bunds and some minor rescue operations for the last few days,'

Das wrote in neat disjointed letters using a waterproof ballpoint pen.[22]

'It is feared that further deterioration of the flood situation will force us to abandon the present camp site. A recce in the nearby areas for an alternative/suitable site was of no avail as almost the whole of Nadia and Murshidabad are under flood waters. Request early suggestions/instruction.'

Tejnagar, a village a few kilometres away, was abandoned a few days later. C2P was shifted a kilometre inland, near the Plassey Monument and the guest house. The men of 2 Sikh LI returned. This time they pitched the camp tents on a four-foot–high, six-foot–wide earthen bund near the factory, built years ago to keep floodwaters out. The flood had turned thousands of acres of sugarcane fields into rotting heaps of mulch. The only crop that would be harvested from the fields of the Ramnugger Cane and Sugar Company Limited would be naval commandos.

The X-men gazed at the rows of brown-bodied youth who had been somewhat miraculously transformed into lithe, sinewy amphibians. Each trainee could swim ten kilometres in the river by day or night, with or without fins, effortlessly run twenty kilometres and could confidently assemble and handle explosives and wield small arms. Their moment of reckoning was approaching that month. Samant had spent the past two months preparing for H-hour. NHQ was only awaiting a nod from the political leadership.

Samant had been trained by the Soviets in the chilly Baltic to manoeuvre his Foxtrot-class submarine in relentless pursuit of warships and merchantmen. When he caught up with them, he would launch torpedoes at them without pity. It was time for him to put all that training down on paper.

---

22 Captain M.N.R. Samant's family archives

Captain Roy's original concept note in April where he called for coordinated strikes to effectively block Chalna/Mongla, Khulna and Chittagong by sinking ships, had laid out the big picture. Sometime in July, Samant sat down in his office in Fort William to minutely detail the mission. He drafted the attack plan on clean unruled sheets of paper in small, disjointed letters, in a handwriting similar to that of the inscrutable Captain Roy's. NCO(X) was going to war.

Situation: The territory of Bangla Desh is under complete occupation by the West Pakistan forces

Own Forces: Mukti Fauj volunteers trained in underwater sabotage techniques and free swimming. Their numbers at the time of writing this order is 357. The volunteers have been selected from different localities in Bangla Desh in order to ensure terrain familiarisation. Further, they have been subdivided into Task Elements (short title: TE) for ease of control.

Intelligence has indicated that West Pakistan forces were firmly established in the main cities of Bangla Desh. Further, it will be reasonable to presume that their organization and security in the principal sea ports of Chittagong, Mongla and Chalna will be extremely efficient, since these ports are the arteries which ensure smooth flow of goods and services to the entire Bangla Desh. Brief state of affairs at Chittagong and Mongla/Chalna are as follows:

a) Chittagong: a small number of jetties and storage sheds for goods have been destroyed. Ninety per cent of the present port workers have been inducted from Karachi. The harbour appears to be functioning normally.

b) Mongla/Chalna: A large quantity of jute awaiting export. Ships continue to be at buoys/anchorage and are carrying out cargo operations using own handling appliances.

The mission during Phase I shall be to cause maximum damage to merchant shipping, irrespective of nationality, in the ports of

Chittagong, Chandpur, Narayanganj and Chalna/Mongla complex by carrying out simultaneous attacks by free swimmers.

The order of performance for destruction of targets shall be as under:

a) Merchant ships, irrespective of nationality.
b) Warships – minor and major, in that order. However, should a situation arise when a minor and major warship be observed alongside each other, then both of them shall be attacked.
c) Auxiliary vessels – such as port trust tugs, pilot/customs boats, lighters, barges and IWT ships.
d) Dry docks, patent slips.
e) Shore installations such as cranes, port power stations, oil dumps.
f) Navigational aids, including shore transits, beacons, lighter, Decca Master and slave stations at Comilla, Mymensingh, Jessore and Chittagong.

Preliminary practical deployment: With a view to inculcating self-confidence, accumulating experience and to weed out organisational lacunae, it is intended to deploy fully trained personnel in small groups to carry out pin-prick raids along the border under the overall direction of the Commander 'C' sector. During these raids, as far as possible, care will be taken to ensure that these groups do not come in contact with major Pakistani regular or paramilitary forces.

Preliminary movement: As against a normal land raid carried out by the Mukti Force personnel, the task elements involved in the naval aspect of Operation Jackpot will have to penetrate deeper into Bangla Desh territory and stay there undetected till D-Day. Further, they will have to carry special naval equipment in addition to the normal small arms. It will therefore be essential to establish a series of safe havens inside Bangla Desh, where the members of task elements can seek shelter.

In this respect, I have been informed by Surgeon Lt Cdr A. Abraham who has met Major Khaled Mosharaff and Major Zafiullah that such havens have already been established at Narayanganj, Chandpur, Naokhali, Nabinagar, Faridpur, Munshiganj, Damra, Narsingdi and Daudkandi.

As is clear, Samant left nothing to chance.

Timing of the attacks: Attacks to be carried out during dark hours with minimum moon conditions. In July, the last quarter commences on the fifteenth, with the new moon occurring on the twenty-second. However, the meteorological data indicates that cloudy skies with torrential rains and about six thunder storms occur in Bangla Desh during the month of July. This may prove to be of advantage as it will slacken vigil kept by sentries.

Method of attack: The attacker must enter the water upstream. This will ensure comparatively effortless arrival at the target. The getaway must be made downstream for similar reasons.

Target allocation: Each Task Element shall engage one target. Ships alongside and at trots must be engaged with utmost co-ordination in order to avoid mutual interference and uncoordinated detonations. (Major warships such as the *PNS Babur* must be engaged with at least two Task Elements.)

Ship attacks: Of merchant ships 'A' brackets[23] and amidships below the water line as possible.

---

23 Triangular bracket that extends from the hull of a powered vessel to give support to the propeller shafts

PNS Babur: 'A' brackets, boiler room area and forepeak[24] – all charges as deep as possible.

Minor war vessels: Amidships. Ships and shore installations with limpets. Buoyage and cables with plastic explosives.

Action on attacking charges: All Task Elements must clear the area of operation on satisfactory attaching of charges or setting of PEK. The route of escape must be downstream, entering land about 4–5 miles downstream. Fins and other equipment used for carrying out attack must be discarded prior to leaving the water. The main aim thereafter is to escape back to India by the quickest means, using earlier havens for safety. The members of the TE are to disclose their identity to the Indian sector commanders on entering Indian territory with request for immediate transportation to Camp Watermanship.

Action on being detected: Immediately ditch fins and naval ordnance; if possible, attach limpet mines to the nearest installations, vehicles – after having set them to minimum delay.

Equipment to be carried: In addition to the standard small arms carried by the army counterparts, each member of the Naval Task Force will carry the following:

1 pair fins per person

3 limpet mines per T.E.

The orders were typed out and put in the green-jacketed file named 'NCO(X)' and locked in the safe in Samant's office. It was so sensitive that the submariner took it by hand to the bosses on the floor above him. It was so hot, he joked with Major General Jacob, that he needed insulated gloves.

---

24 The section of a ship's hold that is within the angle made by the bow, used for trimming or for storage of cargo

Admiral Nanda, meanwhile, was fighting off pressure from General Maneckshaw to send the naval commandos into battle. He would send them into Bangla Desh only if they were trained fully and knew what was required to be done. He was not prepared to risk lives unnecessarily.

The navy chief was clear about the navy's task in the operation, which he conveyed to the X-men on multiple occasions – they were only to train the Bangla Deshi personnel and never to cross the border or join them in operations. For the navy, it was unfamiliar ground across the border. The best people to operate there, he told them, were the Bangla Deshis. He didn't want naval personnel caught and accused of sabotage in a foreign country.[25] Captain Roy's initial briefing gave lieutenants Kapil and Das the impression that they would lead the first wave of clandestine attacks into East Pakistan. Nanda's directives overruled this plan. As they did another one, which dealt with a back-up plan for the diving instructors to lead trans-border operations in case the Mukti Bahini volunteers were not up to standard. By early August, their fears were belied. Lt Cdr Martis had selected an all-Bangla Deshi unit for the mission – a total of 178 naval commandos and leaders. The numbers were close to what DNI Roy had envisaged for Phase I – 150 commandos in five batches of thirty assault swimmers.

NCO(X)'s smallest unit was the 'Task Element' – a team of three naval commandos. Ten task elements made up a 'Task Unit' or a total of thirty combat swimmers. Four task units made up a complete Task Group of 120 commandos. Their primary weapon, the Indian-made limpet mine Mark-I, was now in full production. The half-hemispherical limpets were called 'footballs' in the coded

---

25 Admiral Nanda's interview with Vice Admiral G.M. Hiranandani, Nanda family archives, May 1996

communication that pinged between NHQ and Fort William, Charlie and Delta Sectors, to be used by 'footballers'.

Samant called the first wave of assault swimmers that would strike inside Bangla Desh 'Task Force 54' (or 'TF 54', in their coded communications). They would operate under director of operations (X), Major General Jimmy Sarkar. Samant was commander, Task Group 54.1, with four task units under him, comprising the assault swimmers led by the ex-*Mangro* crew – 54.1.1: Chittagong, under the command of A.W. Chowdhury; 54.1.2: Chandpur, under Badiul Alam; 54.1.3: under M. Ahsanullah in Narayanganj; and Task Unit 54.1.4: for Mongla/Chalna complex was under Mohammad Rahmatulla.

These appointments of the Task Unit commanders, as Samant noted, had been vetted by his naval staff at C2P – Martis, Kapil and Das. The four commanders would be attached to the various Bangla Desh sector commanders in whose geographical area they would operate. The four targets were within a scalene triangle, with a perimeter of nearly 600 kilometres. Narayanganj just twenty kilometres south of Dacca was the northern point, the Mongla-Chalna complex the western point, and Chittagong its eastern extremity. The *Mangro* crew were finally going back to fight for their country. All 178 commandos knew the general target areas of their attack. But 'H-hour', the precise time of attack, was kept a secret from even the Task Force commanders keeping operational secrecy in mind. Even if one of the commandos was captured by the Pakistanis, he would not be able to reveal the plan.

The X-men devised two signals. The first was the stand-by alert – H-hour minus 48, which meant that the attack had to be carried out in forty-eight hours. This signal would be repeated twice. The second, the 'go ahead' signal would be flashed twenty-four hours before the start of the operation. The means to recognize these signals was revealed only to the four Task Unit commanders, each of whom was briefed individually.

Samant wanted the task units to be in their target area 'at least by D minus 2' – two days before D-Day.

The order to move the commandos to their launch pads turned NCO(X) from a training unit into an operational one. The months of training and the familiarity developed at C2P came handy for the X-men to launch their motivated trainees in what the navy believed were suicide missions. All the commandos were lined up and individually photographed in the camp, the mugshots inserted into their personal dossiers in Fort William. Launch pads in Charlie and Delta sectors were activated for the push. At C2P and in Aku Roy's camp at Delta Sector, the X-men conducted the final checks over the first batch of limpet mines, assembling and disassembling them and testing their 'football spikes', the codename for the detonators before handing them over to the naval commandos.

Aku was to select suitable periods for the commandos to attack, guide last-minute checks prior to their cross-border insertion, check their equipment, and to conduct their pre-departure briefings. When the commandos returned after their mission, the aviator was to debrief them and ensure their speedy return to C2P.

Chittagong was to be the fulcrum of the operations. Since May, Captain Rafiqul Islam, the Mukti Bahini commander of Sector I which covered Chittagong as well, had been collecting information about the port, river traffic and duty habits of the sentries guarding it. On 28 July, Captain Islam sat for more than four hours with Brigadier Shabeg Singh, studying maps and charts of the port and the Karnaphulli River, moon timings, meteorological conditions, tide tables, wind speeds, direction speed of water current, and scores of other details deemed critical for this operation.[26]

The commandos would be infiltrated and attached to the various sector commanders in their areas of operation and live in safe houses

---

26 Major M. Rafiqul Islam, *A Tale of Millions* (Dacca: Adeylebros & Co), 1974

provided by the government of free Bangla Desh. Without safe houses and guides, the operation could not succeed.

The commandos were initially divided into groups of three, each armed with one limpet mine. This group was later increased to five when it became evident that three limpet mines were insufficient to seriously cripple a medium-sized merchant ship. This increase also catered for drop-outs by trainees en-route. Each team included at least two locals to ensure familiarity with the terrain.

Every commando was issued one limpet mine, a pair of Abee swim fins, one floating knife and Rs 50 in Pakistani currency – Rs 20 as 'induction money' and Rs 30 as ration money. During prolonged periods in operational areas, the commandos were expected to live off the land. Group leaders were given additional sums of Pakistani rupees to hire boats and for other emergency spends. Each of the four group leaders was also issued a portable National Panasonic 3-band radio with a brown leather cover. The imported plastic-bodied radio sets were eight inches wide, weighed a kilo, and were powered by three 1.5-Volt dry battery cells. Each group was given one 9 mm Sterling carbine, a spare loaded magazine and hard rations – pounded rice and sweet shakarpara.

The commandos were moved to Indian sectors opposite the eastern, southern and south-western parts of Bangla Desh as their launch points. For reaching targets in western Bangla Desh, the infiltration points at Taki, Hasnabad and Jalangi were used.

For Chittagong and Narayanganj, commandos were moved via the IAF courier flight out of Dum Dum airport to Agartala. Here, they were in the care of Aku Roy's naval detachment in Delta Sector from where guides escorted them on foot into Bangla Desh.

In Fort William, Samant had worked out the infiltration plans and the time the naval commandos would take to reach the target. For Chittagong, it took approximately three days. For Narayanganj, around forty-eight hours. The commandos were infiltrated from

Mantoli, about twenty-five kilometres from Agartala in Tripura. From there, they followed a land and water route through Madhapur – Badair Bmpana-Bader Bazar, and on to Narayanganj.

It took two-and-a-half days to reach Chandpur and Daudkandi areas. The infiltration routes were through Bakshinagar in Meghalaya. The commandos had to follow a land and water route that would take them through Debidwar and on to Chandpur. Commandos took the longest – three to four days – to reach target areas in Mongla, Barisal and Khulna. They had to infiltrate via boat, sailing through the unguarded Sundarbans from Hasnabad. Selected Indian Navy officers including Samant were initially deputed to accompany the groups up to the infiltration point. A number of local boats were either purchased or hired to provide riverine transport.

In distant New Delhi, India was putting its pronounced Soviet tilt to paper. On 9 August, Foreign Minister Swaran Singh signed what was to be the single most significant treaty ever signed by the Indian Republic. The most consequential part of the Indo–Soviet Peace and Friendship Treaty initialled by Singh and his visiting counterpart, Foreign Minister Andrei Gromyko in New Delhi, was Article IX: 'In the event of either being subjected to an attack or a threat thereof, the High Contracting Parties shall immediately enter into mutual consultations in order to remove such a threat and to take appropriate effective measures to ensure peace and the security of their countries.'

The treaty, a response to the emerging Washington–Beijing–Islamabad axis, gave Mrs Gandhi a massive insurance policy for the risky course of action her government was now free to pursue. But first, there was the need to save Sheikh Mujibur Rahman, whose execution seemed imminent.

On 10 August, she dashed off a message to world leaders, urging Sheikh Mujib's release, expressing fear that he could be hanged after a secret trial. Foreign Minister Swaran Singh sent out a message to UN Secretary General U. Thant expressing shock over the announcement of his trial and urged the secretary general to take urgent steps to request the Pakistani government to desist.

10 August was also the day that Task Unit 54.1.1 under the command of A.W. Chowdhury was launched across the border into Bangla Desh along with sixty naval commandos. It must have seemed like a remarkable coincidence – the launch order came just a day after the ink had dried on the landmark Indo-Soviet document.

Chowdhury's task unit was divided into three groups of twenty commandos each, all of them disguised in lungis and torn vests. In one hand, the former submariner carried his National Panasonic radio set encased in a brown leather cover, while the other hand held a double-wrapped plastic bag with four small, unmarked, cotton-lined tins. These tins held sixty detonators that were to fit into the limpet mines. The most dangerous man in the Pakistan Navy was on the prowl again.

6
JACKPOT

'*Amar putul aajke pratham jahe susur badi...* '[27]

A rati Mukherjee's voice trilled across the Bengal countryside, the innocent exuberance of a young girl excited about sending dolls to her in-laws' home. But in a small mud hut on the outskirts of Chittagong, A.W. Chowdhury's hair stood on end, the adrenaline pumping through his veins at the start of the song.

It was 6.00 a.m. on 13 August 1971. Chowdhury awakened Shah Alam, who was sleeping on the mud floor beside him. Both of them regarded each other meaningfully and stared at the transistor radio on the floor of the house as Arati sang on.

'Dadu,' Shah Alam whispered, 'the song is playing.'

Chowdhury's thoughts drifted back to the tent in C2P where Lt Cdr Martis and Cdr Samant had played the songs for him and three hand-picked *PNS Mangro* crewmen – every day, for a week. Shah Alam was the only other person in Task Unit 54.1.1 who knew why his commander anxiously tuned in to All India Radio's B station in

---

27 *Chhotoder Gaan*, album of children's songs, composed by Sailen Mukherjee, HMV, 1965

Calcutta at six in the morning and at the same hour in the evening, every single day since they left India.

Arati Mukherjee's song was the signal for 'stand by' – H-hour minus 48 – for the four task unit commanders inside Sector X. Encrypted messages on civilian radio frequencies were a simple but effective tool used extensively by the Allied Forces to direct and coordinate with resistance fighters against the Nazis in Europe during the Second World War. No one knew the importance of coded communication better than Leading Telegraphist Chowdhury, formerly the radio operator on the *PNS Mangro* and, before that, the *PNS Ghazi*.

Across East Pakistan, three of Chowdhury's buddies from the *Mangro* – Badiul Alam in Chandpur, Rahmatullah in Mongla/ Chalna complex and Ahsanullah in Narayanganj – also heard the directives from Naval Commando Operations (X)'s (NCO [X]) unseen commanders, telling them to prepare for the attack.

All the commandos were in deep cover, in safe houses near their target areas across the country. Now, they proceeded with alacrity towards their targets.

The last few days had been a blur. Chowdhury's task unit – with sixty naval commandos – was the largest one. They had bid farewell to the X-men in Camp C2P and boarded an IAF courier flight at the Dum Dum airport in Calcutta. The IAF Fairchild Packet brought them to Delta Sector and its naval detachment headed by Aku Roy. The guides provided by the Sector I commander Captain Rafiqul Islam led Chaudhury's task unit through Srinagar, an Indian border village in the Belonia pocket in Tripura. The group travelled barefoot and in disguise, trekking for nearly three days through Mirsarai and Sitakund to finally reach the outskirts of Chittagong on 9 August.

Now, with less than forty-eight hours to go for the big strike, they were in the safe house hut of an overground worker in a village, Chotto Komira, some eighty kilometres north of Chittagong. They hid in the house by day and stepped out only at night, with Chowdhury diligently tuning into the radio station twice every day. The mines were hidden under a haystack in a shed near their hut.

This was the routine every day, ever since they left Tripura for Chittagong, Bangla Desh's second-largest city. Chowdhury's mother was a native of Chittagong, but she had passed away when he was twelve, and so he rarely visited the city. A little over 200 km south-east of the capital Dacca, the port city of Chittagong, with a population of four million, was the province's maritime gateway – what Bombay was to western India and Karachi was to West Pakistan. In 1971, the city was also the Pakistan Army's lifeline for food, arms and ammunition.

Chittagong port was on the western bank of the Karnaphulli River which began in the Lushai Hills of Mizoram, a state bordering India and Burma. The river formed an S-like loop before emptying into the Bay of Bengal.

Deep-draughted merchant ships sailed fifteen kilometres upriver on the navigation channel before berthing to pick up their cargo of jute, coir and tea. The Pakistan Navy operated off pontoons – floating metal jetties that offered temporary anchoring facilities for its warships and gunboats.

NCO(X) had by now gathered intelligence on the targets. The port was busy with merchant ships and gunboats. The Pakistani freighters *MV Ohrmazd* and *MV Al-Abbas* had pulled into Chittagong just days prior, laden with military supplies. The *Ohrmazd*, with 9,910 tons of military cargo, berthed on Jetty 13, while the *Al-Abbas*, with 10,418 tons, was berthed at Jetty 12. Over 200 tons of arms and ammunition had been offloaded into the dumb barge *Orient No 6* that was now waiting for a tow-tug to take her to Dacca. The naval jetty also had four Pakistan Navy gunboats.

Soon after receiving the H-minus 48 signal, Chowdhury and Shah Alam moved to a safe house in Chittagong's commercial hub, the Agrabad area which was a stone's throw away from the harbour. A third group of twenty commandos were put up in safe houses in Fauzdar Haat, further away from the city.

The city offered the best possible hideouts in close proximity to each other; and so, forty members of the task unit, divided into sub-units of twenty, stayed here in rooms dotting a warren of lanes – Sutarypara, Rangipara and Hajipara.

Inside the city, Chowdhury relied on Khurshed, one of his most resourceful naval commandos, for the lay of the land. Khurshed was a Chittagong native and knew the city like the back of his hand. He was the first commando to be sent in for a recce mission into the city to link up with Maulvi Syed, a key underground resistance leader, and vet the safe houses before Chowdhury and the commandos could enter.

For launching his limpeteers, Chowdhury's task unit would have to go upstream. This meant exiting the city and going over across to the Karnaphulli's eastern bank – a formidable, risk-filled assignment, for Chittagong was crawling with the Pakistan Army, and rumours had already started swirling that the freedom fighters would strike on 14 August, Pakistan National Day, which was also the first since the 25 March uprising. The city was in a complete lockdown. The streets had been barricaded by checkpoints manned by gun-toting Pakistan armymen. Chowdhury's unit had to transport the forty-man strike team out of the city to Charlakhya on the eastern bank of the Karnaphulli without arousing suspicion. But how? They would need motor transport, which was a problem.

Chittagong had hundreds of buses and three-wheeled autorickshaws called 'baby taxis' which negotiated a sea of human-pedalled cycle-rickshaws. There were very few private cars in the city, and certainly none one could drive around without attracting attention.

At 6.00 a.m. on 14 August, NCO(X) relayed the 'go ahead'
signal to its commandos.

Pankaj Mullick's sonorous voice rendered a popular Rabindranath
Tagore song:

Aami tomai joto, shuniye chchilem gaan …
Aami tomai joto
Taar bodole aami, chaa-i-ne kono daan

Bhoolbe shay gaan jodi, nam-huye je-yo bhoole
Uth-bay jokhon taaraa, shonkho-shaagor-kulay

(All my songs sung to you
sought no reward in exchange

If you forget them, do not forget
that they will rise when the stars rise
in the sky over the shores of the evening ocean)

The signal meant that Chowdhury's Task Unit 54.1.1 had to strike
Chittagong at midnight.

That morning, the resourceful Khurshed came up with an
answer to Chowdhury's logistics problems. On 14 August, he
drove up to Chowdhury's safe house with a white two-door Toyota
pickup truck from the Water and Power Development Authority
(WAPDA), the Pakistani utility suppliers. Accompanying Khurshed
was a local contact and resistance worker. The truck was courtesy
A.K. Altaf, an Awami League sympathiser and WAPDA engineer.
Altaf had left the truck with a full tank of fuel in front of the office
for the resistance worker to drive away. If the vehicle was caught,
Altaf reasoned, he could always explain it was stolen. The vehicle
could ply around the city and past the military checkposts without
arousing suspicion.

At 6.00 that evening, '*Amar putul*' played for a second time on AIR. This was the confirmatory signal. Now they had to wait for one more song.

The key personnel of Operation X waited for the rumble on the radio waves that would signal mission accomplished. In NHQ Delhi, the King Cobra, Captain Roy waited for one of his many phones to ring. In the naval detachment in Delta Sector, Aku Roy waited with the Mukti Bahini sector commanders for news from Chittagong. In Fort William, Samant hummed '*Aami tomai joto, shuniye chchilem gaan*' as he typed out his report on the launch of the commandos. The songs had been chosen by Major General Sarkar. The planners had nixed the idea of a third song that would signal 'abort mission'.

Samant hadn't told his task units that there was no turning back on this mission. The naval planner noted, with a tinge of regret, that an estimated 10 per cent of the task units he had sent into the operation were likely be killed or captured.

In Chittagong that morning, Chowdhury's task unit began leaving the city. The commandos were transported in private cars, two and three per car, hired by the local resistance. They were put on boats and guided to a safe house across the river. Khurshed's WAPDA van had left the city in the evening, carrying a large wicker basket of drumsticks to fetch the limpet mines from the shed in Chotto Komira. The vehicle was also stocked with a large supply of locally procured gamchas or thin cotton towels. Chowdhury had paid for all this with the 200 Pakistani rupees he had been given as special allowance for the operation.

Chowdhury's commandos had converged in a village called Anwara Thana across the Karnaphulli that morning. The house belonged to a sympathizer identified only as 'the potter'. In the safe house, Chowdhury and Shah Alam armed forty limpet mines with detonators. They slid pencil detonators into each mine, pushed the soluble plug in behind them, and rolled condoms over the plug to make it waterproof. The charges were now armed and ready for action. There was no sign of the third group of commandos who were staying in Fauzdar Haat. As the precious minutes slipped by, worry lines creased the young sailor's forehead. Finally, he decided to launch the mission with the remaining forty. He lined the commandos along the riverbank for the task.

Across Bangla Desh, close to midnight on 14 August, over a hundred assault swimmers discarded their lungis and vests. They donned swimming trunks, strapped diving knives to their calves, and slid their feet into the Abee rubber fins. They extracted the limpet mines and the gamchas from the bags and baskets and helped each other tie them to their chests. They used large double knots that could be easily opened underwater. The commandos then walked into the water backwards, the most efficient way to walk with fins on land, proceeding to noiselessly launch themselves into the rivers of their beloved country – the Karnaphulli in Chittagong, the Pussur in Chalna/Mongla, the Shitalakshshya in Narayanganj and the Meghna in Chandpur.

The limpeteers swam downstream with the current, backwards and diagonally towards their targets, their hands holding their deadly payload on their stomachs, hips noiselessly scissoring their finned feet, heads barely above the water, steering themselves through the darkness, just as they had been trained at C2P. Some of them had covered their heads with water hyacinth and breathed through bamboo reeds.

In Chittagong, Shah Alam, was the first to hit the water and swim on his back towards the well-lit silhouettes of the merchantmen across the river. The ships were a kilometre away. The swarm attack had been planned for just after midnight for two reasons. It coincided with the beginning of the ebb tide, when the river waters rushed out towards the sea, and also with the changing of the shift among the dock labour. The fast-moving ebb tide that was underway swiftly took the swimmers to their targets in under ten minutes. Shah Alam took a deep breath and lowered himself into the water. Around six feet under, he felt the ship side and reached for his diving knife. He used it to scrape the barnacles off. It was not easy, for he had to rise to the surface for mouthfuls of air and locate the same spot in complete darkness. He then reached for his chest, untied the knot, extracted the limpet mine and tossed away the condom and the gamcha. He dived in again, taking care to keep the deadly explosive away from the ship's hull, and then looked for the cleared spot to place his magnetized charge. The limpet hugged the merchant ship in a fraternal clunk. Deed done, Shah Alam rose to the surface, gasped for air, and flipped around, allowing the Karnaphulli to carry him downstream to the designated pick-up spot downriver where Khurshed and the others would be waiting for him with a fresh set of clothes. The forty commandos sploshed out of the water one after the other. They speedily discarded their fins, knives and swimming trunks, and changed into singlets and dhotis. They needed to leave the target area in a hurry.

The 'Pantle plugs' sat on the sides of the limpet mines, slowly dissolving in the water of the Karnaphulli. A half hour later, when each of the plugs had completely dissolved, the firing sequence was initiated. The thin lead wire in each mine gave way to the tension of the spring and snapped. The spring fired the tiny plunger into the percussion cap, which exploded the small charge explosive pellet in front of it. This, in turn, set off the main TNT charge. At around 1.40 a.m., the first dull, watery explosion resounded across Chittagong.

The *Al-Abbas* shuddered. Soon, the explosive orchestra began. Underwater blasts rattled ship sides, cracked their hulls, and sent up spouts of water in the river. On the harbour front, there was panic. And then gunfire. The army sentries began firing wildly into the water. The explosions continued. The angry waters of the Karnaphulli rushed into the sides of the *Al-Abbas*, the *Ohrmazd* and *Orient Barge Number 6* as the limpet mines punched holes in their sides below the waterline. All three ships settled to the bottom of the harbour, in about twenty feet of water, as if their bottoms had been sliced away. The commandos also seriously damaged five barges, two tugs and one gunboat. Across the Karnaphulli, the commandos counted twenty-three explosions. That night, similar dull blasts reverberated across the harbours of Narayanganj, Chandpur, Chalna and Mongla, crippling merchant ships and sowing confusion.

In Mongla, up the Pussur River, Rahmatulla's Task Unit 54.1.4 seriously damaged two American merchantmen, two Chinese freighters, a Japanese and a Pakistani merchant ship. The group of naval commandos that Humayun Kabir was part of, however, missed their target. They had waited at Heron Point on the Pussur River, waiting for a merchantman that would anchor there. The commandos lost their way and when they finally arrived at the rendezvous, the ship had already begun sailing upstream with the tide into Mongla.

In Narayanganj, Task Unit 54.1.3 under M. Ahsanullah sank four steamers and seriously damaged an inland water transport craft and a pontoon.

In Chandpur, Task Unit 54.1.2 under Badiul Alam sank two steamers of 2,000 and 3,000 tons, and a large cargo barge loaded with rations for the Pakistani military.

NCO(X) had struck furious blows. Its limpeteer assault groups had hit a total of twenty-five vessels in the span of an hour, the largest attack by naval saboteurs since Decima Flottiglia MAS's heyday in 1943.

Fazlul Hoq from Rajshahi, one of the commandos in Chowdhury's task unit, wrote out a post-incident assessment of the Chittagong attack for Cdr Samant. Hoq scrawled his report in Bengali on thirteen foolscap sheets of paper:[28]

Only thirteen targets had been decided upon. In that, the first six merchant ships that had started from near Pakistan Bazaar were there. After that, four gun boats in the naval jetty and three oil tankers in BOC were there but many (swimmers) could not reach their targets and put them in other ships. Especially since the naval jetty did not have any gun boats, they mined the other ships. As a result, almost seventeen–eighteen ships were damaged. Among all these ships, *Al-Abbas* and *Ohrmazd* are worth mention.

After the attack, we were at the banks of the river and the steamers kept blowing their horns in the water. As a result, our aim was to get to the other side of the port. Fortunately, no gun boats came. We left the potter's house almost after an hour and a half, and heard a gun boat's sound, and saw a search light a considerable distance away. Six people from our group lost their way and took shelter at spy Shamshul Alam's house. The rest of us thirty-five people walked all night to get to our old friend Haji Khan merchant's house in Anwara Thaana to take shelter.

---

28 Captain Samant's family archives

In his report, Fazlullah switched to English to highlight these points about the attack:

(a) Camouflage was effective.

(b) Guides were also good.

(c) The plan we were briefed about in Agartala was used.

The Chittagong assault team completed the attack and returned to the safety of the city.

On the sixteenth, at 2.30 in the afternoon, a few of us left Haji Sahib's house to cross the river and took shelter at Shobuj Bagh in Haji Para. The rest reached Hajipara at different hours on the seventeenth.

Panic had gripped the port by then. Crippled merchant ships lay on the riverbed, paralyzing berths and rendering the province's largest port unusable. The Pakistan Army reacted with beast-like fury and turned on the local populace. Captain Rafiqul Islam, the Sector I commander, grimly documented the aftermath:

At day-break, senior officers rushed to the port. Curfew was imposed and helicopters started hovering over the city to locate the Mukti Fouz. As a reprisal, enemy artillery indiscriminately shelled many localities on the eastern bank. The villages close to the river were burnt down. Many innocent villagemen and fishermen were arrested on suspicion. Failing to extract information from them, the Pakistanis became mad with rage. The arrested people were lined up on the river bank and shot down. Their bodies were thrown into the river to drift away.[29]

---

29 Major M. Rafiqul Islam, *A Tale of Millions* (Dacca: Adeylebros & Co.), 1974

The commandos, meanwhile, stayed in Chittagong for two days before exfiltrating towards the Indian border. Fazullah continues:

> We stayed at Hajipara till 8.00 in the morning of the nineteenth and after that took buses in twos from Dewan Haat to reach Daroga Haat. On reaching Daroga, we met Raviul-Alam Sahib again in Samiti Bazaar and twenty-one of us took shelter at a local member's house. The next day, on the twentieth, at 10.00 a.m., we took boats. We reached Isakhali late in the evening. The next day, on the twenty-first, at 2.00 in the afternoon, we left Isakhali for the border. At around 2.00 in the morning, we heard gunfire near the border. We took shelter at Aziz Sahib's house in Koroi Village. The next day, on the twenty-second after 4.00 in the evening, we crossed the border to take shelter at Fongbari before sunset.

They then made their way to Aku's camp in Delta Sector where the naval pilot debriefed them about their incredible mission, before sending them back to Camp C2P in the IAF Packet.

Operation Jackpot had been an unprecedented success for its planners. In Fort William, Cdr Samant toted the figures in the situation report he was preparing for Admiral Nanda and Captain Roy: the 176 commandos launched at Chittagong, Narayanganj, Chandpur and Chalna/Mongla had sunk a total of 44,500 tons of shipping and damaged 14,000 tons.

Inside the province, General Niazi deployed additional troops to guard ports and vital installations along the riverine lifelines. This move took the pressure off the beleaguered Mukti Bahini land forces. The naval commando attacks were a huge morale booster for the guerrilla resistance movement.

'The successful execution of Operation Jackpot made it clear to us that, given proper guidance and leadership, our boys could achieve miracles. They were all sincere and intelligent and ready to grasp any situation quickly. Their mental calibre was undoubtedly superior to that of the illiterate Pakistani soldiers. We were gifted with the largest educated guerrilla force,' Captain Islam noted.[30]

The fight back in Bangla Desh had begun.

30 Major M. Rafiqul Islam, *A Tale of Millions* (Dacca: Adeylebros & Co.), 1974

7

GUNBOATS ON THE GANGA

News of NCO(X)'s 15 August attack pinballed around the world. Suddenly, the Mukti Bahini were no longer the bunch of rag tag fighters battling a professional army. Their cadres had sophisticated skillsets and training to carry out coordinated attacks on targets hundreds of kilometres apart. Not only did the attacks come as a morale booster for the Bengali guerrillas, they directly took the pressure off the desperate war they were fighting as General Niazi pulled troops out from counter-insurgency operations to guard ports, harbours and vital riverine lifelines.

The attacks were Stage I, outlined in DNI Roy's concept note – targeting ships in ports and harbours. It was the start of a covert strategic maritime warfare campaign, what the 19th century US naval strategist Rear Admiral Alfred Thayer Mahan called guerre de course. It literally meant 'war of the chase': a euphemism for commerce raiding, destroying or disrupting the enemy's logistics by attacking merchant shipping rather than engaging its warships or enforcing a naval blockade. In this case, it meant the disruption of the riverine lifelines that sustained the military garrison and exported the tea and jute which nourished West Pakistan's economy with foreign exchange.

The August attacks saw foreign shipping lines increase their war-risk insurance from five shillings to one pound sterling, as also an additional 20 per cent 'risk pay' for the crew. Further, 1,000 dollars per day 'risk money' was paid to each ship that dared to remain in port for a period of more than one week. Even so, foreign shippers shied away from East Pakistani ports, in spite of tight security measures being enforced by martial law administrators. Tea, jute and coir, which brought in much-needed foreign exchange, lay piled up at the ports.[31]

There was alarm in the Pakistan Navy command in Dacca. It didn't take very long for Rear Admiral Mohammad Shariff and his bright staff officer, Captain Zamir Ahmad, to deduce that those neat holes punched into the steel sinews of their warships and merchantmen had come from military-grade explosives. The navy scrambled to counter this new threat. All available river craft were requisitioned to run riverine patrols. Vice Admiral Muzaffar Hussain, C-in-C Pakistan Navy, visited China, Saudi Arabia, Turkey and Egypt to requisition more vessels and maintenance assistance for the Pakistan Navy.

In Fort William, Sammy strode giant strides. NCO(X) had succeeded beyond everyone's wildest dreams. The tiny Indian Navy contingent had earned its spurs and the army's respect. Samant had by then struck a rapport with the temperamental Major General Jacob who would mock ambush him in the corridor, grabbing him by the shoulder for coffee sessions in his office, to his junior's feeble 'murder, murder' protestations. During one of those sessions, Jacob invited Samant home for dinner, where former Army Chief

---

31 Vice Admiral M.K. Roy, *War in the Indian Ocean* (New Delhi: Lancer Publishers), 1995

P.P. Kumaramangalam dropped in. Jacob puffed on his pipe and introduced Samant as 'one of my best staff officers'. He wasn't, but who was to tell Jacob that? Jacob was a gregarious officer and therefore owned everybody.

The legend around C2P, meanwhile, grew and the VIP traffic increased. Major General Sarkar and Major General Jacob made frequent unannounced visits to see with their own eyes how the Mukti Bahini naval commandos had pulled off the feat.

The Pakistan Army remained on high alert in the days that followed the 15 August attack. Then, when days turned into weeks and their vigil slackened, NCO(X) struck again.

On a moonless night in September, 160 assault swimmers launched a second attack on Chittagong. Four naval commandos in buddy pairs – Nur Mohamed and Rehman, both ex-Pakistan Navy personnel dismissed after the Agartala conspiracy case, and Nazrul Islam and Abdur Rehman were launched from Gupta Island in the middle of the Karnaphulli River. Their target were the freighters *Al Murtaza* and *Imtiaz Baksh*. Two other vessels – *Teviot Bank* and the Greek freighter *Avlos* – that were alongside, disembarking supplies for the Pakistan Army, were also targeted. Alan, Ahsanullah, Mondol and Mukherjee attacked the coaster *Dwarka*, two barges and one tug at the Khulna and Chalna ports. Moinuddin Haq, Manzur and Nooruzzaman spearheaded the attack on the river port of Barisal, where they sank the coaster *Shipta Dingha* and also two tugs, a river steamer, a ferry and the buoy-laying vessel, the *Path Finder*. Altaf Mehmood, Hafeez and Swapan led the attack on the inland port of Chandpur and sank one launch, three ferries and a coaster, as also a launch and a terminal pontoon at Aricha Ghat. One pontoon and a ferry were sunk at Golanda Ghat, as also three barges in the Gabkhan Channel. At Ashuganj, one coaster was heavily damaged.

A ferry was set on fire at Jaganghpur Ghat as all limpet mines and explosives had been expended. The toll in September was 6,000 tonnes of shipping sunk and 17,000 tonnes damaged. The figures were confirmed by Lloyds Casualty list as a majority of the vessels were insured with Lloyds of London. [32]

The Pakistan Navy was now in panic. The attacks of August were clearly not one-off. On 20 September, Rear Admiral Shariff issued a two-page note – 'Anti Underwater Saboteurs Instructions'. The letter, intercepted by the Mukti Bahini and passed on to the X Directorate, was copied to commodore Chittagong, commanding officer PNS Titumir, the zonal district officer Narayanganj, and to all of General Niazi's newly re-deployed army companies strung across East Pakistan's riverine delta. The note outlined the Pakistan Navy's version of the counter-sabotage drill, Operation Awkward, which Lt Kapil had overseen in Bombay in early 1971. It was expected, given the common training imparted to both navies by the Royal Navy.

Admiral Shariff's note suggested urgency:

> The measures are to be adopted immediately to meet the present contingency of underwater sabotage attacks on riverine traffic … Impose riverine curfew during dark hours if required and inspect all boats, barges, naukas. Personnel embarking and disembarking boats are required to come alongside ships in the ports of Chittagong, Chalna, Khulna, Dacca and Narayanganj.

Shariff wanted sentries to be placed on the forecastle, midships and quarter deck of all ships, and provided with loaded arms and permission to shoot. Sentries of civilian vessels were to be placed at suitable places and asked to look out for swimmers, frogmen or paddle boats. Sharif indicated what action was to be taken:

---

32 Vice Admiral M.K. Roy, *War in the Indian Ocean* (New Delhi: Lancer Publishers), 1995

If in doubt, open fire … Drop scare charges/grenades at least every half hour, at random. This is applicable to ships holding grenades and depending on the prevailing situation of which the OTC (Officer in Tactical Command) will be the judge. Turn propellers astern, if possible. Carry out ships' bottom searches when tidal conditions permit and at slack water. Underwater swimmers must swim along the ship, searching for mines between the surface and the keel. Both sides must be searched. Inspect all floating articles in the water. Carry out patrol around the jetties and ships berthed. Patrol boats to carry out automatic weapons and hand grenades/scare charges. Patrol boats also to trail fishing hooks to catch swimmers otherwise undetected. Provide flood lights along the ships for underwater line. Stop ditching garbage and refuse over board, particularly wooden/cardboard boxes or similar things which can camouflage underwater swimmers.

There were specific instructions for when a saboteur was caught:

a) Try and apprehend the miscreant and if he tries to dive, drop a scare charge/grenades. Also, engage with automatic fire.
b) Report by the quickest means available the respective operational commanders/nearest army authorities.
c) Order immediate search of the ships' bottoms and dropping of scare charges in the surrounding areas, particularly in the direction of the flow.

The following were the Standard Operating Procedures (SOPs) in case a limpet mine was detected:[33]

---

33 Captain M.N.R. Samant's family archives

- Cordon off the area. Separate the vessels attacked by rowing away from the jetties and other ships, keeping it clear of the main channel.
- Send underwater swimmers to search/inspect the mine if below the water line. Request assistance of bomb disposal teams from nearest Army HQ by signal, with copy to Eastern Command and FOCEP.
- All mines detected and rendered safe are to be reported to the nearest naval authority for inspection and evaluation.

NCO(X) had already anticipated this enhanced vigil. After the shock of the initial wave of attacks, they deduced, their limpeteer commandos would be up against a more determined and vigilant enemy. 'Undetected passage to the targets would become increasingly difficult,' Commander Samant had predicted in his 17 June report to Admiral Nanda. Stage II and Stage III operations, as outlined by DNI Roy, would be impossible without stealthy rebreather sets which recirculated the carbon dioxide exhaled by a diver and left no trail of bubbles. The cash-strapped navy had ruled out using rebreather sets at the start of the operation. It did not have the funds to import them. Besides, it would have meant a longer spell of training the commandos as specialist clearance divers. This meant that the naval commandos would have to carry out missions at even greater personal risk.

On 19 September, Aku Roy, heading the naval detachment in Agartala, sent out an assessment of the developments in Sector X. In his five-page handwritten note sent to Samant in his neat cursive hand, he analyzed the raw intelligence flowing into Delta Sector. With road and rail traffic being increasingly disrupted by the Mukti Bahini and attacks by limpeteer-commandos, the Pakistan Army had begun herding ships carrying their essential supplies into river convoys in order to safely move essential fuel stores, war material and troops by day. The convoys comprised six to ten vessels, comprising some steamers, coasters, coalers and barges. Some vessels, were fitted with three-inch mortars ready to fire, and had sandbagged protection for exposed guards or crew members. Most vessels had between half to a full section of armed guards, possibly a mix of Pakistan Army regulars and a mix of Pakistan police and razakars.[34]

The officer-in-charge of the convoy ensured the usual anti-frogmen and anti-limpet–mine precautions were taken by the convoy and escorts. The escorts were naval or modified gunboats, usually armed with one or two 75 mm recoilless guns and one or two light machine guns (LMGs) or medium machine guns (MMGs). Several civilian motor launches had been converted into gunboats. One of them, the *Tufail*, had been named after a Pakistani officer of the 1965 war.

Vessels did not move at night. They stopped at a protected IWT port where they were herded into a 'safe zone' that was under floodlight and heavily guarded by sentries and armed patrol boats.

Aku advised Sector Commander Brigadier Shabeg Singh and the Mukti Fauj sub-sector commanders to increase riverine warfare activity by laying ambushes against the enemy and countering their new tactics, but it became increasingly clear to his bosses in New Delhi and Fort William that their operation would have to be shifted into a higher gear. New tactics would have to be drawn up. This would mean expanding the scale of the covert naval campaign.

Hydrographer Mitter

'The commander-in-chief wants to see you,' the officer of the day (OOD), Lieutenant K.P. Vidyadharan hailed Lieutenant Suvesh

---

34 Captain M.N.R. Samant's family archives

Kumar Mitter as he walked down the gangplank of the *INS Darshak*. 'Of course he does,' Mitter laughed, acknowledging one of the commonest young officer pranks. Work was hard and the boyishly handsome Mitter, twenty-five-years-old and five feet eight inches tall, juggled two billets. He was hydrographic officer on the survey vessel being refitted at the naval dockyard, Bombay, and also assisted his commanding officer, Captain Frank Leslie Fraser, in the maritime operations room (MOR) ashore in *INS Angre*. The Hydrographic Department prepared the nautical maps and charts for the navy. Survey vessels like the *Darshak* fathomed ocean depths and charted coastal regions for underwater obstacles to make them safe for navigation.

Mitter's 'Old Man', as COs were usually called, wore a second hat – the naval controller of shipping, the official who guided merchant ship movements in war time. It was late September and, in a nod to a war which everyone believed was imminent, the white survey vessel had been painted battle grey. But there was always time for humour. Vidyadharan was insistent. The C-in-C had indeed called – on the OOD's telephone, right on the gangway. Mitter was puzzled. The protocol was to call the CO and not to summon a junior officer directly.

Captain Fraser was away for lunch at his home in Navy Nagar, Colaba. Mitter ignored Vidyadharan's protestations, grabbed a quick meal on the ship and returned to the MOR. 'Did you meet the admiral?' Lt Cdr B.B. Nandy, his senior colleague at the MOR wanted to know. If this was a prank, Mitter sighed, everyone was in on it. Pranksters were everywhere. Three years ago, unseen hands in the dockyard had repainted two key letters on a signboard. 'Naval Warehouse' read 'Whorehouse'. The culprits had never been found. Mitter decided to call this new bluff.

He strode purposefully to the C-in-C's office, a five-minute walk across the road, on the top floor of the five-storeyed Noorbhoy building. He was swiftly ushered before Vice Admiral Surendranath Kohli.

'Are you married?'

'No sir.'

'Are you fluent in Bengali?

'Yes, sir.'

'Good. Report to your commanding officer.'

The strangest interview of Mitter's life lasted under two minutes. He walked back to the naval dockyard. He was informed that the CO, Captain Fraser, had returned and was waiting for him. The suspense was now getting unbearable. The gloomy insides of the *Darshak* resounded with the clang of metal as Mitter ducked in. The CO's cabin was ripped up for the refit. Captain Fraser operated out of the supply officer's cabin.

'Ha! Come in,' he exclaimed as Mitter knocked. Fraser, well over six-feet tall and big built, had folded his frame into the cramped cabin. 'Send for my steward.'

The Old Man was a terror. One of the naval hydrographic service's brightest, but a man who bore a fearsome temper. If he ever stood on the *Darshak*'s starboard, ran a joke on the ship, you could find the entire crew on the port side. On the *Darshak* that afternoon, the crew paused expectantly outside his cabin, awaiting Mitter's grim fate. The suspense broke when the steward raced past, his tray rattling with two glasses of gin and lime. There was going to be no public execution. The crew went back to their stations.

'Son,' Captain Fraser began, 'you have been selected for a classified task. It's risky, a very risky mission … would you be willing to go?' Mitter looked at him quizzically. 'Of course, if you're not interested, it won't reflect badly on you,' Fraser added.

The CO sounded relieved when Mitter agreed to take on the task. He nodded in appreciation. He asked the young officer to hand over all his duties and await his movement orders.

सत्यमेव जयतें

Calendar art created during the Bangladesh war in 1971, showing Mrs Gandhi, Sheikh Mujibur Rahman, a burning Yahya Khan and an exploding merchant ship.

Admiral S.M. Nanda with Captain M.K. Roy on the quarterdeck of a warship in 1971.

Lt Cdr Mihir Roy (extreme left) with his crew from INAS 310 squadron, Op Vijay, Goa, 1961.

Admiral S.M. Nanda and Mrs Gandhi on board the *INS Vikrant*.

Admiral S.M. Nanda.

Cdr Samant as commanding officer, *INS Karanj*.

Abee fins.

Humayun Kabir and others in C2P. Before them are disassembled limpet mines.

Refugees in Calcutta; display at the Genocide Museum, Khulna.

1969 OVERSEAS LONG M C D OFFICERS COURSE

Lt Kapil, standing, second from left and Lt Das, sitting, second from left, during their training at the HMS Vernon in the UK in 1969.

Tejnagar sugar cane farm – Site of Camp C2P on the Plassey battlefield, Nadia district, West Bengal.

Frogmen: Indian Naval clearance divers jump off a ship for ships' bottom searches in dry (rubberised) suits, CDBA (closed circuit / rebreather) sets and Churchill fins.

A Mukti Bahini poster during the liberation war depicts General Yahya Khan; 'These are animals. Kill these animals.'

Condoms – used as covers on the soluble plugs in the limpet mines – in production at the Hindustan Latex Ltd plant, Trivandrum, in 1969.

নিরাপত্তা পাস

যে কোন মিলিটারী/পুলিস ফোর্ড অথবা শান্তি কর্মিটি এই কার্ড ধারীকে গ্রহণ করিবেন।

এবং

তাহার উপর কোন প্রকার শারীরিক নির্যাতন করা যাইবে না। তাহাকে পাকিস্তানী হিসাবে পুনরায় গ্রহণ করিতে হইবে যেহেতু সে পরের প্রবোচনায় পথভ্রষ্ট হইয়াছিল।

حفاظتی پاس

اس پاس کے حامل کو کسی بھی فوجی جوڑی پولیس جوڑی یا پیس کمیٹی میں قبول کیا جائیگا

اور

اسے جسمانی ضرر نہیں پہنچایا جائیگا ۔ اسے پاکستانی کی حیثیت سے واپس قبول کیا جائیگا جو غلط رہنمائی کی وجہ سے گمراہ ہو گیا ہے اور اسنے اپنی پی کھٹا نہ تھی ۔

AAK Niazi

*Lieutenant General
Commander Eastern Command
(Amir Abdullah Khan Niazi)*

Niazi Leaflet – Bilingual Pakistan Army leaflets signed by Lt General A.A.K. Niazi instructing the Mukti Bahini forces how to conduct their surrender.

Recreation of a torture chamber used by the Pakistan Army at the Genocide Museum, Khulna.

Naval commandos with their trainers. Standing (L to R): Badiul Alam (guide), unidentified, Shah Alam, Abdur Rashid, unidentified. Sitting (L to R): L. Singh, Sub Lt. B.S. Thakur, Lt Cdr George Martis, Leading Seaman M.S. Gupta. Sitting on floor (L to R): Imdad Hussain Matin, Khurshed Alam. This photograph was taken in Chittagong in December 1971 after the war.

Sub Lt Zamir Ahmed (standing, second from right) right behind his roommate Sub Lt Samant (seated), Whale Island, Portsmouth, UK, during their gunnery course in 1953.

Photo wall of international media coverage of the attacks on ships by naval commandos.

Naval commandos in operation inside Bangla Desh, holding Mark 1 limpet mines in their right hands, Abee fins in their left. Commandos are Khalil-ur-Rahman, Akhtar, Emdad, Khasru and Arun Bhatt.

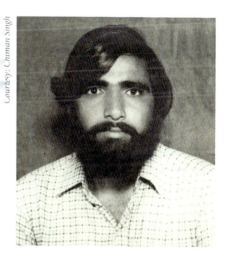

Chiman Singh, MVC, in Delta Sector, Agartala, Tripura, October 1971.

Signal reporting Chiman Singh missing.

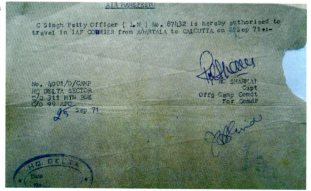

Air manifest authorizing Chiman Singh's flight from Delta Sector to Calcutta.

Lt Cdr Ashok 'Aku' Roy, the officer-in-charge of the naval detachment in Delta Sector.

Lt Suvesh Mitter (centre) with Captain Fraser (second from left) on the deck of the *INS Darshak*.

The salvaged hulk of the *MV Akram* at the Shahen Shah dockyard by the Shitalakhya river in Narayanganj in 2017. The *Akram* resupplied the Pakistan Army until it was sunk by naval commandos in Chandpur on 30 October 1971.

Sunken merchantship at Chittagong during Operation Jackpot.

Cdr Subir Paul – CO *INS Kavaratti*.

Capt Samant with Sheikh Mujibur Rahman and the first Bangladeshi acting navy chief Capt Nurul Haque.

L to R: Cdr Vijai Kapil, Chiman Singh and Capt M.N.R. Samant.

L to R: Commodore A.W. Chowdhury with Cdr Kapil on a floating jetty in Chittagong in front of the ship berths attacked by Chowdhury's assault swimmers during Operation Jackpot on 15/16 August 1971.

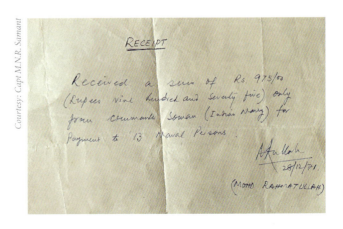

Handwritten receipt from Rahamtulla to Capt M.N.R. Samant.

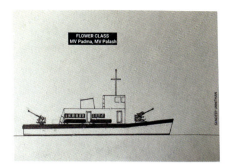

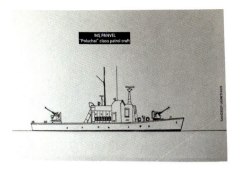

Artist's impression of a thirty–metre–long 'Flower-class' harbour utility craft from Calcutta Port. These were converted into the Mukti Bahini gunboats *MV Padma* and *MV Palash*. (Dimensions: displacement approx 100 tons, full load; length x width x draft: 100ft x 18ft x 6ft)

Artist's impression of *INS Panvel*, a thirty–metre–long, ninety-ton Soviet-built 'Poluchat'-class patrol boat from the Eastern Naval Command. (Dimensions: length x width x draft: 98ft x 15ft x 4.8 ft)

Mark VII airdropped mine.

The Petya-II class corvette *INS Kavaratti* in the Bay of Bengal during the 1971 war. Her pennant number has been painted out.

C-in-C of the Bangladesh armed forces, Colonel M.A.G. Osmani with his commanders.

Lt General Niazi signs the instrument of surrender at the Dacca racecourse, 16 December 1971.
Sitting (L to R) Lt General J.S. Aurora, GoC-in-C Eastern Army Command; Lt General A.A.K. Niazi, Commander, Eastern Command.

Standing (L to R) Vice Admiral N. Krishnan, Flag Officer Commanding-in-Chief Eastern Naval Command; Air Marshal H.C. Dewan, AoC-in-C Eastern Command; Lt General Sagat Singh, Commander 4 Corps; Major General J.F.R. Jacob, Chief of Staff Eastern Command.

Newspaper headlines announcing the defeat of Pakistan and the birth of Bangladesh.

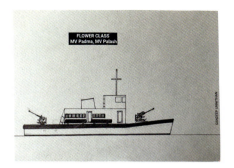

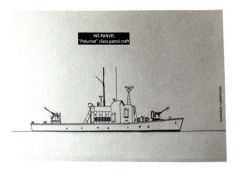

Artist's impression of a thirty–metre–long 'Flower-class' harbour utility craft from Calcutta Port. These were converted into the Mukti Bahini gunboats *MV Padma* and *MV Palash*. (Dimensions: displacement approx 100 tons, full load; length x width x draft: 100ft x 18ft x 6ft)

Artist's impression of *INS Panvel*, a thirty–metre–long, ninety-ton Soviet-built 'Poluchat'-class patrol boat from the Eastern Naval Command. (Dimensions: length x width x draft: 98ft x 15ft x 4.8 ft)

Mark VII airdropped mine.

The Petya-II class corvette *INS Kavaratti* in the Bay of Bengal during the 1971 war. Her pennant number has been painted out.

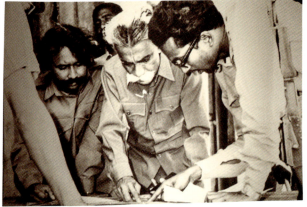

C-in-C of the Bangladesh armed forces, Colonel M.A.G. Osmani with his commanders.

Lt General Niazi signs the instrument of surrender at the Dacca racecourse, 16 December 1971.
Sitting (L to R) Lt General J.S. Aurora, GoC-in-C Eastern Army Command; Lt General A.A.K. Niazi, Commander, Eastern Command.

Standing (L to R) Vice Admiral N. Krishnan, Flag Officer Commanding-in-Chief Eastern Naval Command; Air Marshal H.C. Dewan, AoC-in-C Eastern Command; Lt General Sagat Singh, Commander 4 Corps; Major General J.F.R. Jacob, Chief of Staff Eastern Command.

Newspaper headlines announcing the defeat of Pakistan and the birth of Bangladesh.

'Until then,' he said, 'have a good time.' It sounded like a condemned man being granted his last wish, but it didn't occur to the young officer then. But his curiosity was piqued by what the captain said next: 'No one on the ship must know what happened.' It was an order. And the CO had even figured out Mitter's alibi. 'Tell them you were hauled up because of some complaints from your girlfriend,' he grinned.

Two days later, there was a knock at Mitter's cabin door on the ship. A top secret signal was handed to him. He was to report to INS Hooghly in Calcutta as soon as possible. The following evening, the young officer with five years of service under his belt and years away from his first command, was on the train. His mind rattled with questions.

Mitter reported to Fort William the morning after he arrived in the eastern metropolis. The city had birthed two generations of his family. His grandfather, scion of a rich zamindar family from Govindapur, one of the five villages around Fort William, had moved into the city in the late 18th century and set up a printing press which had built the family fortunes, a three-storeyed house and several acres of land. The fortunes, the press and the land were squandered away in the early 20th century when an alcoholic uncle ran up gambling debts. Mitter's mother, Shobhana, pawned her jewellery to save the family house from being sold. The older of two siblings, Mitter was fascinated by the uniform, a passion encouraged by his convent-educated mother. Shobhana pushed her young son to join the Boy Scouts in school and the NCC in college. As a Class IX student, he had even slipped into a nearby naval recruitment centre to try and join the navy as a boy entry, but was turned away by a kindly recruiting officer. In 1965, soon after his graduation, he finally enrolled in the navy as a short service commissioned officer. His father Gunendranath Mitter, a deputy secretary in the Eastern

Railways, was shocked. He had arranged a job for his son as an accounts clerk in the railways.

Mitter had dutifully reported to Commodore R.P. 'Squeaky' Khanna, the naval officer in charge (NOIC) at INS Hooghly. Squeaky Khanna, whose high-pitched voice was the source of his nickname, directed him to meet Commander Samant in Fort William just two kilometres away.

The young lieutenant strode in through the Plassey Gate at the eastern end of the fort in his crisp naval whites. He crossed the dry moat, entered the main gate and walked into the Command Headquarters – the twin-storeyed colonial-era Indo-Gothic structure with large arches and high ceilings. He was ushered into the nondescript two-room set – Samant's nerve centre.

Mitter knew Samant in the way a subaltern would know a senior officer – from afar. He had once bumped into the pioneering submariner at the naval dockyard, Bombay, in 1969 when the *INS Karanj* was berthed for repairs. Any thoughts of reminding him of that brief meeting in the washroom rapidly vanished. His putative boss sat in civvies and studied him from across the table. His face was contemplative, his lips pursed as he shot a series of questions.

'Have you been circumcised?'

'No, Sir.'

'Do you know how to perform namaaz?'

'No, Sir.'

Samant looked disappointed.

'Where are you staying?'

'In my family home, Ballygunge.'

'Good. I want you to continue staying there. I don't want anyone seeing you around here.' An Ambassador car and driver, what the military called 'civilian hired transport', would be at Mitter's disposal. He then shot a reproachful look at Mitter's uniform before dismissing him: 'Don't be seen in uniform again.'

The second strangest meeting of Mitter's life ended in a few minutes. It was not to the be the last. The next morning was a milestone in his life and he didn't even have a clue about it. He reported in civilian clothes to the NCO(X) office. Lt Cdr Menon was waiting. The two men hopped into the Ambassador and drove to the Ordnance Club just two kilometres away. The car entered a bungalow in the complex. A strapping figure in civil clothes was waiting for them there. Mitter was introduced to Major General Jimmy Sarkar. His hand nearly raised to salute until he realized the general was also in a cotton shirt and trousers. His hand dropped back. Didn't anyone in Calcutta wear a uniform?

The trio boarded the Ambassador. Menon directed the driver to take them to the Garden Reach Shipbuilders and Engineers (GRSE), three kilometres away. GRSE had been founded in 1884 as a privately owned ship repair yard on the east bank of the Hooghly. It was now a government-owned defence shipyard.

Menon led them to a slipway inside the GRSE where Mitter saw two of the strangest looking warships under refit. The blunt-nosed boats were each nearly 100-feet long and eighteen feet wide. Two 40 mm L-60 ack-ack guns, with their distinctive conical flash hiders, poked out, one in the fore and another in the aft. They were very clearly gunboats, but of a kind Mitter had never seen before.

Sarkar turned to Mitter. 'You are going to command one of them,' he said, pointing at the boats. 'I hope you have a happy command.'

'Depends on the task you give me,' the young officer shrugged.

The general looked miffed at the young officer's impertinence, but didn't say anything.

Mitter had been given a naval subaltern's dream. A first command. His hesitation was because he had correctly figured this was unlike any regular naval operation. He was right. He was a key figure in a clandestine naval force – Sammy's navy.

The attacks of August had validated the first phase of NCO(X) and Samant's ability to lead it. In September, Admiral Nanda authorized the formation of a naval wing under the commander. Wheels had turned at the very highest levels of government. The West Bengal government had offered two harbour craft. The navy's Warship Overseeing Team, a small liaison team of shipwrights and engineers within GRSE, had surveyed four utility craft operated by the Calcutta Port Trust – the *Palash*, *Parijat*, *Parul* and *Padma*. The hull and machinery of the *Palash* and *Padma* were found to be sturdier. The *Palash* was of course named for the Butea monosperma flower and the *Padma*, for the lotus flower. Samant had taken the two vessels from the Calcutta Port Trust on 22 September and handed them over to the GRSE for refit and trials. 'Intend fitting two 40/60s,' he wrote to Captain Roy in Delhi on 23 September. 'Request position one suitable lieutenant (executive branch) to commence training immediately.' This is the signal that had led to Mitter's deputation.

The truism in the growing Indian Navy was that lieutenants and lieutenant commanders ran the show. In October 1971, Mitter was possibly the navy's most overburdened subaltern, his life a daily lurch between his house in Ballygunge and GRSE. Over the next few weeks, he had to not just supervise the refit, but select his crew, finish sea trials and ensure that both ship and crew were fighting fit.

It was Mitter's longest stay at home after he joined the navy. His mother Shobhana was pleased. Gunendranath Mitter, for whom a Calcutta Municipal Corporation clerk had a higher value in the marriage market than a naval officer, saw this as the return of the prodigal son.

Mitter was solely focused on the refit. Informally called the 'Flower Class', the four boats were built at the GRSE in the 1950s and 1960 to service Calcutta port. Merchant ships began their journey at Sandheads where the Hooghly emptied into the Bay of Bengal and sailed 232 km upstream through one of the world's longest shipping channels, into India's only major riverine port. The Flower class were like river taxis, which transported crews to and from merchant ships and the pilots who boarded and guided vessels into port. This explained the roomy cabin on deck for the ship's master, equipped with a toilet and shower of the kind one would find in an apartment.

The boats were not certified for open sea sailing; in fact, they were not even permitted to ply beyond harbour limits. They were bereft of communication sets, sextants, radar or gyro compasses which would indicate water depth, direction, or above-water obstacles. Their saving grace were the two robust German-built MAN W6V diesels which generated 380 horsepower and a modest top speed of 11.5 knots. In their original form, they would be pretty much useless as warships. Hence, they were back to their birthplace for a role change. The process of converting them into sea-going war vessels would take two months and cost the Jackpot approximately thirty-eight lakh rupees. The refit was supervised by GRSE's Warship Overseeing Team (WOT) headed by Cdr Subramanian, a gangly, grey-haired shipwright with over twenty years of experience. Assisting him was Lt Cdr Vishnu Kumar Raizada, an electrical officer on a three-month temporary duty from the Directorate of Naval Design in Delhi. Raizada supervised the installation of the compasses and rudimentary battery-operated echo sounders which indicated water depth. Each ship was given a Japanese-made portable walkie-talkie with a five-kilometre range. The WOT also welded two twenty-foot–long rails on the port and starboard side of each boat. The rails sat six inches off the deck. Possibly meant for inflatable life-rafts, Mitter thought.

A few days later, the captain-designate of the *Palash* showed up. It was Lt Cdr Jayanto Kumar Roy Choudhury. 'Kiddo' Roy Choudhury stood at 5 feet 2 inches and had just made it past the navy's physical standards. He was stoutly built, had light green eyes and like several other Bengali armed forces officers, belonged to a zamindar family with roots in East Pakistan. Roy Choudhury seemed an apt choice – he was currently gunnery instructor in Gunnery School in Cochin and, as senior officer, would be squadron commander. Roy Choudhury was commissioned into the navy in 1957. In Fort William, he had been reunited with a steely officer who was his first interaction with the navy on the destroyer *INS Godavari*. 'Do this bloody thing chop' the words of the sharp, no-nonsense RN-trained executive officer Lt M.N.R. Samant still rang in his ears. But, that month, Roy Choudhury had other things to worry about. Sheila Roy Choudhury was in her eighth month of pregnancy at the family home in Jadhavpur, South Calcutta, and so, her dutiful husband divided time between the family and work.

The hunt for boat crews had already begun in early September. In the following months, the number of deserters from the Pakistan Navy swelled, giving the Indian Navy a steady source of maritime-trained, war-usable manpower. The ex-navy personnel had a choice of either joining the naval commandos at C2P or joining the Mukti Bahini land forces. Only a miniscule number opted for the army. Most reported to C2P. The army had selected a group of forty-five naval volunteers and sent them to the Kalyani Camp, and from there to Calcutta. Mohammed Jalaluddin was part of the group. He had heard of the formation of a new gunboat arm and wanted a piece of the action.

Mitter had taken an instant liking to the short, lanky Pakistan naval sailor. Jalaluddin was technically competent, and interested and eager to help. He became the *Padma*'s de-facto second-in-command and Mitter assigned him to crew selection. Jalaluddin screened the volunteers for the crew – gunnery crew, telegraphists, signalmen and artificers who would be vital to run the little warships. Their crew of forty-five comprised of deserters and naval commandos from

C2P camp. Among the deserters was Mohammad Ruhul Amin, former engine room artificer of the gunboat *PNS Comilla*. On 25 March, Amin, a sailor with twenty years of service, had escaped from Chittagong, where his gunboat was stationed. He crossed over to India through Agartala in May that year.

Jalal selected nineteen crew for the *Padma*. Nineteen others, including Amin, were deputed for the *Palash*. The remaining five crewmen were to stay on as a reserve crew ashore.

The Warship Overseeing Team stripped all identification marks off the vessels. Anything on the hull and machinery which could link the boats to India were removed or ground away. The black and yellow colours of the Port Trust utility vessels were completely scraped away. The boats were given a coat of menacing battleship grey. In the last week of September, the boats slid into the water from the slipway, one after the other, and were secured on the GRSE pontoon jetty.

To Lt Cdr Roy Choudhury, the floral names given to the boats were unbecoming of the role he believed they would play in the liberation of Bangla Desh. He changed the name of the *Palash* to *Bhuli Nai* (unforgettable), a nod to a 1948 Bengali film about a band of revolutionaries battling Lord Curzon's partition of Bengal. Mitter clapped his head in disbelief as he saw the new name plate go up on the *Palash*. 'Dada,' he hissed, 'we are just 60 kilometres from the border and this place is crawling with spies. A name like this would be a dead giveaway ... they will know we are making it for the Bangla Deshis.' Roy Choudhury was insistent. *Bhuli Nai* it would be.

This was not the first time that Calcutta Port Trust auxiliaries had been used for a covert operation. In 1943, an intrepid group of British reservists, the Calcutta Light Horse, had sailed a battered hopper barge, the *Phoebe*, designed never to leave the Hooghly river, 1,819 nautical miles away, to neutral Goa. Here, the Lighthorsemen boarded and sank the German merchantman, the *Ehrenfels*, which was transmitting movements of Allied merchantmen from within its anchorage in the Mormugao Port to Kriegsmarine U-boats prowling in the Indian Ocean. The deniable mission for Britain's Special Operations Executive (SOE) had shut down this transmitting station without antagonizing Portugal, whose neutrality was vital for British interests in Europe.

Nearly a quarter century later, these two unmarked Calcutta Port Trust auxiliaries, crewed by Mukti Bahini, signalled the next phase of Nanda and Roy's covert and deniable war. They would directly target merchant ships bringing arms, ammunition and supplies to the Pakistani forces through its riverine lifelines. And thus, in early October, the Bangla Desh Navy was born on a pierside at the GRSE. The boats were prefixed with MV for Motor Vessel – the *MV Palash* and the *MV Padma*. *Bhuli Nai* had evidently been just a momentary thought. The professional soldier inside Lt Cdr Roy Choudhury had taken over. The brief commissioning ceremony was the only time the Mukti Bahini crew saw their commanding officers in naval whites. Raizada's facial features – he belonged to a Kashmiri Pandit family from Jammu with origins in Afghanistan – had by then piqued the interest of the *Palash*'s Bangla Deshi crew. Roy Choudhury pulled him aside one day to discuss the crew grapevine. Raizada, they believed, was in fact a Pakistani naval officer they knew from their time in that navy. He was Lt Cdr Khalid Hussain of the Pakistan Navy, working undercover. The electrical officer laughed it off and went back to work.

After the commissioning, the gunboats shifted to the Calcutta Port Trust's Man-of-War jetty along the city's riverfront. In the jetty often used by the navy, the boats loaded up with L-60 ammunition, fuel and water, and discretely sailed down the channel to their new home. Sammy was not going to let his precious gunboats be seen near one of India's busiest ports. He had already identified a redoubt – Camp 2 Haldia. C2H was located at roughly half the distance between Calcutta and Sandheads, on the western bank of the Haldi river, close to the spot where it met the Hooghly. The gunboats were anchored on a pontoon jetty – a 100-foot–long floating metal pier tethered to the shore. C2H sat on the edge of flat barren fields dotted with wild shrubs. Not a blade of grass grew, no cattle grazed, and hence no curious villagers would approach the camp. The camp was sited on a five-acre plot of land on the seafront. A deserted asphalt road was its only landward access. A small residential complex – a clump of single-storeyed single rooms, set in two neat rows – sat across the road. The buildings were owned by the Calcutta Port Trust and were for the use of port trust officials as their camp office and lodgings when they visited the under-construction Haldia Port. The boats were moored were just 250 metres away from the Haldia Coast Battery manned by the navy to protect the port and refineries from sea or air attack.

About a dozen naval personnel lived in a tin shed near the waterline and manned the lone 3.7-inch mountain howitzer and two L-60 ack-ack guns borrowed from the army.

A large army tent housed four spare Mukti Bahini crew – Chief Writer Ataul Haque, the record keeper, Master-at-Arms M.A. Quddus, Leading Technical Operator Mufazzal Husain and cook Amir Husain. Three rooms of the port trust complex were also used – as a battery charging room, as ship's store, and as a guest house for officers visiting the camp.

Sammy now had two camps, both on the same stretch of river – C2P on the Bhagirathi and C2H, downriver, on the Hooghly.

Over the next few days, his gunboats sailed out of C2H each day to carry out their familiarization, training and work up in complete secrecy. They conducted sea trials and gun trials at Sandheads, a stretch of open sea over 100 km south of Haldia. Roy Choudhury and Mitter wanted to test their boats and, more importantly, the ability of their crews to fight as a cohesive unit. Army gunnery experts who came in from Calcutta aligned their gun sights. A few days later, the gunboats chugged out to Sandheads, the dark blue Indian ensigns on their masts flapping in the breeze. They were going to test their 40 mm Bofors guns, a weapon designed by Swedish firm Bofors AB during the 1930s. The Eastern Command had borrowed the four '40/60s' from the 107 Territorial Army Unit at Ballygunj camp, not far from Mitter's home. The guns were the ground-based, aircraft-killing mainstay of all three services. In the hands of an expertly trained crew, they could belch out an intense volley of fire – nearly eighty rounds per minute – out to nearly seven kilometres.

At Sandheads, the crews fired at improvised floating targets – oil barrels marked by flags. Each gun had a six-man crew. The captain of the gun sat on the left of the turret, aimed and fired. The trainer sitting next to him manoeuvred the gun, and a third crewman – the loader – stood in the centre to push four-round clips into the breech. The magazine was located in the forward storage compartment near the boat's bow. A three-man relay team of loaders passed fresh clips by hand through a hatch in the compartment.

When the L/60's seven-foot–long barrel was cranked down horizontally into the direct-fire mode, it became a devastating naval cannon. Each shell carrying one pound of high explosive fired a projectile which could pierce mild steel and concrete. The results at Sandheads, however, were not spectacular. The rolling and pitching of the ships made accurate firing a difficult task.

Even as the gunboats continued their workup, NCO(X) readied its assault swimmers for a second wave of attacks. Pakistani sentries had begun to tire from their day and night vigil on the waterways they had maintained since the attacks of 15 August. In early September, Samant despatched Lt Das and Leading Seaman

Chiman Singh to Agartala to arm the fresh batch of limpet mines in Delta Sector. The duo flew in a military courier flight, a Packet aircraft which skimmed the East Pakistan periphery, before landing in Agartala. The duo headed for Delta Sector and the chief of the naval detachment, Lt Cdr Aku Roy.

The launch pad in Agartala was five kilometres from the border, on a hillside and co-located with the headquarters of Delta Sector. The Indian Navy detachment was an austere setup housed in three tents – the officers in one, the sailors in another and limpet mines, detonators and Sterling submachine guns stored in the armoury tent. Six other tents housed the naval commandos. It had just a small clearing with a volleyball court attached. The detachment was a launch pad where trained naval commandos – around two dozen at a time – would be brought in and housed. When the time was right, they would be briefed about their final mission in Bengali by Aku Roy before being launched into East Pakistan. The camp was also a recovery station – commandos returning from operations were debriefed here by Aku and sent back to C2P via the IAF courier flight.

Aku was far cry from his rambunctious self in Bombay. The months of isolation had begun taking their toll on the sociable naval aviator. The enormity of the task at hand was clearly weighing on his mind. He had to launch a second wave of commandos with limpets for their three-day journey to their target areas in Chittagong port. Steeped in work, drafting reports and studying intelligence briefs, the pilot occasionally left his tent only occasionally to join in occasional volleyball games with the naval commandos. Das, meanwhile, armed the limpet mines and returned to C2P, leaving Chiman Singh for nearly a month in Delta Sector.

Delta Sector launched its second batch of assault swimmers on 13 September. The 'Chit Gang' of twenty-three 'footballers', as Aku called them in a handwritten note to Samant. 'Results awaited'. 'Other results achieved available in Eastern Command + Delta Sector sitreps.'

Aku breathlessly recounted the events of the past few days in his report. Lt General Aurora had visited the Delta Sector camp on 14 September. The C-in-C wanted all the 'footballers' now operating in the area to stay within the camp and not be sent back to Calcutta. Supplies of limpet mines and fins were a problem and Lt General Aurora assured Roy that he would soon send forty-eight footballs (limpets) and forty-eight footwear (fins) as soon as possible. Roy wrote of his present inventory: 'Regarding present stocks held, there are at present nineteen footballs held but no delay firing pistols for them. There are twenty-six footballers at the camp here now. Director (GS-X) has asked commander D-Sector to keep sixteen footballers for a special task and has asked for sixteen pairs of footwear which have not yet been received.'

The thirteenth of September was also when the police constable turned naval commando Humayun Kabir was blooded in combat. He and several other commandos laid a riverine ambush in Harinagar, Khulna district. A Pakistani convoy of one gun boat and several troop-carrying launches was fired upon by the team. 'In the firing, the gun crew of the escorting gun boat was killed and the radar antenna was destroyed,' the Bangla Desh government in exile noted in a press release.

NCO(X)'s second wave of assault swimmers struck on 18 September. These attacks in Chittagong and Chalna were as audacious as the ones the previous month. 'At Chalna, in three consecutive attacks on alternate nights between 18 and 22 September, commandos armed with limpet mines damaged or destroyed *SS Lightning, SS Teviot Biock, SS AC Murtaza, SS Imtiaz Baksh*, the oil tanker *Sibtadinga*, one barge and two flat barges were set on fire, blocking the export of jute,' Major General Fazal Muqeem Khan wrote in 'Pakistan's Crisis in Leadership'.[35]

The Mukti Bahini had by now stepped into a second phase. As Niazi's advisor Brigadier Salik noted,[36] between August and September, the 'Mukti Bahini showed improvement in their training and a method in their operations. They seemed to be more confident, better motivated and better led. Now their exploits included ambushing army convoys, raiding police stations, blowing up vital installations, sinking river-craft and assassinating prominent political leaders. Their operations extended right up to Dacca.'

The encomiums continued to pour in for the naval commandos. The commander of Delta Sector, Brigadier Shabeg Singh, had by then grudgingly accepted their importance in at least one aspect – he occasionally sent for them to retrieve his golf balls from water hazards – a pond in the army golf course. Aku, much to the relief of his pilot pals, had no time to indulge in his favourite sport – hunting wild hare and boar from the back of a Vespa scooter. Years ago, a hare hunt inside the Hakimpet airbase ended when the impulsive Roy fired at, and fortunately missed, his friend Lt Medioma 'Mike' Bhada.

In Delta Sector, the mercurial pilot had trained his sights on bigger game – the inland shipping pulsing through East Pakistan's waterways. Aku sifted through the intelligence pouring into Delta Sector and had already outlined his convoy disruption game plan to his bosses in NCO(X).

---

35 Major General Fazal Muqeem Khan, *Pakistan's Crisis in Leadership* (Islamabad: National Book Foundation), 1973

36 Siddiq Salik, *Witness to Surrender* (New Delhi: Lancer Publishers), 1977

In his report of 19 September to Samant,[37] Aku suggested continuing the attacks against IWT shipping at ports 'by small groups of footballers on opportunity basis'. They were to pick off stragglers and unwary units which did not operate in convoys. 'Use frogmen with air breathing sets to attack major enemy ports – Chalna and Chittagong. Engage enemy boats wherever possible by using gunboats and laying ambushes using MMG/ LMG fire and automatic fire directed at waterline to sink boats'. They were to blow up ghats, jetties and cargo facilities used by the enemy wherever possible using the demolition explosives available, grenades or even arson.

He suggested laying 'carefully prepared ambushes for IWT convoys and escorts at suitable points on the river/channel banks in daytime using 57 mm Recoilless Rifles (a type of anti-tank weapon) to hit targets and using MMGs and LMGs for covering and continuous fire also'.

He noted deficiencies which were hurting the covert war effort. 'Though there were plenty of willing men in these sectors,' Aku wrote 'arms, explosives and special equipment was sadly lacking for these projects.' Training could be organized locally with an underwater demolitions expert from the navy to advise in the assembly and laying of mines, provided the materials were available to them. 'If materials, arms and advisers are made available at the sectors, more positive results could be achieved,' he wrote in his report.

Aku emphasised the need to employ a particularly nasty naval weapon – the naval anti-ship mine – to ambush inland shipping. These containers, packed with high explosives and dropped on the seabed, were classified according to their trigger mechanisms. Contact mines were triggered off when the target touched them;

---

37 Captain M.N.R. Samant's family archives

acoustic mines by the noise of a ship's propellers; and influence mines by the magnetic field generated by the hull of a ship.

He suggested placing mines on the river beds at suitable points and considering the depth of the water, the 'Mine river/channel bottoms at suitable points giving regard for the probability of vessels passing over the mined point. Consideration being given to depth of water, the ship's draft and the narrowness of the channel. The mines should be anchored to the bottom by a country anchor/heavy weight to prevent drifting. Suitable external 'fixing' marks on banks or channel should be chosen to mark the mines. The mine should be wired (before dropping). The wire leading to a dynamo exploder at a concealed point ashore. When a suitable vessel passes over the mined point, the mine should be exploded.'

He added:

The mine can be dropped at a suitable point by a country boat and from that point the pre-attached wire can be led to the concealed point ashore. The above procedure can also be used to mine the river/channel bottom adjacent to a ghat/jetty when no vessel is alongside. When a vessel comes along, the mine under it can be similarly exploded. The quantity of explosive in such a mine should be about 200 lbs to do effective damage (assuming average water depth of 10–15 feet and draught of 6–10 feet). The mine can be used singly on a single vessel or two or more mines can be used separately and suitably placed to do heavy damage on a convoy.

He recommended the use of the 250-lb aerial depth charge (dropped by the Alizé to hunt submarines) as the ideal weapon.

Aku's report was also copied to the DNI, Captain Roy in Delhi. It triggered off a chain of events that would play out in the weeks ahead. One pleasant September morning in Calcutta, Samant sent Lt Mitter to the military dispersal area of Calcutta airport to receive a military consignment from Bombay. Mitter left for Dum Dum airport after leaving the camp in his gunnery officer and chief boatswains' mate Jalal's care. The airport, north of Calcutta, was named after the 18th century British cantonment and arsenal where the eponymous 'expanding bullets' were invented.

The IAF flight was delayed, so Mitter spent his time looking over the IAF fighter jets parked between the runways. The six Folland Gnats of Number 22 Squadron sat under camouflage netting and sandbags – improvised blast pens that would protect them from enemy attack. A sign of the coming war. Everybody knew the Gnat – the tiny subsonic fighter aircraft – that had burnished its reputation in the 1965 Indo–Pak war as the 'Sabre Slayer' for shooting down Pakistani jets. With their swept-back wings, the IAF's primary air defence aircraft resembled the little insects they had been named after, resting in their nests. Then, at 6.30 p.m., a Fairchild Packet roared into view. The transport aircraft which had been the IAF's primary heavy lifter since the 1962 war with China manoeuvred past the Gnats and rolled into the military dispersal area. It resembled a giant metal box with wings – the reason why it was called the Flying Boxcar. As the cargo hold swung open, he saw the boxes he had been waiting for all day. There were ten wooden boxes secured in the hold, each around ten feet long, with 'Naval Armament Depot, Bombay' stencilled on them. A forklift hauled the boxes out of the aircraft and onto the truck.

'Handle the consignment with care,' Samant had told Mitter the previous day. 'It contains explosives.' Of what kind, he hadn't specified. The boxes were loaded onto the truck and, escorted by Mitter, began the slow and long drive south to Camp C2H where they were unloaded by cranes.

Meanwhile, on 28 September, it was Chiman Singh's turn to leave Delta Sector. The skirmishes between Indian and Pakistani troops along the border were a daily occurrence by now, and the sounds of gunfire could be heard in the distance. As the young sailor reported to Lt Cdr Aku Roy, he detected a trace of emotion in his voice: 'So, Chiman Singh … you're leaving too…'

The camp's isolation had begun to tell on Roy. In Delta Sector's jungles, he was a caged bird, launching naval commandos, writing intelligence reports and supervising the dreary task the 'Pongos'[38] ought to have been doing. The roar of aircraft over his tent were a constant reminder that he had not clocked the thirty-six flying hours per year that were mandated for aviators posted in non-flying billets. The accelerated tempo of naval air operations since April meant that if war broke out, he would be stranded without an aircraft because all the aviators with more current flying experience would get ahead. This had in fact already happened in June, before his current assignment, when NHQ recalled all Alizé and Sea Hawk pilots with current flying hours back to the Fleet Air Arm. In Delta Sector, the grounded pilot's mind buzzed with escape plans. He had heard Pakistani Sabres flying out of East Pakistan making strafing runs of Agartala airport.

Clearly not a war he would sit out of, he had joked with his boss visiting from Calcutta: 'Sir, another attack and I'm just going to grab a Dakota from the runway and get out of here.' He had also requested Samant and Roy that he be sent back to the Fleet Air Arm, for his fellow Cobras – Dhir, Ramsagar and Bhada– cornering all the glory on the *Vikrant* was not something he was looking forward to.

Chiman Singh didn't know of all this, but from that brief conversation it was clear to him that the aviator was unlikely to stay in Delta Sector for long.

There was another strange reason for Aku wanting to leave. In his final report to Samant, he mentioned his car in Bombay needing attention. Women came and went in the handsome bachelor's life,

---

38 Naval slang for the army

but the Standard Ten with the white roof and fins, was his only permanent love. On a solitary white-knuckle drive to Ooty from Cochin, some years ago, his car had tumbled down two steep road bends, flipping over on its hood on the first and landing on its four wheels on the next. The bruised pilot drove the car with the compacted roof down to Coimbatore for a very expensive repair.

For naval headquarters, X-men like Aku were on Temporary or 'TY' duty, working for a maximum of three months under the British-era rules. Any longer and the individual would have to return to where he was originally posted, even if just for twenty-four hours, record his position, and turnaround with a fresh three-month extension. As far as Aku was concerned, he had done his bit for the country with Operation Jackpot and the September attacks. He now wanted out.

When Chiman Singh reported to C2P on 30 September, the camp was enveloped in gloom. It had been four days since Lt Cdr Martis broke the tragic news. Lt Samir Das had died in a road accident on the night of 26 September. Accompanied by Major Nazmul Haque, commander, Mukti Bahini Sector VII, Lt Samir Das had been sent by Cdr Samant on a recce-plus-launch operation towards north Bengal. The duo was returning to Malda by jeep after a detailed meeting with Commander 101 Communication Zone Major General Gurbax Singh Gill in Siliguri, when their jeep was hit by a truck on the Purnea–Siliguri Road. Both Das and Haque died in the crash, and the driver miraculously survived. Das's body was cremated on the banks of the Brahmaputra and his ashes were scattered in the river.

Back at the camp which Das helped set up, there was no let-up in operations. Under Martis, NCO(X) was churning out recruits at a furious pace. Naval commandos were being trained and pushed across the border through the launch pads. Once they had crossed into the riverine areas of Sector X, they set to work on their targets like angry bees.

Curiously for a covert operation, Operation Jackpot left an enormous paper trail. That was because even though the money came out of secret funds, they had to be audited by the defence ministry. Officers at every level meticulously prepared reports of every item of expenditure, which would later be perused by the government auditors.

'The paperwork thrust on all of us,' Captain M. Rafiqul Islam, commander of the Mukti Bahini's Sector I (Chittagong) confided, was, 'frustrating and time-consuming'. 'Bangla Desh Forces HQ and the Indian sector HQ both demanded separate reports and returns for every item, every action, in duplicate even triplicate, and nicely typed and without any mistake to boot. There were times when for days together we had to prepare reports, leaving all operations at a standstill and the troops slumbering. If a galaxy of officers were available, such paperwork could have been properly distributed without overtaxing anyone or affecting the battle. But with only two officers at the sector HQ, out of whom the commanding officer ran from one subsector to another and the administrative officer scurried around for supplies, this luxurious paperwork annoyed us terribly. But we had to keep mum. Our supplies could be stopped without those reports. There were scores of those reports with hundreds of pages to be typed, checked and signed.'[39]

Rafiqul Islam was not the only one exasperated by filing reports. Naval commandos were expected to file detailed after-action debriefs and their expenses even while on the run from the enemy. On 9 September, for example, Badiul Alam, operation leader of Task Unit 54.1.2 that attacked Chandpur the previous month, filled out his

---

39 Major M. Rafiqul Islam, *A Tale of Millions* (Dacca: Adeylebros & Co.), 1974

expense sheet. Under three columns – date, description, amount – Alam, the former *Mangro* crewman, filled in what his men had spent on boat fare, food and tiffin and bus fare between 16 August and 2 September 1971. The escape from Chandpur had cost the group a total of 520 rupees and 25 paise.

Back in Fort William, Samant and Lt Cdr C.S. Menon were doing the same. All of NCO(X)'s activities were neatly documented and typed out on foolscap sheets. These reports included assessments, targeting information and, finally, detailed after-action analyses of attacks. Samant typed out the most sensitive reports himself. His assessments and action plans travelled up NCO(X)'s short command chain to Delhi and to his bosses Captain Roy and Admiral Nanda. DNI Roy might have been in Delhi, but nothing in NCO(X) moved without his approval. He was the spider sitting at the centre of an elaborate web he had spun. He knew every strand – the number of commandos being trained, where they were, their targets, what they planned to do next, and even the number of mines, swim fins and knives held in the camp. He kept tabs on the operation through frequent trips to Calcutta.

The Roy family grapevine, meanwhile, buzzed with stories of how their naval relative had begun spending a lot of time in Sheuli Bari, the two-storeyed family mansion at the intersection of two tree-lined roads in South Calcutta. The DNI was in plainclothes, wore muddy rubber boots and, unusually, was escorted by a submachine gun toting bodyguard. He could be spotted sprawled on the carpet in the living room, poring over nautical charts of East Pakistan. Back in Delhi, his ten-year-old son Probir wondered why his father would be doing any of this. Why, indeed?

In New Delhi, meanwhile, the navy had firmed up all its operational plans for the coming war. Sometime in October 1971, Admiral Nanda went to brief the prime minister. It was more than just a briefing. Nanda had gone to ensure the government would not issue another absurd directive like it had in 1965, to tie down its maritime sword arm. Would the government have any political objections to the navy attacking Karachi, Nanda asked her. The PM asked her navy chief for the reason behind his question. Admiral Nanda reminded her of the orders in 1965 per which the navy was told not to operate north of Indian territorial waters, meaning both East and West Pakistan. The decision had put the navy in a spot. The military aspects of the maritime encounter were the responsibility of the chief of naval staff, but the political aspects needed her clearance. The PM thought a bit and then responded: 'Well, admiral, if there is a war, there is a war.'[40]

'Madam, I have my answer.'

'After this clearance,' Admiral Nanda wrote in his autobiography, 'I was convinced that there was no further need of a dialogue on how precisely the navy was going to conduct its operations.'

In October, soon after this significant meeting with the PM, Admiral Nanda decided to pay C2P another visit. Like the first visit, he was accompanied by the Eastern Army Commander Aurora and Captain M.K. Roy. They were all in plainclothes and had flown in an Army Aviation Corps helicopter from Calcutta to observe a full day's training, including practical demonstration of explosives and hand grenades.

The camp was still a slushy mire from the monsoons. Nanda squished around the camp, inspecting it in his rubber Wellington boots. They moved to the officers' tent for tea before leaving. Nanda sat down and found the gumboots wouldn't come loose. Lt Cdr Martis sat down at his feet. 'Sir,' he said, looking straight-faced at Nanda, 'I think this is the first and the last time I'll be pulling a chief's leg.' The gathering dissolved into laughter as Martis yanked

<hr>

40 Admiral S.M. Nanda, *The Man Who Bombed Karachi* (New Delhi: HarperCollins *Publishers* India), 2004

Nanda's boots off. The VIPs then headed towards the green Alouette III crouched motionless on the helipad like a meditating dragonfly.

'Samant, come join us,' Admiral Nanda said, motioning towards the spare seat on board the chopper. Samant seemed relieved. It would save him the drudgery of the six-hour–long jeep ride back to Calcutta. The Alouette III lifted off with the high-pitched whine of its single 4447kw Turbomeca Artouste turboshaft engine and Plassey receded into the distance. About twenty minutes into the flight, Captain Roy's eyes widened with disbelief when he saw the lube oil pressure on the helicopter dropping fast. The pilot Major G.S. 'Gusty' Sihota responded to the emergency with alacrity. He immediately landed the helicopter in the middle of an open field, much to Captain Roy's relief. Roy had survived two crashes earlier – an Alizé off the coast of Hyeres, South of France in 1960 and, years before that, in a Royal Naval Firefly in the English Channel.

Hundreds of curious villagers gathered around the machine. Samant, who wasn't sure which side of the border they were on, ordered the pilots to brandish their revolvers. The crowd stayed at a respectful distance. He established that they were roughly ten miles from the border, on the Indian side. Samant was relieved the Pakistanis hadn't listened in to their distress call.

Now the problem was how to communicate the location of the crashed VIP flight to Calcutta as discreetly and as rapidly as possible. The nearest local police station was located some ten kilometres away. There was no mechanical transport in sight. As the brass sat around the helicopter, Samant, the junior-most of the group, swiftly sized up the situation. He left the army pilots behind to guard the crashed helicopter, waylaid a lungi-clad cyclist, then rode the ramshackle bicycle with the owner on the pillion all the way to the police station. The unlikely bicycle team landed at a nearby police station, where Samant reported the matter to the officer in charge. The police officer, in turn, commandeered a passing truck. Samant hopped on board with the driver and the cleaner and guided them to where the helicopter had landed. The pilots stayed behind to guard the helicopter and Admiral Nanda, Lt General Aurora, Captain Roy and Commander Samant boarded the cabin of the vehicle. Samant directed the driver to take them to the headquarters of 42 Infantry Brigade in Krishnanagar.

The atmosphere on board the truck was tense. The VVIPs were quiet. Memories of India's worst-ever military crash – November 1963, when four lieutenant generals, one air vice marshal, a brigadier and a flight lieutenant died in an Alouette crash in Poonch, Jammu and Kashmir – were still fresh in their minds. Today, it seemed, providence was on the Indian side.

Nanda's gruff exterior masked his quirky gallows humour. It usually took a crisis to reveal it. 'Jaan bachi to laakho paaye' (it's worth millions if everybody is safe) Nanda chuckled at a common Hindi aphorism as the truck drew closer to the Bhagirathi. He was displaying the same humour he had exhibited when he ribbed a naval commander who had knocked five frontline warships out of action in a freak berthing accident in Bombay earlier that year: 'You have achieved in five minutes what the Pakistan Navy has been trying to do for two decades.'

'Ghar ke buddhu waapas aaye,' (the prodigal fools have returned) General Aurora piped in. The group in the driver's cabin smiled and relaxed a little.

When they reached the riverfront, Samant darted out and commandeered a large thirty-foot long nauka, riverine Bengal's standard transport. The boat was powered by six oarsmen, three on either side. 'C'mon, you pull,' Nanda grinned and directed Samant to one of the oars. Nanda played coxswain, throatily urging the six oarsmen on as they crossed the river. The navy chief had found a way to bust his stress over the incident.

The police communication network had meanwhile informed the army unit. The brigade's rescue teams with transport and equipment were waiting on the opposite bank. The VVIPs were swiftly driven to the Headquarters Mess where Brigadier Gharaya headed the reception committee, waiting with glasses of frothing cold beer. 'Here! Samant!' Admiral Nanda picked his glass up and offered it to the commander who grabbed it and gulped it down without question. After a brief halt at the Brigade Mess, the party embarked in jeeps with escort riders for Fort William. Lieutenant General Aurora personally drove the jeep with Admiral Nanda seated next to him, weaving through Calcutta's chaotic traffic. This was one adventure the architects of the coming war would remember for the rest of their lives.

'Soman' resumed his work, moving wraithlike, briefcase in hand, between his camps C2P, C2H and his Fort William redoubt. His force was well prepared and itching to get into combat. Back at C2P, Lt Kapil was nursing an itch of a different kind. The poor living conditions in the camp had kicked in, first, as red patches around his groin and soon, the lower half of his body was covered in red sores. It was a fungal infection called 'Dhobi's Itch'. A tube of quick fix local ointment from the Palashi market only turned the sores into open wounds. Walking was an ordeal. The military doctors prescribed a stay at the army command hospital in Barrackpore. The cantonment where a sepoy, Mangal Pandey, had fired the first shot of the 1857 First War of Independence, was a salubrious recovery spot. Kapil blended into the army hospital, playing daily games of Bridge and rummy with the dozen other army officers in the large dormitory-sized ward. Another game he played was evasion – deflecting curious queries from army roommates about what he was doing here: ashore, so far away from the maritime theatre. It was a game his boss Commander Samant was also playing with him. Kapil, for instance, had no idea about Sammy's gunboats. NCO(X) was a tightly-run operation. Information was on a strict need-to-know basis. Only Admiral Nanda, Captain Roy and Commander Samant knew the big picture.

Samant was also laying the foundation for the future Bangla Desh Navy. On 4 October, on the request of the Bangla Desh Forces HQ, he despatched a list with the names of seventy-one naval commandos, between nineteen and twenty-five years old. The group had a mean age of twenty – there were five graduates, two post-graduates, a second year MBBS student, an engineering diploma holder and one associate mechanical engineer. All others had passed their intermediate examinations, held engineering diplomas or had been undergraduates for science, arts and commerce degrees. These were the men in whom Samant had spotted officer-like qualities and education levels suitable for induction as Bangla Deshi naval officers.

October brought deliverance for Aku Roy. Captain M.K. Roy had grudgingly approved his request for a transfer back to the 310 Squadron. Aku had not known, perhaps, of the raising of 'Kilo-Flight', the Mukti Bahini Air Force on 4 October, with one Dakota, one Otter and an armed Alouette helicopter. But it was unlikely that would have lured him away from the opportunity to get back in the left seat of the Alizé. An ecstatic Aku, three months away from his thirty-second birthday, emerged from Delta Sector, boarded the ferry flight to Calcutta and reported to Cdr Samant in Fort William. The young aviator was soon winging his way back to Bombay to be in the thick of the coming war.

October was also when the tide had once again started turning against the Mukti Bahini and the Indian forces supporting them. The after-effects of the Independence Day attack had quickly worn off. The flow of maritime trade from the ports of Bangla Desh and their subsequent distribution into the hinterland by inland water transport resumed despite the attacks by C2P's naval commandos.

Samant had analyzed the reasons for this. The Pakistani authorities had started offering lucrative compensation rates to foreign shipping companies. The Pakistan Army and Navy had stepped up gunboat patrols. Now, Nanda, Roy and Samant had shifted NCO(X) into a twin-pronged strategy of massive simultaneous attacks on the main and riverine ports. The gunboats, the second prong of their strategy were not ready for action yet. But they had someone who was – Major General J.F.R. Jacob. In October, Jacob was the country's most important two-star officer. He wore two hats as chief of staff Eastern Command and director operations (X) controlling Mukti Bahini actions. He had taken over from Major General Jimmy Sarkar who had moved to the army headquarters as the quarter master general, the office responsible for providing transport and supplies for the entire army.

On 8 October, Jacob's intelligence chief Colonel A.C. Vora invited Commander Samant home for dinner. He had someone very important to introduce – M. Rehman, former general manager of Inland Waterways in East Pakistan, who had crossed over into India after the military crackdown. Rehman was a goldmine of information and seemed to know a lot about the naval set up in East Pakistan. Prior to May 1971, Rehman said, only one naval establishment, *PNS Bakhtiar*, existed in Chittagong. After the outbreak of trouble in the province, the government realized the importance of the inland waterways to move troops and logistics and the fact that they needed to strengthen their navy for operations against India. Until 1971, the navy in East Pakistan was headed by the commodore commanding East Pakistan (COMCEP). In May 1971, it was upgraded to flag officer commanding East Pakistan at Dacca headed by Rear Admiral Mohammad Shariff.

But the show in Shariff's office, Rehman said, was being run by Shariff's chief of staff. Samant froze as he heard the name –

Captain Zamir Ahmad – his cabinmate from the British Naval Academy, Dartmouth. Zamir had risen fast in the Pakistan Navy and had already got his fourth stripe. 'He is extremely hard working, shrewd and in the good books of Pakistan Naval HQ,' Rehman told Samant. Since 1 June that year, Captain Zamir had set up an amphibious warfare unit, the Pakistan Marines. The Marines, a battalion-sized formation headquartered in Dacca, were meant to defend the waterways and the ports of Khulna and Chittagong from the enemy. Fate, it would seem, had placed the cabinmates from Dartmouth on opposite sides.

I wonder if Zamir knows who he is fighting, Samant thought to himself. Captain Zamir's businessman father Nazir Ahmad Qureshi who lived in pre-Partition New Delhi's Karol Bagh was a member of the Khilafat Movement and a prominent member of the All India Muslim League Council. This is the same council that finally approved the Partition Plan held in Delhi's Imperial Hotel on 3 June 1947. The decisions were a result of what came to be known as the two-nation theory – the Hindus and Muslims of India could not live together and hence needed separate homelands based on religion. The thread connecting the disparate ends of Pakistan was religious identity. If East Pakistan broke away, the two-nation theory would collapse. For Zamir Ahmad, Samant reasoned, the struggle to defend East Pakistan was also an intensely personal one.

Samant was by now no longer concerned about the failure to locate former SSU personnel – he now had hundreds of naval commandos. Phase II would need 114 commandos, a mix of new recruits from C2P and those returning from Operation Jackpot. Unlike Phase I, which involved precisely targeted, massive attacks on four designated port targets, Phase II would consist of dispersed attacks of less intensity across four Mukti Bahini sectors. Phase II was going to be a war of a thousand cuts, designed to bleed out the adversary 'in the true spirit of guerrilla operations', as Samant noted in his plans.[41] His commandos would not be deterred by the enhanced vigil on the waterways, they would attack whatever targets they could. 'Opportunity targets that present themselves will be made full use of. Teams will comprise of two individuals. Teams will form part of the Mukti Bahini forces operating in their respective areas and will seek the best opportunity to ensure successful attacks. They will, however, operate under the control of their respective sector commanders who will decide the targets and organize the infiltration.'

To ensure all-round coverage of Bangla Desh, eleven important ports and loading sites were selected. Using intelligence gathered from the Mukti Bahini, NCO(X) had assessed the nature of targets in each port and drawn up a list of the number of teams required to achieve the mission.

Each two-man team would carry two limpet mines, 4 kgs of PEK explosives with a detonator and fuse, two diving knives, survival rations for transit depending on the distance they would have to travel, two pairs of fins and four hand grenades.

He wrote out a list of targets in the four sectors:

Charlie Sector

1. Khulna – Jute and Inland Water Traffic (IWT), Chalna, Gunboats at PNS Titumir
2. Barisal – (i) floating dock (120'x 45') (ii) Hovercraft service – called rocket service (iii) possible gunboat and IWT
3. Morrelganj – (i) occasional tanker/barges (ii) possible gunboat (iii) IWT – does not halt at night
4. Madaripur – (i) possible gunboat (ii) two IWT ships
5. Goalundo Ghat – IWT shipping – one ship and two ferries

---

41 Captain M.N.R. Samant's family archives

Delta Sector

6. Narsingdi – five to six large IWT ships carrying jute
7. Munshiganj to Narayanganj area (i) two big steamers (ii) one Muslim League boat (iii) over ten medium/small IWT launches (iv) barges
8. Brahmanbaria – four to five IWT ships – is a focal point of supply

Foxtrot/Juliet Sectors

9. Sirajganj –IWT shipping and gunboat
10. Phulchari – IWT shipping and gunboat
11. Chilmari – IWT shipping and gunboat

In October, a third wave of assault swimmers got ready to strike deep inside eastern Bangla Desh. The operation would use eighty-two commandos to strike at Narayanganj, Chandpur and the islands of Hathia and Sandwip. The infiltration plan through Delta Sector was named for a force of nature – Operation Cloud Burst.

C2P's officer strength was severely depleted. Lt Cdr Martis was away on leave of absence and Lt Kapil nursing his sores in Barrackpore. Samant addressed his letter to Sub Lieutenant B.S. Thakur, the person in charge of C2P: 'I require a total of eighty-two. But since thirty-nine are already available in Delta Sector, I am asking for forty-three now from the camp. So select the best ones. Tell others not to worry, for we will be sending them too.'

Thakur was asked to move the commandos from his camp, equip them with knives, fins, seventy-four complete soluble plug assemblies and personal clothing, including bedding. The selected group was to report to Major Manzoor at Kalyani camp in Charlie Sector. In his letter, Samant couldn't resist listing NCO(X)'s achievements from Phase II of the operations. 'You will be happy to know that our boys have done the following. Mid-October, the coaster *MV Siptadingha* was sunk in Barisal area. On 27 October, two Pakistani gunboats had been damaged in the Phulchari Ghat area of B Sector.'

Among the commando task force leaders launched in Phase II was Abdur Rakib Mian. The twenty-four-year-old electrical mechanic of the *PNS Mangro* had accompanied A.W. Chowdhury and six others in their escape from Europe. He was given his first mission to sink river steamers carrying provisions for the Pakistan Army at Phulchhori Ghat, which fell under Foxtrot/Juliet Sectors. Rakib, the native of Tangail district, had infiltrated the border through Mahendraganj in Meghalaya with eight naval commandos. On the night of 25 October, there were five steamers in port when the nine commandos entered the river from south of Bahadurabad Ghat. Each commando had a limpet mine strapped to his chest. The river was in spate. The ships were on high alert as two ships had been damaged in an earlier attack. One of the steamers they had targeted started up its engines just as Rakib approached, its giant propellers shredding his body. Abdur Rakib had paid the highest price in the liberation struggle.

The October 1971 kill sheet was sent to Captain Roy in three horizontal pages, headlined, 'Naval Commando Operations during October 1971 – Maritime Shipping Attacked'. The legends were marked 'C' for captured, 'D' for damaged and 'S' for sunk. The activity sheet was divided into five columns – date, port of targets, number and type of targets, details and remarks. On 8 October, the Pakistani coasters *MV Nasim* and *MV Rashid*, each displacing around 800 tons had been sunk. 'Information based on Lloyds, Calcutta, and own sources' the remarks read. In the second week of October, in the Barisal area, an 800-ton Greek tanker had been sunk: 'Information based on intercepts'. On 28 October, a Greek tanker had been damaged in an attack in Chittagong. 'Damaged.

Information confirmed vide ADSI Log…' On 30 October, in Chandpur, the US-origin coaster *MV Loren*, displacing around 2500 tons had been sunk. In the Barisal area on 31 October, another coaster of US-origin had been damaged.

On October 29, Samant's new staff officer Lt Cdr G.D. Mukherjee who had replaced Cdr C.S. Menon that month, escorted ninety commandos from C2P to Kalyani Camp. He brought them to Kalyani Camp on 29 October to launch them with the Mukti Bahini's Major Manzoor. They were split in two groups – eighty-four commandos belonging to Khulna, Barisal, Arichaghat, Golando Ghat and Gab Khan canal would be launched from Barisal. Six commandos for the Nagarbari area would be launched from Jalangi in Murshidabad district.

On 1 November, the eighty-four commandos arrived at Major Nazrul Huda's camp bordering Jessore district. It was close to the Kapotoko river which demarcated the international boundary. Sixty commandos were launched into Bangla Desh by ferry at 9.30 p.m. The Khulna party comprising twenty-four commandos could not be launched on that day because guides were not available. 'A protection party of twenty-four boys were provided for these sixty boys. In addition, the leader and sub leader of each party was issued with one carbine and two hundred rounds. The boys were fairly motivated and the launching was fairly organized and the entire operation went on very smoothly,' Lt Cdr Mukherjee typed out in his report to his boss.

Among Mukherjee's launch crew was a tall, lanky, long-haired diver with chest-length beard, in a checked shirt and lungi – Leading Seaman Chiman Singh slinging a 9 mm Sterling carbine – on another launch mission. Chiman Singh was to escort his naval commando understudies to the border, remove all identification from them, and then, after ensuring they had gone, turn back. After the successful launch, called an 'induction', the launch team was to report to Lt Cdr Martis at C2P. Chiman Singh walked into the darkness with the naval commandos but did not return.

The news travelled back to Samant in Fort William almost immediately. Chiman Singh had most likely entered East Pakistan with the naval commando party he had escorted for the induction. Samant tensed up. Singh's capture by the Pakistanis could lead to an international incident. He sprinted up the stairs of Command HQ and rapidly knocked on Major General Jacob's door. He entered and began without a preface: 'I'd like to report one of my boys missing sir.'

Jacob was sitting in a cloud of pipe smoke. He appeared unflustered. 'Who?'

'Chiman Singh.'

'What was he doing?'

'He had gone to induct a naval commando party … he hasn't returned…'

'Oh F**k!' Jacob exclaimed, but he dismissed Samant's apprehensions. 'He must have been carrying a gun which he hadn't used in years and must've decided to go in …' he guffawed, adding, 'don't worry, he'll be back.' A few days later, NCO(X) declared Leading Seaman Chiman Singh missing in action.

Colonel
M.A.G. OSMANI

COMMANDER-IN-CHIEF
BANGLADESH
ARMED FORCES

Admiral S.M. NANDA
CHIEF OF NAVAL STAFF

Gene

Captain M.K. ROY
DIRECTOR
NAVAL
INTELLIGENCE

STA

C2P
PLASSEY
NAVAL COMMANDOS

Lt Cdr GEORGE MARTIS
CAMP IN-CHARGE

Lt V.P. KAPIL
SECOND-IN-COMMAND

Lt SAMIR DAS
TRAINING COORDINATOR

NAVAL TRAINING CREW

CHIMAN SINGH

E.J. PRINCHAN

KARAN SINGH

P.K. BHATTACHARJE

MANGRO 8

L to R: Abdur Rehman, Abdur Rakib Mian, Ahsanullah, Aminullah Sheikh, A.W. Chowdhury, Badiul Alam, Rah

al S.H.F.J. MANECKSHAW
CHIEF OF ARMY STAFF

Lt Gen J.S. AURORA
GOC-IN-CHIEF
EAST

Major Gen J.F.R. JACOB
CHIEF STAFF OFFICER
EASTERN COMMAND

Cdr M.N.R. SAMANT
F OFFICER-1 (NAVAL OPERATIONS X)

Major Gen B.N. SARKAR
DIRECTOR OPERATIONS (X)

C2H
HALDIA
GUNBOATS

Lt Cdr J.K. ROY
CHOUDHARY
MV PALASH

Lt Cdr ASHOK ROY
NAVAL DET
(TRIPURA D SECTOR)

Lt Cdr J.P.A.
NORONHA
'FORCE ALFA'
DEC 6–11,1971
INS PANVEL

Lt SUVESH KUMAR MITTER

M.S. GUPTA

P.K. DHOLE

E

432 *NAVAL COMMANDOS/ ASSAULT SWIMMERS*
TRAINED BETWEEN MAY–NOV 1971

natullah and Syed Mosharaff Hussain.

A (ALFA)
Murti
West Bengal

We

Panchag

Thakurgaon

S

Dinaj

B (BRAVO)
Raiganj
West Bengal

Ganga River

Bhagirathi River

Ra

Plassey
C2P

West Bengal

Brigadier
N.A. SALIK
CHARLIE SECTOR

C (CHARLIE
Kalyani
West Benga

Calcu

C2H

Haldia

Hooghly River

Sandheads

DISCLAIMER: Sketch is not drawn

8

BEHIND ENEMY LINES

The khaki-clad postman cycled his way through the village post office and stopped at the house of Nand Kishore Yadav, deep inside Gokulgarh village in Haryana's Gurgaon district. The village had sent its sons in all the wars of the 20th century, several of them, never to return. Homes shared an uneasy relationship with postmen. It was no different this time. The postman bore a telegram from the Indian Navy for a bewildered twenty-three-year-old Vidya Yadav.

'Regret to inform your husband C. Singh, leading seaman, service number 87600, reported missing in operation 1 November. Further information will be sent immediately on receipt.'

The wails that emanated from the small brick home drew the rest of the village women in. Gokulgarh, it seemed, had given another son to the cause of India's defence. It was a war the village hadn't heard of yet.

News of the twenty-five-year-old's MIA status had already ricocheted around Fort William and Camp Plassey a few days earlier. Chiman Singh had last been spotted with the Mukti Bahini team he had gone to send off and Lt Cdr Mukherjee's debrief of Cloud Burst to NCO(X) had somewhat allayed their fears:

171

One naval sailor L/S Chiman Singh had also crossed over on the other side and has not come back. He is not a traitor. I think he got conditionally involved and he thinks if he is there, he will be able to carry out the operation properly. Before he left, he had left his identity card, Indian currency and his belongings in the transport.

It was not easy for NCO(X) to contact commandos once they had been launched. But what had happened to Chiman Singh?

'Saheb, come with us.'

Chiman Singh smiled at Nazrul Islam and his men as he continued to collect all their valuables. The group of men stood at the point that marked the border between India and East Pakistan. From there on, it was enemy territory. The NCO(X) personnel were under strict instructions not to cross the invisible line. Their death or worse, capture, could reveal India's hand in the covert war.

But Nazrul Islam persisted. 'Saheb, come with us.' Chiman Singh carried their valuables with him to the truck and kept them inside.

The X-men were meant to train, motivate and finally launch the naval commandos across the border for what could easily be the last mission of their lives. There was no question of emotional involvement. But after six months of hearing stories of atrocities committed on their trainees and their families, their dedication to their cause had moved him. Singh left his diver's watch, his identity card and cash along with the belongings of the naval commandos and then turned around and headed into the darkness, towards the border. 'C. Singh … C. Singh!' the voices rang out in the distance. Singh's heart was pounding. The voices grew fainter as the group strode into East Pakistan. There was no turning back now. The smiles travelled through the group as they saw their instructor joining them. Chiman Singh was disobeying orders for the first time in his ten-year-long career, risking a court-martial, dismissal or, given the nature of the operation, certain imprisonment.

The group merged into the pitch-dark countryside of Khulna.

Surrounding him were little Davids who carried in their cloth bags a dozen limpet mines, thirty-six hand grenades, five kilograms of plastic explosives, detonators, delay pencils, cortex and safety fuses.

Nazrul Islam, a twenty-two-year-old engine mechanic first class from Barisal had deserted the Pakistan Navy a few months earlier. He was among the eleven names that Samant had recommended for officer training in the Bangla Desh military that month. In an official note, dated 5 October, to the Headquarters Eastern Army Command, Samant had listed Nazrul Islam as a candidate for officer training. 'Ex ME (I) from Pak Navy submarine service who is at present away on a naval commando mission.' He was, in Samant's words, 'a young sailor with a cheerful disposition, above average ability to lead and organize.'

Nazrul's small group, including Chiman, crossed Khulna district led by the Mukti Bahini guide provided by Major Huda. Their guide knew his way around the less-travelled routes and the location of the safe havens arranged for them by the Bangla Desh government in exile. Their destination was Barisal, East Pakistan's second-largest riverine port and a district in south-central Bangla Desh. The district was sandwiched between Khulna, Dacca and Chittagong, and bound by the Bay of Bengal in the south.

Even in the darkness, Singh could make out how green the region was: full of coconut trees, quite like the backwaters of Kerala where he had spent five years of his career.

The group walked only by night, crossing the waterways by boat and seeking refuge in designated safe houses on the periphery of villages. Here, they slept through daylight, taking care not to step out of their shelter. As they headed deeper inside Khulna, fearful thoughts began to cloud Singh's mind. He was dressed like the rest, in a lungi and vest, but he could never blend in – his six-foot frame, thick beard, complexion, and distinct features always attracted a second look from locals. The group shielded him from conversation lest his cover be blown. Chatty strangers they encountered en route were told they were attending social gatherings or family celebrations in the village after next.

Their expert local guides were well-versed in the routes and the safe havens along these routes. They had also been advised to only reveal the next stop along the route to locals if ever the question of their destination arose, and never the final destination.

Singh resolved to be extra vigilant. Any misstep would not only grievously endanger his life, it would also bring disgrace to his country. He had already decided not to risk capture. If it came to that, he would turn the barrel of his 9 mm Sterling into his mouth and pull the trigger. The carbine never left his side. Even when he bathed in ponds, it was always kept right beneath his clothes, within easy reach.

The walks were arduous. They covered over twenty kilometres each night, halting at safe houses by 5 a.m. and leaving at 6 p.m. They never spent more than a night in each safe house. Every village they passed had Awami League supporters, but also Muslim League sympathisers and razakars who were on the alert for Mukti Bahini fighters. In village after village, the group heard stories about skirmishes between the two groups. The razakars, armed and given free hand by the Pakistani authorities, terrorized the villagers, settled old scores and, finally, walked away with their opponents' most precious possessions – their cattle.

After ten days of walking, the group reached Barisal district. Their guide took them to the designated safe house near a village –

a mud hut covered with corrugated tin sheets and paddy husk. It was the house of the village headmaster, an Awami League activist.

The headmaster, a short, middle-aged man with a greying beard in a lungi and gamcha, welcomed the group and made a beeline for Singh. He struck up a conversation in broken Urdu.

'You don't look Bengali … how are you supporting us?'

He was a foreigner, Singh admitted. He had come from the UK to join the freedom struggle. The headmaster was impressed. A little later, villagers began streaming into the house. Two men brought in a calf; they were washing its toes. One of them offered prayers to the bleating animal. Singh leaned towards Nazrul and asked him what was going on.

'They are sacrificing a calf,' Nazrul whispered, 'in your honour.' The calf was led away for the slaughter. Its throat would be slit, all the blood drained out of its body before it was cut up and served to their honoured guests. Singh was aghast. He was not a beef eater.

Hours later, when the food arrived, Chiman Singh sprang up, holding his stomach, and darted out of the small gathering outside. 'He has a stomach upset,' Nazrul informed his host. When Singh returned after a visit to the fields, there was a strange-looking man waiting for him. It was the village hakim whom his hosts had swiftly summoned.

The hakim seemed to notice how different Chiman Singh was from the rest of the group. Singh was on alert, his pulse racing as the physician came closer for an examination. Singh resumed his act. He clenched his jaw as if in extreme pain. Nazrul explained his symptoms – stomach cramps.

The hakim nodded and asked Singh to open his mouth even as his hosts crowded around. Singh winced at his touch, and didn't meet his eye. But the hakim seemed convinced of his ailment. He handed Singh a pouch of medicines and left.

Lest the village doctor recount his strange encounter to someone else, the group decided to leave earlier than planned. Singh kept up the act. A deliriously hungry diver remembered to grab a handful of puffed rice before heading into the cold winter night with his crew.

Before leaving, they handed their host some Pakistani currency and something far more valuable – a certificate of appreciation recording their contribution to the struggle for Bangla Desh. Each Mukti Bahini team launched between August and November distributed such letters to anyone who provided them safe haven.

As the naval commandos neared Barisal district, the group came across a large power pylon along a riverbank located right next to a jetty. There were no vessels in sight, but this was a tempting opportunity target. Chiman Singh packed some plastic explosive on one leg of the tower, rolled the cordex 300 metres away and lit a match. The spark hissed down the line. There was a sharp crack. The pylon groaned and toppled over, smashing the jetty and snapping the high-tension wires. They had risked alerting the enemy but this target seemed worth that risk.

The group continued their trek. After a few nights, each evening marked by a stop at a new village and a new safe house, the group reached Barisal. The town was located amidst a latticework of rivers. The fury of the monsoons had subsided. The Kirtankhola river had receded, exposing its sandy bed at places. At one such spot, Singh spotted the white skeletons. There were hundreds of them – stripped of clothes and flesh, each one tied to a brown earthenware pot and lodged on the sands like some ghostly frieze. His diver's mind broke the carnage down as he hurried past. The pots were sinkers used to drown those hapless people and to keep their bodies on the riverbed when they bloated up. It was, he noted, an inexpensive way to kill a lot of people in a riverine country.

In Barisal, the group met the local Mukti Bahini commander, Captain Shahjahan Omar. The officer was in his mid-twenties, well-educated and impressively built, and lived on a small motor boat berthed on the river. He proudly showed Singh his prized possession – a Type 56, a Chinese clone of the AK-47. Captain Omar then briefed them on the local situation and pointed to targets of opportunity. There were barges and ferry boats used for supporting the Pakistan Army in Barisal. Chiman Singh, Nazrul Islam and the commandos waited for the next five days for a target to emerge. Singh stayed on Omar's boat, sleeping on one of the twin bunks.

Meanwhile, the countryside around them had risen in revolt. Mukti Bahini guerrilla activities hit a crescendo in November. Each day of the calendar was marked by attacks as guerrillas ambushed Pakistani troops across the country almost at will. On 4 November, a team of assault swimmers sank a 700-ton oil tanker *Mahtab Jabed* in Chittagong, killing seven crewmen. On a single day, 12 November, the guerrillas struck in eight different locations across the country – Kushtia, Chuadanga, Sylhet, Dacca, Chailashia, Juri-Goalbari, Chittagong and Rajshahi – killing over fifty Pakistani soldiers. Between October and November, the Pakistan Army lost 236 officers, 136 JCOs and 3,559 soldiers in counter-insurgency operations. The insurgency was slowly bleeding Niazi.

On the eastern side of Barisal, a few kilometres away from where Chiman Singh and his team were, naval commando Atharuddin Talukder took his spectacles off. He was ready for his first mission. He had been launched from C2P in September and was now in a three-man task unit that included the team leader Syed Abdul Basher and naval commando Shah Alom. They were hiding in Kornokathi village on the eastern bank of the Kirtonkhola, about four kilometres from Barisal. Talukder had spent the month of Ramzan hiding in the home of Abdur Rashid, a local sympathizer. On 12 November, an opportunity target emerged. A local sympathizer, Chunnu Talukder, had spotted two riverine ships called coasters moored near a floating dock. Shah Alom was to dive into the river at Napterhat, plant his limpets on a ship anchored near the Telegraph & Telephone Office and escape to the house of another sympathizer Rustam Sardar. Talukder was to join him there after striking at the second ship.

Talukder had left his spectacles behind in Abdur Rashid's home for he felt that wearing it would attract attention. What troubled him was his missing diver's knife. A police constable who had defected to the Mukti Bahini had borrowed it from him while Talukder stayed at Captain Omar's camp, never to return.

The commandos had decided to attack at 2 a.m., when the 400-metre wide Kirtonkhola was ebbing. The attack would be carried out exactly as they had been trained. The commandos would enter the river upstream, float down to their targets – two oil tankers and a foreign vessel carrying relief goods – and then float away downstream with the ebb tide.

Talukder would dive into the small canal at Naptarhat flowing by the northern side of the Kauwarchor Madrasa, affix his limpet mines to the ships anchored beside each other near the floating dock. Shah Alom too would enter the river at Naptarhat and exit near Rustam Sardar's house.

The group arrived at the location at 1 a.m. along with their local guides – three young boys carrying a kerosene lamp. The boys were to go to a designated spot downriver and shine a lamp to identify the spot where the commandos had to exit the water.

At Naptarhat, Talukder began his part-transformation from an ordinary Bengali civilian into riverine guerrilla. He slipped on his swimming trunks as the boys tied the limpet to his chest. He carried his Abee fins in his hand and walked along the riverbank, looking for a spot to cross the river. The boys, meanwhile, raced down the riverbank ahead of him.

He walked for nearly 700 metres on the riverbank between Naptarhat and Kauwarchor Madrasa. Around 100 metres away, he saw the searchlight from a patrol boat anchored midstream criss-crossing the river. A counter-saboteur drill was underway. His target, the coaster carrying food supplies, was under heavy guard. Talukder paused to understand the search pattern. It swept past the riverbank every three minutes. He lay down and waited for it to pass over and then started walking again. His exposed body trembled in the cold November night but he ignored the sensation. His only concern was to reach his target, which he realized would be impossible without being spotted. It was already 2 a.m. He had to hit the water before the tide turned.

He tore the wrapping off the condom, rolling the rubber over the soluble plug. He put on his rubber Abee fins and walked backwards into the river, balancing the weight of the mine on his chest. As soon as he hit the water, the weight of the mine disappeared.

The beam of the searchlight stabbed the water. Talukder dived beneath the surface to avoid its gaze. The fast-moving ebb tide took him further down, away from his target. That was when he spotted the silhouette of an oil tanker moored by the riverbank. He took a deep breath and dived beneath the water, going down around six feet along the shipside. He used his bare hands to scrape the moss off its hull, unfastened the limpet and pressed it against the hull. He rolled the condom off the soluble plug. The rubber sped away with the current.

He then turned around and let the current take him to the eastern shore of the river. A load was now off his chest and mind.

The search light returned. He dipped his forehead, eyes and nose beneath the water. In the inky blackness of the river, there was silence all around. The words of Prime Minister Tajuddin Ahmed visiting C2P echoed in his ears: 'This is a suicide squad … only those who can sacrifice their lives for the country should take this training.'

If the searchlight caught him, Talukder thought, martyrdom would be near. He stuck his face out of the water and saw the light shimmering at Naptarhat. The boys were waiting and waving the kerosene lamp. Then, he felt a trembling sensation under the water, it was the shock wave from the blast. In the distance, he saw a narrow plume of water rise up from the river to a height of ten feet. It was the greatest moment of his life.

Just then, he felt a net close in around him. He thrashed about. He had swum right into the net of a fisherman walking on the riverbed, against the current. The fisherman, who thought he had snagged a crocodile, panicked and scampered ashore. Talukder extricated himself from the net, walked out of the water and calmed the trembling man in Bengali: 'Don't worry, I am a freedom fighter.'

Almost in response, a fusillade of bullets crackled from the western bank, raking the river like light rain. The duo lay prone on the ground. After a few minutes, the firing stopped. Talukder rose, thanked the fisherman and walked towards Naptarhat. The boys were waiting for him. They couldn't conceal their excitement. 'I saw the water leaping out the highest,' one of them chortled.

In his moment of triumph, one thing became clear to Talukder. His battle was not a solitary one. It was a people's war. His host Abdur Rashid and his family had fed and sheltered him at great personal risk. Without these young boys, he could never have got to the target and back. A naval commando risked only his life, Talukder mused. Locals who assisted them, imperilled their families. He dried himself with a towel borrowed from one of the boys, discarded the swim trunks and wore a lungi and shirt they had brought with them. He was now a civilian again. He walked towards the safe house of Rustam Sardar where the team was to assemble. The November chill had started to kick in.

The group reached Sardar's house by around 4 a.m. Talukder was feted as a hero by the team leader, Sayed Abul Bashar. His comrade Shah Alam who had arrived there before him was crestfallen. He had failed to target the foreign merchant vessel laden with food.

The ship had switched its engines on and the propellers were churning the water. Shah Alam could not plant his mines. Talukder discovered the next day that the oil from the ship he had crippled had travelled nearly thirty kilometres downstream to neighbouring Jhalakhati district.

Talukder was part of the last major wave of naval commando attacks before the outbreak of full-fledged war. The attacks came at a cost. By the end of November, at least a dozen naval commandos were killed in the line of duty, some of them after being brutally tortured by the Pakistan Army and their razakar collaborators. Kabiruzzaman was spotted by a searchlight while planting a limpet mine on a ship at Takerhat in Barisal. He was shot and killed on the spot. Siddiqur Rahman died of injuries sustained after being shot by razakars. Mohammad Hossain Farid was captured by the Pakistan Army during the second attack on Chittagong. The chilling story had it that he was stuffed into a manhole and bent over until his back broke. For NCO(X)'s planners, an attrition rate of less than 2 per cent for an overall strength of over 450 trainees was deemed acceptable. It was far less than the 10 per cent attrition rate that Commander Samant had estimated in May. He was happy to have been proven wrong.

9
SAMMY'S TURTLES

On 4 November 1971, Mrs Indira Gandhi met President Richard Nixon in the Oval Office of the White House. The visit was part of India's outreach to tell the world about the atrocities in Bangla Desh and the millions of refugees pouring into India.

The meeting was a disaster, marked by mutual suspicion, acrimony and, as emerged in Nixon's White House tapes declassified three decades later, explosive anger and frustration.

The two heads of state sat down for an informal chat in the Oval Office with their aides National Security Adviser Henry Kissinger and Principal Secretary P.N. Haksar seated close by. Nixon denounced the Bengali insurgents for interfering with the supplies on ships near Chittagong harbour. That kind of guerrilla warfare, the president suggested, had to rely on sophisticated training and equipment. Mrs Gandhi dodged the accusation, foggily responding that 'India had been accused of supporting guerrilla activity but the situation was not that clear.' Nobody sitting in the Oval Office believed that, least of all Gandhi and Haksar. She perplexingly compared the insurgency to Cuban exiles in Florida striking against Cuba.[42]

---

42 Gary J. Bass, *The Blood Telegram: India's Secret War in East Pakistan* (India: Vintage), July 2014

Nixon's private conversation with Kissinger recorded on tape at the Oval Office the day after meeting Mrs Gandhi was an explosive, expletive-filled rant – the duo called the Indian prime minister a 'bitch' and 'an old witch'. Kissinger repeated what the President had said about the Mukti Bahini guerrillas getting sophisticated military training.

Kissinger: She didn't know [unclear exchange] about the guerrillas in East Pakistan. [unclear]. One thing that really struck me, the blown up [unclear] and that takes a lot of technical training. I wonder where they got that...[43]

What would the US power duo have thought about the even bolder phase of operations that was underway in India even as they spoke?

On Monday, 8 November, at around 3 p.m., C2H exploded in frenzied activity. NCO(X)'s gunboats had finally got their green signal. Operation Hot Pants was underway. The *Palash* and the *Padma*, their engines thrumming, fore and aft Bofors hooded in canvas, cast off.

Commander Samant was on board the *Padma*, briefcase filled with his top-secret mission charts and his mind troubled. The *Padma* was running on one engine. Her port engine had broken down while she was in the Middleton Channel. The crew struggled but couldn't rectify the defect. The operation already had two false starts earlier that month. The first one when reports of a cyclone postponed the sail out. Then, on the night of 5 November, a steel wire used to tether the *Padma* was sucked into the boat's churning propellers. The boat had to be towed to the GRSE by the *Palash* where, after a few hours, workmen un-entangled the propellers. Today, however,

---

43 National Security Archive Electronic Briefing; September 1970–July 1971

there was no time to go back to the yard. Samant had taken the call – the *Padma* on one engine. He had mentally lined up three options for engineering assistance – from a naval escort ship that was to meet them at Sandheads, from the pilot vessel there, or from a hydrographic survey vessel operating in the area. This mission was too critical to be held back by a busted engine.

Nanda, Roy and Samant's maritime campaign was aimed at interdicting the merchant shipping that sustained East Pakistan's military garrison. The three waves of NCO(X)'s assault swimmers launched from C2P since August were meant to turn East Pakistan into an unsafe destination and drive ships away from its critical ports. By early November, NCO(X) was battling the god of maritime commerce: Mammon. Pakistani authorities had hiked freight rates and were also paying the war risk insurance premiums, along with additional wages for crew on cargo being brought in and out of its rebellious province. Carrying cargo to East Pakistan was now an attractive proposition for short-term gains.

The lure of financial gains had their effect. A number of foreign merchant vessels disregarded radio broadcasts by Swadhin Bangla Betar Kendra[44] asking them to stay away from Bangla Desh and not resupply the Pakistani military garrison. It was business as usual. And there was Captain Zamir Ahmed. By October, the Pakistan Army and Navy's enhanced vigil on the waterways made it tougher to target merchant shipping. Captain Roy's kill sheets showed a steady declining trend since August.

In mid-October, Samant drew up a plan to wrest back the initiative – an offensive plan that would deal a hammer blow to maritime shipping in the eastern province. His name for the operation – Hot

---

44 The Calcutta-based radio station of the Bangla Desh government in exile

Pants[45] – raised a chuckle when he took it to Major General Jimmy Sarkar. General Sarkar read through the plan and swiftly signed off on it. Samant then stuffed his briefcase with operational details and charts and boarded a flight to Delhi. He spent the day with Captain Roy in his office detailing the plan threadbare. The mission objective was clear – choke maritime traffic to the eastern province with a gunboat attack. Samant answered all of the DNI's queries – the time, duration, the risks involved. Admiral Nanda dropped in on their meeting post lunch. He looked through the plans and, realizing their sensitivity, said he had to brief the prime minister about the operation.

Samant returned to Calcutta, still working on the plan. He added an Indian naval warship to it, dashing off a coded message to Captain Roy: 'Request confirm availability of one Petya for distant support during commitments. Position and time will be signalled.' *INS Kavaratti*, one of two Petya-II-class corvettes deployed under Rear Admiral S.H. Sharma's Eastern Fleet in Vizag, appeared in Calcutta soon after that signal. A few days later, Samant convened a final operational meeting in the conference room of the INS Hooghly. Captain Roy flew in from Delhi to attend. In the hush-hush meeting that Squeaky Khanna was kept out of, Hot Pants was discussed in detail. Participants included the *Kavaratti*'s CO, Commander Subir Paul, who had been a term junior to Samant in Dartmouth, Lt Cdr Roy Chowdhury, Lt Mitter and Lt Cdr C.S. Menon. Only these men knew that the coded phrase for the mission – 'Turtles to lay eggs in the approaches to Anwar' – was not about marine biology.

Now, a week after that meeting, Samant waited for his old college mate to show up. Two hours later, the knife-like silhouette

---

45 Very short shorts with no waistband, a term coined by *Women's Wear Daily* in 1970

of the *Kavaratti* came into view in the mid-channel. The Soviet-built Petya-class corvette was unlike the Indian Navy's British-built steamships. It ran a single diesel engine for normal cruising but also had a Soviet innovation of the 1960s – twin gas turbines derived from aircraft jet engines – for sprint speeds of close to 33 knots. It was equipped with a powerful, nose-mounted sonar to detect subs and a battery of rockets and torpedoes to chase and hunt submarines.

Today, the *Kavaratti* would play sheepdog, escorting the *Palash* and the *Padma* into East Pakistan using its 'Fut-N' air search radar to detect enemy aircraft and, if needed, use its two 57 mm twin cannons to protect the flotilla.

Cdr Samant walked to the *Padma*'s forward deck with a loud hailer in hand and spoke out his brief message. 'Warship! Warship! Our port engine packed up. Please help us to repair': From the command bridge,[46] Cdr Paul asked the *Padma* to come alongside. As soon as the boat was abreast, Lieutenant S. Parulekar and two engine room artificers from the *Kavaratti* hopped on board. Mitter briefed them about the engine room trouble and they went below decks.

By 8 p.m., after close to five hours of work, the *Kavaratti*'s engineers had zeroed in on the problem – a faulty fifth cylinder in the *Padma*'s engine. The cylinder was isolated and the engine coughed back to life. The revival of the engine calmed Samant. He could now focus on the mission ahead and reach his rendezvous point in twenty-four hours. The force now headed towards Pakistani territorial waters, the whine of the Petya's gas turbines, accompanied by the 'I-can-do-it, I-can-do-it' thump of the *Palash* and *Panvel*'s diesels.

Just then, a stream of Punjabi abuses invoking wives, mothers and sisters punched through the radio waves. The enemy had detected the transmissions of the task force and now a shore-based

---

46 Raised platform from where a ship is steered

transmission butted in on their VHF voice frequencies and on the portable walkies the *Padma* and *Palash* used to communicate amongst themselves. The Pakistan Navy's shore-based transmission was a bait. If the ships responded, they could risk revealing their position. The task group laughed the abuse off, resisted the urge to respond, and continued on its mission.

At around 9 p.m., the force reached the edge of Indian territorial waters, the approaches to Sandheads. The three ships anchored for the night at a spot called the Eastern channel light vessel. The *Padma* advanced towards the *Kavaratti* once again and Commander Samant vaulted across the guardrail to board the warship from where he would supervise the operation. While approving the plan, NHQ had insisted that the force commander not risk capture during the mission. For Samant, capture would mean coming face to face with Captain Zamir Ahmad, a scenario he did not even want to consider.

At 8 a.m. on the morning of 9 November, the flotilla resumed its voyage. The weather was calm, the visibility, excellent, and the seas, mirror-like. To add to that, electronic anomalous propagation conditions or anaprop, a temperature inversion condition which enhanced the range of normal radar waves, boosted the range of the Petya's search radar. The coast was clear so far and, to keep it that way, they maintained strict radio silence. The ships used their signalling lamps to wink messages in Morse code at each other. The squadron commander Lt Cdr Roy Chowdhury sailed for the target area in a single line formation followed by the *Palash*. The *Kavaratti*, meanwhile, weighed anchor and disappeared over the horizon.

The crew of both gunboats were at defence stations, one step below action stations – the forward gun covers of both ships ready to be removed swiftly in case of an emergency. The two boats sailed by the fathom line, a smooth and uneventful passage with clear weather.

At around 3.30 p.m., the task force crossed the longitude of 090 degree east, which marked the start of East Pakistan's territorial waters. As the boats crossed into enemy waters, there was a thrill of excitement. The gunboat crews brought out the Bangla Desh flag – a red disc in the centre of a green field, with a map of their beloved country in the centre, in orange. They ripped the tarpaulins off the guns and off the rails to expose four black cylindrical objects, strapped on their decks, two on each side. Sammy's gunboats were on the prowl.

The task force listened in on VHF to Khulna Port Control as a merchant ship gave its expected time of arrival at the Fairway Buoy (at the mouth of the Pussur river entrance) as 2.30 a.m. The contact was classified as 'Rhino Charlie',[47] a possible target.

At around 4 p.m., the *Kavaratti* picked up three radar contacts towards the north, north east and south–southeast. The force altered course southwards. In the meantime, 'Rhino Charlie', which appeared to be a small merchant ship, was spotted three nautical miles away. The sun set around 5 p.m., cloaking the area in darkness. Between 5.45 and 6.45 p.m., the *Kavaratti*'s Fut-N radar began picking up a number of aerial contacts. The ship's company went to action stations – gun crews in the gun mounts, radar operators at their display units, engineering crew in the engine room, watchkeeping officers on the deck, and ammunition supply parties in the magazines. The corvette began taking evasive zig-zag manoeuvres to throw off any possible air attack.

All contacts faded by 7 p.m. Samant and Paul reviewed the situation once again and decided to continue with the mission. The evasive manoeuvres had cost them time. The original plan was slightly modified as it was now evident that the boats could not

---

47 In operational plot terminology, Rhino indicated a radar contact, and Alpha through Zulu served as alphabetical nomenclature for a particular surface ship as identified

possibly arrive off the entrance of the Pussur at the pre-planned H-hour of 8 p.m.

On the bridge of the *Padma*, Mitter's thoughts raced back to the events of the previous few days. Three days after he had received the boxes from Bombay, a private Ambassador car had brought in a short, plump gentleman into Camp C2H. Lt V.S. Chitale, a fleet air arm engineer from Bombay, had been sent to the camp by Commander Sainant on a mission. Chitale carried a small box of hand tools with him. He asked for a crowbar and cracked the wooden boxes open to expose their mysterious contents. Mitter peeped inside to see a dull black cylindrical object sitting on a cradle inside. Each box held a British-made A-Mk VII influence mine, each weighing around 175 kgs. The mines were part of the ordnance that Micky Roy had inducted with the 310 squadron of the Alizé in 1961. Each Alizé could carry one air-dropped A-Mk VII mine in its bomb bay, which would drop out like a bomb but deployed a parachute in its tail to ensure a slow, near-vertical descent into the water to lie in wait for its prey. The nose of the mine was 'chamfered' – the symmetrical sloping edge ensured the mine would not bounce off the surface of the water.

Lt Chitale walked around the mines using a small screwdriver to set the ship count mechanism. He looked like a surgeon on a field visit and happily explained the working of the mine to Mitter as he went about his task. Contact mines, he explained, activated when the mine touched the target – a Hertz horn on the mine broke and completed a circuit to explode the mine. Acoustic mines were triggered by the noise of a ship's propeller. The Mark VIIs, however, were the deadliest kind – influence mines. The giant magnetic field of a ship passing overhead would trigger off nearly 100 kgs of high explosives, the expanding gas bubble smashing into the hull of the vessel sailing above.

The Indian Navy had never deployed the Mark VIIs, but three key X-men knew its deadly potential. Captain Roy had, as a midshipman on board the minesweeper *HMS Mariner* in 1946, cleared air-dropped German mines laid between Iceland and Murmansk. Aku Roy's Alizés had flown practice missions with dummy Mark VIIs, and Samant, as staff officer in NHQ in 1965, had drafted a plan to use IAF Canberra bombers to sow Mark VIIs at the approaches to an enemy port.

The ship count mechanism on each Mark VII determined how many ships would pass above it before it exploded. A ship count of four meant the mine would explode when the fourth vessel passed overhead. Chitale primed six mines with ship counts – eight, four and two – to make them unpredictable.

An army crane and personnel from Fort William lowered four mines per gunboat, two on each side. The deadly ordnance was strapped down with two-inch–wide steel brackets, secured with a thin steel rope onto the deck and then covered with tarpaulin.

The stability of the boats with the gun mounts, each weighing nearly a ton, had worried Mitter. The Warship Overseeing Team chief Cdr Subramanian assured the young officer that the boat's meta centric height and centre of gravity were well within limits. But, he stipulated, the forward draft should not exceed five feet and the aft not exceed six feet. The ship had to maintain the positive trim of one foot at all costs and had to be cautious before taking on a full load of rations and ammunition. The mines added nearly a ton to each vessel, pushing them towards the edge of their design envelope.

Captain Roy's briefing in INS Hooghly had laid out Operation Hot Pants for all three commanding officers. The operation would directly target Mongla Port, East Pakistan's second busiest seaport after Chittagong. Mongla, surrounded by the dense Sundarbans mangrove forest, was located on the Pussur river and, was East

Pakistan's maritime jugular. If Mongla Port was closed, the Pakistan Army would choke.

At around 9 p.m., a contact flashed on the radar screen of the *Kavaratti*. The contact, nine miles away, was the Pussur river buoy that marked the mouth of the riverine channel and also the point where the operation would start from. Each gunboat would arrive at the Anwar Fairway buoy[48] which was eighty-six nautical miles away. They would then enter the channel, keeping a one nautical mile distance from each other.

The *Kavaratti* stood in close proximity without entering the fairway, watching from a distance over the south-easterly horizon as the gunboats set about their task. The coast was clear except for two trawlers and a mother vessel which the task force sighted at about 2 p.m. at a great distance away. At about 4.30 p.m., when dusk began setting in, the ship's company were ordered to eat an early dinner. All lights on board were switched off and the vessels now sailed in total darkness. The lack of a radar meant they were totally blind. Intelligence alerts they had received before sail out warned them about a Pakistani gunboat stationed on Hiran Island at the mouth of the Pussur.

Mitter placed a former Pakistan Navy sailor Mohammad Abdul Haque as a lookout on starboard side of the bridge with a pair of binoculars.

'Haque, kicchu dekhte pacho?' (Haque, do you see anything?) Mitter asked.

'Kuchey toh dekhi na … chokushu te jhapsa dekhin.' (Everything is blurred. I can't see anything.) Haque took the binoculars off his eyes and reported, his voice trembling.

'Dada tumhar patha dekhao!' (Elder brother, show position.) Mitter spoke into the walkie-talkie. A pinprick of light shone in the

---

48 A floating object that marks the beginning of a navigation channel

distance. A crewman on the *Palash* shone back an improvised, low-powered masked torch light with a 5-mm vertical slit.

At about 9.30 p.m., the two ships reached the fairway buoy lights marking the beginning of the maritime highway that guided merchant ships all the way up to Khulna. Mitter sounded action stations. All crew rushed and manned their guns, ready to fire on command. A half-hour later, they spotted the twinkling lights of the port and the starboard buoys straddling the quarter-mile wide channel – the ones on port were odd numbered on the nautical chart: P2, P4, P6 and P8; the starboard buoys, even numbered: S1, S3, S5, S7, and so on.

Two nautical miles away, the *Kavaratti* winked her red yardarm lights twice for a split second. It was the signal for the turtles to lay their eggs.

'Start dumping the garbage,' Lt Cdr Roy Choudhury's voice rasped over the walkie talkie.

Palash altered course and cut speed to five knots. Then, starting from P6, began laying her four mines at regular intervals on a diagonal course heading to S7. On the *Padma*, the mine launch team of two sailors led by Majumder stood at ready. As the boat approached buoy P4, they unfastened the canvas-sheathed brace, removed the steel wire that held the mine in place and yanked the metal ring at one end of the mine, arming it. They then braced themselves against the ship's side and kicked each of the four mines at one-minute intervals. From the bridge, Mitter counted the four splashes in the water. A few minutes later, Majumder reported to Mitter on the bridge, grinned, and proudly held out four six-inch–long safety cables, each with a ring attached.

By around 11.30 p.m., the boats had laid a diagonal double line of explosives at the mouth of East Pakistan's second-largest port.

The *Kavaratti* stayed on its position within Indian waters. Close to midnight, she picked up a radar contact fifteen nautical miles south-west of the task force. The contact, the task force deduced, could be 'Rhino Charlie', which they now knew to be a British merchant ship *MV City of St. Albans* headed for Khulna.

Why not attack Rhino Charlie, just to send another message, Samant suggested. Cdr Subir Paul did not want any of it. He wanted to leave the scene immediately, for it was imprudent for a naval warship to be in the vicinity of a deniable operation.

'Subir, I understand your problem and I wouldn't want to be in your shoes right now, but allow me to send out one signal to my boats,' Samant requested. The CO agreed. The *Kavaratti* flashed out the range and bearing of the approaching contact to *MV Palash* using its signalling lamp. 'Engage target closest to you.' And with that order, the darkened *Kavaratti* rapidly accelerated and turned away on a south-eastern course for Vizag.

Fifty minutes past midnight, the *City of St. Albans* was running a straight course towards the fairway buoy when two dark shapes crossed her port side.

Roy Choudhury's voice crackled on his walkie-talkie: 'Maar shala ke!' (Kill the blighter!). It was an order for both gunboats.

Four L-60 guns swung towards the merchant and started firing, their tracer shells punching a dotted line of fire. The 40 mm shells exploded on the ship's hull and superstructure. On the *Kavaratti*, Samant saw the distant flashes of the engagement. The airwaves burst radio signals on the international distress frequency. 'This is a British merchantman. We are under attack.'

The *City of St. Albans* immediately altered her course to starboard and began heading south. On the *Padma* and the *Palash*, nearly 300 brass empties rolled on the deck. Gun smoke swirled in the night air. The crews were exuberant. It was the first engagement of the Mukti Bahini's naval wing.

Mitter now wanted to leave the scene as quickly as possible. It was only a matter of time before they attracted a roving Pakistani gunboat.

He needn't have worried. The distress signals from the *City of St. Albans* went unanswered. The vessel steered away from the Khulna channel and, at around 1 a.m. headed towards Calcutta. The two gunboats too followed in its wake. Both the hunters and the hunted were heading for the same port.

Two hours later, at around 3 a.m., the Khulna channel resounded with a thunderous roar. A column of water grew out of the water and fell back with a splash. The first turtle egg had hatched. The International Distress Frequency 500 KHz crackled with the frantic message of the merchantman *MV Berlian* and reported an explosion in her stern.

Hearing the *Berlian*'s SOS, another merchantman, the *MV Merkara* refused to enter the channel. It changed course and headed eastwards towards Chittagong Port.

The *Padma* and the *Palash*, meanwhile, lowered the Bangla Desh flag and hoisted the Indian ensign, covered their guns with tarpaulins and headed into the pre-dawn surge of fishing trawlers heading into the Bay of Bengal. Their gunwales considerably lightened without the mines, the gunboats sped through the water. After first light, Mitter gave the order for tea and breakfast for the crew. They arrived at Sandheads at 8.30 a.m. the next morning. Phase I of Operation Hot Pants was over.

The disguised gunboats saw merchant ships at anchorage waiting for harbour pilots at Sandheads to guide them into Calcutta port. At around 10 a.m., the *Padma* floated some 200 metres past a merchant ship with tell-tale pockmarks and holes on the hull and superstructure. It was the *City of St. Albans*, flying a red British ensign. Both the boats rounded the stern of the ship and sailed past her port side to see more damage to her port bow hull. The ship had hoisted a white and red flag which read 'pilot on board' and was evidently waiting to enter the Hooghly with the rising tide.

The *Padma* and the *Palash* did not wait for the river to start flooding and began sailing towards Haldia and their C2H anchorage. At about 5 p.m., they entered their anchorage and secured themselves alongside their jetty at C2H. Lieutenant Chitale was waiting by the jetty. Mitter walked up to him and handed him the four safety wires of the mines. Chitale smiled. 'Pray to God that they explode at the right time,' he said. 'These are World War II vintage mines ... at least some, if not all, should go off,' Chitale chortled.

When the story of the havoc wrought by the Mark VII mines became known the next day, Samant dashed off a signal to NHQ from Vizag, where the *Kavaratti* had brought him. 'Hot Pants dropped' Samant radioed his coded 'mission accomplished' signal to NHQ and Eastern Command. It created some confusion in Delhi. Dropped? Did he mean that the operation had been cancelled? Army chief, General S.H.F.J. Maneckshaw wanted to know.

The Indian Navy, meanwhile, was fire-fighting an international incident. News had spread that a British flagged merchantman had been shelled by Mukti Bahini gunboats who may have sought refuge in India. On Thursday, 11 November, the day after the attack, the gunboat crews rose late. Soon after they had reached C2H the previous evening, squadron commander Roychowdhury had ordered a late hands call in the morning for the ship's weary company. This meant a relaxed 'Sunday routine', followed by a late breakfast.

At around 10.30 a.m., however, a white Ambassador came to a screeching halt in front of the gangway. Captain Khanna – NOIC Calcutta, in civilian clothes – leaped out of the back seat of the car and began shouting at the officers. 'Go to Nabadweep, go to Nabadweep at once, and hide yourselves there.' Khanna breathlessly informed Roychowdhury and Mitter about the possibility that the British Deputy High Commission will bring the media to C2H. They had to clear out of the berth at once. Roychowdhury and

Mitter explained why they were confused – Nabadweep was about 120 nautical miles upriver on the Bhagirathi. The boats didn't have any charts beyond Howrah Bridge. This only infuriated Capt. Khanna more and he began swearing. Just then, another Ambassador car pulled up, carrying two officers Mitter and Roychowdhury recognized. They were Lieutenants R.C. Paul and Sharma of Calcutta Port Trust, both officers from the Indian Naval Volunteer Reserve. Sharma stood at the gangway, raised an assuring hand and winked at the gunboat COs. Captain Khanna shot a look at them. 'Take them to Nabadweep at once,' he reiterated before hopping back into his car and speeding off towards Calcutta.

Sharma and Paul informed the boat commanders of a better sanctuary – Kakdwip, on the eastern bank of the Hooghly. They would pilot the boats to a spot which would hide them from the prying eyes of the press and the public. Shortly afterwards, both gunboats boats sailed for Kakdwip and anchored in Ranglafala Channel off Harwood Point.

On 13 November, a second turtle egg hatched in the Khulna channel. The gunboat *PNS Tufail* was flung up, killing several of its naval crew.

Six more eggs lay on the sandy riverbed, their shells primed to crack open when a giant metal object passed above. Soon after the loss of the *Tufail*, Indian Military Intelligence (MI) intercepted a tele-conversation between a Captain Nawab of Khulna and Karachi Port Control. The port director, Khulna Port, had suspended all ship movements with effect from 13 November. The Pakistan Navy, stretched as it was thanks to the task of patrolling the waterways, clearly lacked the resources to undertake a minesweeping operation. All shipping along the nautical channel that stretched from Akram Point to Khulna, ground to a halt. Operation Hot Pants had paralyzed another one of Niazi's arteries. Sammy's turtles had accomplished their mission. The nascent Bangla Desh Navy had come of age.

The boats, meanwhile, spent three uneventful days in their hiding place before returning to C2H on 14 November. The two pilots left for Calcutta. Mrs Roychowdhury was in an advanced stage of pregnancy. So her husband once again handed over charge of the squadron to Mitter to visit home and take her for her medical check-ups.

By mid-November, the maritime balance had tipped towards NCO(X). East Pakistan had become a no-go zone as far as global shipping was concerned. The military leadership was not getting charters for love or for money. Especially for money. Ship owners had evaluated the massive risk of losing their ship, the high insurance premium against the hazard, and decided that the high freight rates were simply not worth the risk.

Stage III of Roy's concept note – the complete paralysis of East Pakistan's waterways – was fast turning into a reality. And at such a low cost. All the assets the NCO(X) used were limpeteers and make-shift gunboats. And the best part was, it was all deniable.

On 28 November, the Calcutta-based English daily *Hindustan Standard* headlined its story 'Logistic Deficiencies Hurting Pak Troops'.

By large-scale destruction of roads and rail bridges, culverts and minor bridges, the guerrillas have presented the Pakistani forces with a serious headache. It has far more than a nuisance value since local labour to assist in repairing the damage is scarce. But it is not the destruction of the road and rail bridges that has done the greatest damage. Attacks on ships in harbours and other inland watercrafts in places such as Chittagong, Chalna, the Mongla area and Chandpur have placed a severe strain on the Pakistani supply routes. Grain and munition ships and a tanker have been sunk. Even so, there was an emergency supply route using Chalna port. Mukti Bahini frogmen, however, early this week sank a 'Greek vessel' in this route. The supply throughout is, therefore, affected.

The position of Chittagong is apparently not much better. Mukti Bahini commandos have been very active in this area from the commencement of operations. They have put out of commission all but two of the moorings. The port's ability to handle military hardware has been severely curtailed, and there is the ever-present fear that ships moored to them will be subjected to attacks by the frogmen. Ships flying foreign flags have been sunk and their owners are now very firm that they will not visit Chittagong port. Perhaps that is not an irreparable loss, as the overland route connecting Chittagong with Chandpur or Dhaka has not been severed. In order to repair its severely battered lifeline, Pakistan has tried hard to develop an inland waterway to Chandpur. This has not, however, been very successful as Chandpur has been receiving the attention of the commandos. Four vessels carrying food and supplies for the Army were recently sunk there, including a vessel recently acquired from China. In desperation, the Pakistan authorities have issued orders to their gunboats to shoot and destroy all country boats plying in the Chalna and Satkhira areas. This is likely to have widespread repercussions as the people of the delta region have always used the waterways for travel and cargo carrying. It could result in the locals of the area facing starvation in the course of time.

The only disappointment in November, Samant noted in his reports, was the failure of his commandos to target Bangla Desh's longest river-spanning structure, the 1.8-km–long Hardinge Bridge over the Padma, located a little over 80 kilometres north-east of C2P. The bridge, constructed by the British in 1912, was a vital rail link between the districts of Khulna and Jessore.

In fact, an operation – Operation Grey Cat – had been launched on 30 August to target it. Eight commandos trained in boatmanship and the use of special explosives called Herrick Charges, had been launched downstream in a country boat from BSF posts at Jalangi.

It was the post-monsoon period and the river was swollen. The team, however, failed to tie the boat to one of the bridge's sixteen piers. A second attempt made on the night of 31 August failed too. Both times, the country craft was launched after being towed up to Raita Point, which was located about eight nautical miles upstream from the bridge. On the third attempt in October, the boat was detected by Pakistani sentries patrolling the bridge and fired upon. Two naval commandos were captured and presumed killed during this mission.

Samant's analysis of the failures pointed to a reason other than the strong current – an undercurrent within the Bangla Desh government in exile of wanting to preserve national assets like the bridge for use after independence. This feeling, he observed in his reports, appeared to inhibit some of the commandos. In October, the commandos destroyed the Arani Bridge, another vital link approximately twenty kilometres south of Rajshahi. But the Hardinge Bridge continued standing.

As Niazi's troops unleashed a reign of terror, Operation Jackpot was inflicting a thousand cuts. In the month of November, C2P launched 271 assault swimmers into Bangla Desh, the largest since their 15 August strike. Cloud Burst was now raining naval commandos through Charlie and Delta sectors, from where they swarmed across the riverine nation, striking targets at will. If ships were hard to hit, they targeted maritime infrastructure – jetties, barges and pylons. The naval commando offensive coincided with those of the Mukti Bahini land forces that month which, as Brigadier Salik noted, seemed to be Phase III – the third and final phase of their operations.

'It saw them fairly active on both sides of the border and in the interior. Backed by Indian troops and artillery, they mounted pressure on the border outposts and fomented trouble in important towns and cities. This dual attack overtaxed our resources and strained our mental energies. It is during this phase that the Indian Army established some important bridgeheads which they profitably used during the war.'[49]

At daybreak on 21 November, thirty-four soldiers of the 1st battalion of the Maratha Light Infantry (MLI) waited near the tracks for a military train. The location was over forty kilometres inside enemy-controlled Bangla Desh. The soldiers were clad in scruffy civilian clothes and military boots, and included a demolition team. The thirty-four–man raiding party led by Lieutenant R.S.V. Dafle and 2nd Lieutenant Basant Kumar 'Pony' Ponwar had jogged through the night to reach the railway line over 200 kilometres north-west of Dacca. They had placed forty-five kilograms of explosives along the track and a culvert. The Pakistan Army train they were targeting was a lifeline to Rangapur district – it offloaded troops and stores at the railhead for trans-shipment by ferry to Phulchari Ghat on the Jamuna river. A river steamer which plied between Bhadurabad Ghat and Phulchari Ghat was the other target, chosen because it was used for riverine patrols and was fitted with a powerful searchlight which lit up the riverbank, making night raids difficult. The MLI unit based in Tura, Meghalaya, had planned a hybrid attack with the Mukti Bahini – naval commandos would sink the steamer, after which Dafle and Ponwar would hit the train.

Earlier in the night, the MLI had rendezvoused with four naval commandos who had infiltrated into Bangla Desh through Foxtrot Sector. The naval commandos from C2P were led by the local Mukti Bahini commander. At around 3 a.m., the commandos dived into the water and swam towards the steamer moored at Bhadurabad Ghat. Three dull blasts signalled it had been hit. The Pakistan Army

---

49 Siddiq Salik, *Witness to Surrender* (New Delhi: Lancer Publishers), 1977

immediately towed out the crippled vessel into the middle of the river, allowing it to sink without obstructing the jetty.[50]

The naval commandos had accomplished their mission risking their lives. Now, three hours later, the MLI soldiers had to do their bit. But there was a problem. At daybreak, civilians had started walking on the railway tracks and there was a possibility they would raise an alarm when they spotted the explosive charges. There was a railway bridge about 500 metres away, guarded by the Pakistan Army. Dafle and Ponwar triggered off the charges on the track, destroying the culvert and ripping up a 100-metre track section. They then lobbed a few rounds from a two-inch mortar in the direction of the soldiers guarding the bridge. Mission accomplished, the MLI soldiers began speed marching back towards Meghalaya.

'By mid-November,' Major General Fazal Muqeem Khan wrote in *Pakistan's Crisis in Leadership*, 'the strategic and tactical mobility of the Eastern Command had been reduced to a minimum due to extensive guerrilla activities in the rear and numerous road bridges, ferries, river-craft and ships, which were the sole means of transport for shifting troops and logistics from one place to another and from one geographical compartment to another across river obstacles.' How this disabling of Sector X – the nucleus of the Bangla Deshi riverine network – would make the difference between victory and defeat would be apparent the following month.

---

50 SOP, as suggested in Rear Admiral Shariff's note on what to do in case a vessel was hit

10
FORCE ALFA

The paralysis of riverine traffic in Sector X delighted Operation X's planners Roy and Samant. Stage III of the operation had been a success. The subcontinent, meanwhile, continued its downslide towards war. DNI's gush of alerts about Pakistani frogmen planning attacks continued. This time, they suggested, the enemy would strike at the *Palash* and the *Padma* on 21 November. On that day, Samant drove down to Garden Reach Shipyard where the two ships were berthed. He wanted them to sail for the safety of C2H on the 23rd.

Lt Cdr J.K. Roy Choudhury was away attending to his wife. Mitter, who was holding charge, assured Samant that he was aware of the Operation Awkward counter-sabotage drills. Samant appeared relieved. 'Then it's all yours'. He wished him luck and left. Mitter consulted the Hooghly River Tide Table and judged that enemy frogmen could launch an attack from upstream, when the tide started ebbing. Frogmen would either launch themselves from a passing boat upstream or from Bichali Ghat, a public ferry terminus approximately 100 metres upstream just outside the boundary wall of the GRSE factory complex. The attack would be executed under cover of darkness. Hence, lookouts equipped with binoculars scanned the river with searchlights.

One sailor, armed with a Sterling carbine, was posted on each ship with orders to fire at anyone swimming towards the ships. As the boats were on shore supply, the engine room crew were instructed to start the diesel generator of the ship immediately in case of a power failure. Duty rosters for sentries and lookouts were prepared and six-hour watches were kept from 6 p.m. through the night. 'Clear lower decks' was ordered before sunset each day and the ships' company were briefed about the situation.

One day, Mitter took rounds of both the ships, found sentries and lookouts on the alert, the beams of the searchlight illuminating the riverfront before them. He instructed the lookout on the *Padma* to wake him up at 2.30 a.m., around the time of the middle watch. He then set his alarm and went to sleep in his cabin. He awoke to take rounds of both ships, the *Palash* being the first. Both the bridge lookout and sentry were awake and alert. Next, he walked to the bridge of his ship, the *Padma*. The duty sentry was missing. Mitter thumbed through the duty roster and found his name. Mohammad Rafiqulla was nowhere to be seen.

A sentry missing with his weapon was a serious matter. Mitter took out his small pocket torch and shone it on the faces of the crew who were sleeping on deck. He walked to the forward gun. A metal object caught the glint of the torch. It was the muzzle of a carbine. Head and neck warmly ensconced in a woollen scarf, a crewman was asleep on a bed behind the forward gun cover. It was Rafiqulla, snoring fitfully, the carbine tucked under his pillow. Mitter pocketed his torch, yanked the scarf and grabbed Rafiqulla up by his hair.

'Kitha koren? Kitha koren?' the crewman shrieked, dazed and wondering what he had done wrong. He sheepishly picked up his carbine and resumed sentry duty. The next morning, he was the butt of the jokes of the crew. It brought them a brief moment of levity from the monotony of their daily routine.

On 23 November, the two Flower-class boats sailed down the Hooghly back to their home port C2H, waiting for further orders.

With the subcontinent perched on the precipice of war in November, the navy had moved up the *INS Panvel*, a Soviet-built 'Poluchat'-class patrol boat up from Visakhapatnam to Calcutta on 1 November. She was now patrolling the Ichamati river near Sandeshkhali, a town 73 kilometres east of Calcutta. The town was where the Padma's distributary, the Ichamati, meandered through India and Pakistan before flowing through the Sundarbans into the Bay of Bengal. The *Panvel*, roughly the length of two city buses, was the smallest of the Soviet warship acquisitions. She and her four sister ships had arrived as deck-cargo on Russian heavy-lift merchant ships in 1967[51] and named for a town near Bombay.

The *Panvel*'s CO, Lt Cr Joseph Pius Alfred Noronha – square jawed, hawk-nosed with a protruding lower lip – had started growing a sea beard. Alfred to his friends and family, was the sixth of seven children of a postmaster from Mysore. The family were devout Roman Catholics, and all four boys bore the prefix Joseph Pius thanks to a religious vow. Noronha was a man in search of an elusive destiny. He had led an unremarkable life until then, joining the navy in 1959 after a brief stint as a medical salesman in Bombay.

The *Panvel*, Noronha's first command, was an opportunity to prove his mettle. He treated the 90-ton vessel like he would a 10,000-ton cruiser. His insistence on strict discipline on the

---

51 *Transition to Triumph*, Vice Admiral G.H. Hiranandani, 2004

cramped patrol boat amused his young second-in-command, Sub Lieutenant A.R. Vijaygopal. The *Panvel* had a single toilet, shower stall and kitchen, shared by officers and men alike. Noronha had got the command through a strange twist – the previous CO had got himself transferred out that September because he never saw the tiny boat ever going to war. How wrong that officer was, Noronha thought on 30 October when he was asked to steer it to Calcutta, closer to the Eastern theatre. The *Panvel* made a perilous passage across the Bay of Bengal, just a day after a very severe cyclonic storm crashed into the Orissa coast, killing over 7,000 persons. The aftermath of the killer storm tossed the *Panvel* above, breaking waves on her deck, mangling her anchor cable chain.

The patrol boat sailed up the tranquil Hooghly two days later, passing C2H's secret anchorage, alarming Lt Mitter who briefly mistook her to be a Pakistani gunboat. Like the Flower class, the *Panvel* had been retrofitted in Visakhapatnam with two Bofors 40/60 guns, fore and aft. The addition of the gun crews doubled the ship's strength to nearly thirty personnel.

Noronha had anchored at the Man of War jetty near the INS Hooghly for over a fortnight, awaiting orders. As November drew to a close, the eastern Naval Command directed him to patrol the international maritime boundary at Sandeshkhali.

The *Panvel*'s administrative base was thirty-eight kilometres north along the river, in the village of Hasnabad. The village was also the base for a BSF waterborne battalion which policed the boundary. The naval gunboat relied on Hasnabad for both food and fuel. The diesel for her twin M50 engines came from a fuel bowser onshore.

The *Panvel* chugged up and down the broad expanse of the Ichamati. A few crewmen from the discontinued Dacca-Calcutta steamer service occasionally came on board the gunboat to act as guides through the waterways. The river was almost one kilometre wide in places, but just over four metres deep. These were uncharted waters, which meant the navy wouldn't take disciplinary action against a captain if he grounded his ship. Noronha had by now mastered the art of beaching his vessel on the soft riverbank to draw fresh water supplies.

The beaching drill was carefully carried out. He only had to ensure that the ship's twin propellers remained clear of the soft mud even as it ran up the beach at a 45-degree angle. His crew leaped ashore, dragging the boat's twelve-metre–long fire hose to hand pumps ashore. The *Panvel* lay up on the riverbank like a giant crocodile, the crew hand-cranking fresh water into her tanks. When the tanks were full, the order to unbeach was given. The boat's twin M-50 V12s which generated over 2400 HP easily pulled it free of the riverbank.

Chiman Singh returns

Meanwhile, deep inside Bangla Desh, Chiman Singh, the MIA naval diver, was distraught. Captain Omar had not come up with any targets for his group to attack. His patience on end, Singh decided to return to India. In late November, he left his limpet mines and explosives with the Mukti Bahini officer for attacks when the opportunity arose.

By 22 November, he was slinging his carbine and walking back towards the Indian border at Boyra accompanied by Nazrul Islam and the ten naval commandos. The exfiltration drill was for the commandos to walk back to their launch pad. Here, they would be met by the sector commanders and debriefed. What Singh didn't know was that, by then, the Indian Army was already ten kilometres inside East Pakistan. The previous day, the Pakistan Army had launched an offensive backed by tanks, artillery and fighter jets to repel what they called was 'an enemy attack supported by MiGs, armour and artillery.' Niazi in fact[52] wanted to evict Indian troops who had occupied the area since 13 November.

The naval commandos had stumbled into the midst of a full-scale war.

A sentry in olive green sprang out of a trench and aimed a rifle at them. Chiman Singh and Nazrul Islam lowered their weapons, raised their hands and identified themselves. They were in the battle line positions of the 22nd battalion of the Rajput Regiment.

Just then, an air raid siren went off. Every eye on the ground looked skywards at the source of the thunderous roar in the skies. The first aerial duel of the India–Pakistan war had begun in the skies over Boyra. Three IAF Gnats had streaked in from Dum Dum to tackle three F-86 Sabre jets from Dacca who were flying in support of the Pakistan Army's ground offensive. Singh and Islam took cover in the L-shaped trenches. They were kicked out – the trenches were for Indian soldiers only, the soldiers snarled. The dogfight continued. The aircraft twisted, pirouetted and fired cannons at each other. The dogfight lasted barely a few minutes. The nimble Gnats won the day. Two Sabres crashed out of the sky, trailing smoke. A third turned tail and sped back to Dacca. Two parachutes blossomed in the skies.

Some of the Rajput soldiers sprang out of the trenches and set out after the downed pilots. Chiman Singh and the naval commandos were rounded up and escorted to their commanding officer for questioning.

Lt Colonel Bhopal Singh seemed pleasantly surprised at first to hear of a navy man so far inland. He fondly recounted his visit to the *INS Vikrant*. But then, the man in the lungi and gamcha who claimed to be from Gurgaon district and spoke the local Haryanvi

---

52 Siddiq Salik, *Witness to Surrender* (New Delhi: Lancer Publishers), 1977

dialect didn't have a shred of identity on him. His battalion kept up with the interrogation. Could he just be a Pakistani spy trying to gather field intelligence, Lt Colonel Singh wondered. Then, the unit's education NCO Havildar Yadav from Gurgaon remembered the unit sweeper was from Gokulgarh village. Ram Singh was called in, but again, he flatly denied having ever seen the bedraggled, bearded man. But Chiman Singh saw a familiar face in the scrawny young man – Ram Singh was his younger brother Chetram's classmate. The excited conversation of recognition saved the day for Chiman Singh. The battalion called their brigade, which in turn called the division which then checked with Fort William. Yes, a naval sailor named Chiman Singh had been reported MIA.

A wave of relief swept through C2P when Chiman Singh reported to the camp the next day. That evening, Lt Cdr Martis broadcast a brief radio message to Cdr Samant.

> Glad to report C Singh reported C2P PM 23 safely. Propose forgive and forget if possible. More in person.[53]

The next day, Lt Cdr Martis escorted Chiman Singh to the brigade commander, Charlie Sector. Brigadier Salik decided to follow the standard operating procedure. Chiman Singh was sent to Headquarters, Eastern Naval Command, for a proper debriefing and screening by Military Intelligence.

The 22 November Battle of Boyra, which Chiman Singh had a ringside view of, was a turning point. It signalled the start of war in the eastern theatre. India and Pakistan were now in a full-fledged,

---

53 Captain M.N.R. Samant's family archives

albeit undeclared, military contest using tanks, artillery and fighter jets.

The next day, the Pakistan government declared an emergency, putting all its naval units out to sea. Indian warships and submarines followed suit, sailing out of harbours to assume their wartime positions. The only window the frogmen saboteurs of Pakistan's Special Services Group had to strike at the Indian Navy had now closed.

At the Command Hospital in Barrackpore, Lt Kapil was swiftly discharged. His sores had not healed fully, but the army wasn't going to wait – the hospital had to make room for the Boyra battle casualties.

The Indian Navy moved its personnel around with alacrity. Lt Cdr Martis and Sub Lieutenant B.S. Thakur were recalled and placed under the Eastern Fleet. Recruitment and training of the naval commandos at Camp Plassey ground to a halt. The camp was now manned only by a skeletal navy crew who looked after the equipment and explosives. Every available man – officer, trainer and trainee – was drafted for the war effort. Most of the naval commandos had already been infiltrated inside Bangla Desh. They were asked not to return to their base in India. Once they had carried out their missions, Samant ordered, they had to stay behind to fight with the local Mukti Bahini wherever they were.

Samant had meanwhile informed Major General Jacob and the Eastern Command's intelligence chief Colonel M.S. Khara of Chiman Singh's return. Singh would have to be deloused, Khara told him grimly, delousing being military speak for screening spies. Samant relented. But they were not to use third degree.

Chiman Singh was detained in Fort William's Military Intelligence section and subjected to rigorous questioning. The military spooks wanted to be sure he was telling the truth and that he hadn't revealed details of the top-secret operation he was part of. The questioning went on for six, sometimes eight hours a day. The Military Intelligence operatives took copious notes and then went over his statement, hoping to detect a loophole. Chiman Singh stuck to his story – the passage, the people he had met, the power pylon and jetty he had destroyed, the Mukti Bahini's Captain Omar whom he had operated with.

Lt Kapil, who had by then moved to Fort William, hovered around Singh, interacting with the Military Police to ensure all was well. The interrogation ended when MI corroborated his story with the Mukti Bahini. Chiman Singh was telling the truth. He was finally given an all-clear by the Military Police and billeted in the NCO Mess. It was a day that marked a turning point in the subcontinent's history: 3 December.

War

At 5.40 p.m. on 3 December 1971, Pakistan Air Force jets bombed IAF airbases in Amritsar, Pathankot, Srinagar, Avantipur, Utterlai, Jodhpur, Ambala and Agra. The Pakistan Army opened with an artillery barrage on Indian positions in Poonch, Sulemankhi and Khemkaran. Indira Gandhi, who was visiting Calcutta that day, cut her visit short and flew back to New Delhi.

Shortly after midnight, her calm voice rang out over the radio waves across the country.

I speak to you at a moment of grave peril to our country and our people ... Some hours ago, soon after 5:30 p.m. on 3 December, Pakistan launched full-scale war against us.

It was an electrifying address. Everyone stopped what they were doing to listen. Inside Fort William, Samant interrupted the discussion of war plans with Lt Cdr Roy Choudhury and Lt Mitter. On the dimly lit bridge of the *Panvel* in Sandeshkhali, sub lieutenants Ashok Kumar and Vijaygopal paused a late-night tipple as the transistor set played out Mrs Gandhi's voice.

The PM berated Pakistan's 'wanton and unprovoked aggression' and summed up the past nine months into her terse three-minute speech. India had withstood the greatest of pressures 'in preventing the annihilation of an entire people whose only crime was to vote democratically' she asserted, even as she praised the 'courageous band of freedom fighters who had been staking their all in defence of the values for which we also have struggled and which are basic to our way of life'. She concluded with a call to arms. 'So today we fight, not merely for territorial integrity, but for the basic ideals which have given strength to this country.'

She meant war.

In distant Vizag, sometime after midnight on 3 December, Nirmala Samant was shaken awake by the sound of a massive, window-rattling blast. The force of the explosion shook the beds of her children Ujwala and Natasha Samant and woke up their neighbours in the naval base. 'An earthquake ... a school holiday!' little Ujwala exulted even as the adults around her grew fearful. The blast was from the direction of the Ramakrishna beach, one-and-a-half kilometres from their home. Navy lookouts at the coast battery near the harbour mouth saw a flash and a huge plume of water shoot up out of the water. The explosion was quickly forgotten in the din of war.

The astute Mrs Gandhi had staked her country's prestige on the war. India was ranged against two of the five superpowers, the United States and China, one of whom was egging the other on to intervene with a 1962-style border action in favour of its beleaguered ally, Pakistan. All India had was an assurance of support from the Soviet Union. And gutsy, bull-headed military leaders.

Hours after the PM spoke, Admiral Nanda's left hook emerged in the north Arabian Sea. Three darkened silhouettes raced through the waters, picked up three targets on their fire control radars[54] and fired. The barrage of anti-ship missiles launched by the Soviet-built Osa-1-class boats, *INS Nirghat*, *INS Nipat* and the *INS Veer* – locked on to their targets, sinking the destroyer *PNS Khaibar*, the minesweeper the *PNS Muhafiz* and the merchant vessel the *SS Venus Challenger*. The Battle of Karachi was over in less than thirty minutes as the boats disengaged and sped back to Indian waters. Nanda had lit a bonfire in Karachi, as he had promised.

In New York, the US called for an emergency meeting of the UN Security Council and sponsored a draft resolution calling for a ceasefire. It was the day the Soviet Union imposed the first of three vetoes on the US resolution, the third one being on 14 December. The Soviet vetoes prevented a ceasefire, which would call for the Indian Army's withdrawal from East Pakistan, from being passed. Pakistan Army columns in the west mounted an armoured thrust towards India's vulnerable Chhamb town even as the IAF and PAF duelled in the skies.

On the morning of 5 December, Nanda's right hook began turning into the wind off south-eastern Bangla Desh. A dozen Sea Hawk fighter jets roared off the deck of the *INS Vikrant*. Eight hawks sped towards Cox's Bazar, rocketing and strafing the airfield, ATC tower, damaging the power house and setting fuel tanks on fire. The *Vikrant* and her escorts had sailed through the night from their hidden palm-fronded anchorage in the Nicobar Islands and steamed north towards Bangla Desh.

Later that evening, the Sea Hawks appeared off Chittagong, attacking the hangar and control tower of the airfield and setting a

---

54 Radars that detect targets for guns and missiles to hit

fuel dump on fire. Two gunboats were strafed, one of them caught
fire. Six merchant ships in the outer anchorage were attacked.[55]

Off the entrance of Visakhapatnam harbour on 5 December, a
small team of naval divers led by Lt Cdr Sajjan Kumar was probing
the source of oil and flotsam reported by fishermen. The long
black form of the PNS Ghazi sat on the seabed sixty metres below,
oozing black oil, her mouth blown out in a calamitous explosion of
mines and torpedoes, her flooded interiors packed with the bodies
of ninety-three crewmen. The Ghazi's second hunt for the Vikrant
had ended in catastrophe, just two kilometres off the mouth of
the harbour where she thought her target was. There was at that
moment, no end to the Pakistan Navy's misery.

Samant, meanwhile, was eager to join the war in Bangla Desh.
His covert unit, including the gunboats, were now directly under Lt
General Aurora's Eastern Command. Samant's main contribution
to his parent service since the formal declaration of war had been
to fly down the former Mangro crew Mohammad Rahmatulla and
A.W. Chowdhury to INS Virbahu, the submarine base in Vizag.
Chowdhury chalked out the Ghazi's layout on a blackboard in
the base. He had served two years on the Ghazi and knew his
way around her blindfolded. Rahmatulla and Chowdhury cleared
whatever doubts the navy might have had that the sub lying inert on
the seabed was indeed the fearsome underwater predator.

On 5 December, Commander Samant was back in Major
General Jacob's office in Fort William for his orders. Jacob was by
then in the thick of the war he had planned for all year and could
spare only a few minutes. He gave the naval officer a situation report
– the Indian Army had begun a three-pronged offensive into Bangla
Desh and intended to reach Dacca by bypassing all the strong points
in the towns and cities that Niazi had created. The Indian Army's 2

---

55 Vice Admiral G.M. Hiranandani, *Transition to Triumph* (New Delhi:
Lancer Publishers), 2000

Corps had advanced to Jessore district on the south-western flank of Bangla Desh. The 9th Infantry Division's 41 Brigade was attacking Khulna held by the Pakistan Army's 107 brigade. Lt General Aurora and Major General Jacob wanted Samant to mount an attack from the river, to dislocate the Pakistani troops.

Samant readily agreed. He planned a gunboat raid, naming his force 'Alfa', a nod to Lt General J.S. Aurora's name.

'Force Alfa', he proposed, would strike at the Khulna–Mongla industrial complex along the Pussur river, attack Pakistani shipping and gunboats, and throw the Pakistan Army off balance. The offensive plan excited Jacob. 'Go and beat up everything on the Pussur,' he told the naval officer.

Samant had flashed one last coded message to his boss Captain Roy before leaving – he was away for a mission expected to last about a week. His covert unit was now an overt military force.

NCO(X)'s key mover had drafted the only two naval divers available – Lt Kapil and Leading Seaman Chiman Singh – into the attack. The duo had prepared for the mission by testing their diving sets, the same ones that were donated by Bangla Deshi expatriates earlier that year. They had dived into a pond in front of Victoria Terminus, in the heart of Calcutta, in full view of a curious crowd.

On 8 December, Samant, Kapil and Chiman Singh left Calcutta to cover the eighty-kilometre distance to Hasnabad where the *Palash*, *Padma* and the *Panvel* were waiting.

On the car ride, Samant revealed to Kapil the existence of the gunboats, Camp C2H, and their plans for the raid. When they arrived at the ramshackle pier at Hasnabad, Kapil's face creased into a smile as he saw Lt Mitter, his shipmate from the *INS Ganga* waiting there. His thoughts went back to their last covert mission together –when sub lieutenants Mitter and Kapil had painted 'Whorehouse' over the naval storehouse. They were now a team again, on a deep-penetration gunboat raid into the heart of enemy territory.

The crews of the three boats were a study in contrast. The *Panvel* crew were in khaki naval work rig. The Flower-class gunboat crews looked like they were turned out for a weekend excursion. Samant, the force commander, was in trousers, a full-sleeve shirt, canvas boots, and slinging his 9 mm carbine. Mitter was in khaki trousers and a collared T-shirt and brown leather shoes. Kapil, who hadn't worn a uniform since April, was in blue and yellow Bermudas, a yellow T-shirt and rubber-soled corduroy shoes.

The formal declaration of war had boosted Samant's officer strength. Lt Cdr Raizada, who had supervised the refit of the boats in Calcutta and Lt J.V. Natu, a naval engineer from the INS Shivaji Technical Institute in Lonavla who was briefly base engineer officer in-charge in C2-H were roped into Force Alfa. A third officer, Sub-Lieutenant Bandopadhyay, a tall and lanky young officer who worked as Samant's junior staff officer in Fort William, refused to be left behind – he had hopped on board the *Padma* just as it sailed out from the GRSE.

Hasnabad was Force Alfa's first stop in a 200-km journey to their next stop, Akram Point in East Pakistan. The commandant of the BSF battalion there was Lt Commander H.K. Mukherjee, a retired Indian naval officer, now re-employed by the BSF. He was clearly delighted to be of assistance to his former naval colleagues.

The *Padma* and the *Palash* had shed their Mark VII mines in C2H and were lightened for their riverine passage. The boat crews then painted over and strung out a 10-ft by 8-ft yellow awning athwartships over the three boats. These yellow cloth panels were the coded 'air recognition signals' agreed upon with the IAF for easy identification as friendly vehicles to the IAF jets buzzing above.

The BSF had deputed the *MV Chitrangada* only riverine patrol craft it had in the area to accompany Force Alfa.

Samant divided his team amongst the four boats. His staff officer Lt Cdr G.D. Mukherjee and Leading Telegraphist Chatterjee went on board the *Chitrangada*. Lt Cdr V.K. Raizada and Lt Kapil were to be on the *Palash* with Lt Cdr Roy Choudhury. Lt Natu, Sub Lieutenant A.K. Bandopadhyay and Leading Seaman Chiman Singh were on the *Padma*. The task unit also carried ten naval commando recruits from C2P, a dozen limpet mines and seven scuba diving sets, fully charged with air. They also carried along plenty of demolition stores for diving operation from the gunboats – scuttling and boarding operations or underwater demolition tasks.

Samant also borrowed two 7.62 light machine guns from the BSF. These guns were fitted above the bridge of the *Padma* and *Palash* and manned by one BSF trooper each.

Commander Mukherjee spared no effort to ensure their timely departure. He stocked the boats with stores, fuel, water and provisions which could not be procured locally through the regular service channels. The task force did not have the latest navigational charts of the riverine areas – they relied on World War II-era British Army maps. Mukherjee overcame this by providing each boat with a guide who knew the Sundarbans like the back of his hand. He also alerted the local BSF outposts and Mukti Bahini army units of their presence to avoid a possible 'blue on blue' – service slang for friendly fire engagements.

Samant discovered that the *Chitrangada*, commanded by a BSF officer, had a top speed of barely seven kilometres an hour. The BSF boat was hence given an eight-hour head start and sailed out by 11 p.m. on 6 December.

At 6 a.m. on 7 December, Force Alfa sailed out of the Hasnabad anchorage in a straight line formation. Commander Samant was on board the command vessel, the *INS Panvel*, the prospect of his first brush with combat weighing on his mind.

The appearance of this mysterious man in plainclothes who passed instructions to Noronha, piqued crew interest. Vijaygopal already had a nickname for their plainclothes-wearing task force commander who only brusquely identified himself in two words – 'naval intelligence'. He was 'the Spy'.

Samant peered out from the *Panvel*'s bridge as the black river snaked out before them. The tiny enclosed bridge with the five rectangular portholes was cramped like the conning tower of his last command, the submarine *INS Karanj*. There was just enough standing room for four crewmen. He recognized the platform's Soviet-philosophy – austere crew comforts but superlative operational features. The 'Mius' X band surface search and navigation radar mounted in front of the open bridge could pick up targets eighty kilometres away. The radar feed appeared on a display unit in the bridge – a circular orange screen with a raised rubber eyepiece. The Plan Position Indicator screen had four concentric circles which measured distance; a radius line in the centre swung around like a one-handed clock to follow the radar's sweep. The bridge also housed the ship's high-frequency radio set and a chart table across which they had laid the World War II vintage survey maps of Bengal.

The *Panvel*'s twin engines were under the charge of Kapalli Sai Raju, a leading electrical mechanician from East Godavari district. From his position in the engine room below the deck, the twenty-four-year-old 'Generator' Raju ensured the V-12s kept ticking and that the power supply to the wireless equipment and radars was in order.

The river was calm but, as it turned out, deceptively so. The *Palash* ran aground while manoeuvring around a soft bottom shoal soon after departure. Roy Choudhury's efforts to extricate her from the shoal proved futile. The tide was rapidly receding, which meant she could be stuck there for a long time. The *Padma* was called in and tied a tow rope to its sister ship and yanked it free from the sandbank. The boats resumed their passage. They were headed towards the khals – narrow tidal channels that offered a navigation route through the dense impenetrable mangrove forests of the Sundarbans. The Mukti Bahini guide took them through Garani Khal the shortest, most secure route to Akram Point. The task force sailed through the khal, which was twenty metres at its narrowest and 200 metres at its widest. They sailed past exotic wildlife – a tiger, wild deer and thousands of wild duck.

Communication secrecy for the operation was paramount. Samant had ordered that all out-bound signal traffic between the boats and base would be initiated only by him.

He had prepared a special high-definition crypto code for the mission with the INS Hooghly's signal officer. The only exception to his order would be unforeseen requirements or when on a detached mission.

Just then, a clear burst of transmission in Morse code identified itself using NOIC Calcutta's alphanumeric callsign. The message asked the *INS Panvel* to transmit continuously. The *Panvel's* radio operator instantly identified it as a ruse. This was because the high-frequency transmission was far clearer and more powerful than the ones they were receiving from the INS Hooghly. It was very likely the Pakistan Army's Signal Intelligence Monitoring organization in Khulna, trying to get a direction fix on the *Panvel*. Samant ordered radio silence for the rest of the passage.

The task force rendezvoused with *MV Chitrangada* across the Garani Khal at about 4.30 p.m. that day. It was already pitch dark. Samant held a commanding officers' conference in the *Panvel's* tiny wardroom below the bridge. Over a map, he explained that they would head for Akram Point, the Pakistani position closest to the Indian side, after midnight. From here, they could ambush ships trying to escape into the Bay of Bengal through the Pussur river.

The three gunboats arrived off Akram Point, at 1 a.m. on 9 December. Akram Point was the conflux of the Sibsa and the Pussur rivers, with the Sundarbans jutting out like a thick mangrove fist between the two rivers. The *Panvel* anchored at Akram Point, its radar sweeping the Pussur. The radar operator was studying two large radar blips that were moving southwards – downriver and past them. The contacts could not be seen visually from the open bridge of the *Panvel*. They had obviously been darkened. They appeared to be two medium-sized merchant vessels. Force Commander Samant was called up to the bridge. Samant peered into the plan position indicator of the Mius. The targets were beyond the gun range of his task force. He decided not to waste time and precious fuel in a stern chase. He briefly broke radio silence to transmit a coded message to Headquarters Eastern Naval Command, Visakhapatnam: 'Have observed two unidentified darkened contacts leaving harbour and proceeding to open sea. Request intercept.'

The Pakistan Army's retreat from Bangla Desh had begun. The radar contacts were the Pakistani merchant ships the 7,235-ton *MV Anwar Baksh* and the 9,326-ton *MV Baqir*. They were packed with Pakistan Army personnel and their families who were making a break from Mongla for the Bay of Bengal. Several hours later, the vessels were intercepted by the destroyer *INS Rajput*, enforcing a naval blockade near the mouth of the Pussur. The navy boarded the ships and diverted them to Sandheads, Calcutta, where they became war prizes.

Force Alfa anchored in the lee of Akram Point for the rest of the night. They had travelled a distance of over 240 kilometres since leaving Hasnabad on 6 December. The *Panvel*'s Mius remained active, sweeping through the night, looking for more activity. There was none. The next morning, the boats carried out a reconnaissance sweep of a twelve-kilometre stretch from Akram Point towards Hirani Point. There was nothing. At about 9 a.m. on 9 December, the flotilla retired to the sanctuary of a sheltered anchorage not visible from the river. Six hours later, they weighed anchor and set sail to arrive at the Mongla anchorage by nightfall. They planned to surprise the enemy. Samant had already flashed coded high-frequency messages to the navy through his communications node at INS Hooghly.

The *Panvel, Padma, Palash* and *Chitrangada* travelled up the Pussur river channel in complete darkness. When they were within twenty kilometres of Mongla port, an orange glow lit up the horizon and the eastern coastline near it. The Force advanced to about five kilometres off Mongla. The glow was from ships at anchorage that had been attacked and set ablaze. They reached their destination by 10.30 p.m. and anchored for the night. They planned to enter the Mongla anchorage at dawn the next day.

Back in the Arabian Sea, a massive orange flash lit up the night sky. The *INS Khukri*, an anti-submarine warfare frigate had been hit by a Pakistani submarine it had been hunting for. The *PNS Hangor* had replaced the *PNS Mangro* on a patrol station codenamed 'Bravo 123456' – a stretch of sea from Diu head to Dabhol. The *Hangor*'s skipper Lt Cdr Ahmad Tasnim had fired a torpedo which had homed in on the *Khukri*'s propellers and exploded under her keel, triggering off nearly twenty tons of high explosives stored in the aft magazine. In the chaos on board, the supremely calm Captain Mahendranath Mulla turned to his executive officer and calmly spoke the toughest words a commanding officer can ever utter: 'Number 1, abandon ship'.

Captain Mulla then shouted at his wavering crew: 'Paani mein jao, yahan nahin bachogey. Jahaz par nahin bachogey! Paani mein jao! Life-raft mil jayega! Jao! Jao!'(Get in to the water. You won't survive on the ship. You'll get the life raft. Go!)[56]

---

56 Source of Captain Mulla's conversation: Lt Cdr Madanjit Singh Ahluwalia, *Torpedoed at Sea* (Chennai: Notion Press), 2016

Nearly 200 of his men were still trapped below decks. Captain Mulla could have saved himself, but the deeply empathetic naval lawyer who took on impossible-to-win cases for the men had already made up his mind. Less than three minutes after she was hit, the *Khukri* disappeared beneath the Arabian Sea, the gallant Captain Mulla still on the bridge.

Force Alfa, meanwhile, entered the war's second theatre at first light on 10 December. There was a deathly calm at the Mongla anchorage. Mongla Port, established on the left bank of the Pussur river was East Pakistan's second maritime gateway after Chittagong. The port had been shifted 18 km south from its original location at Chalna, to accommodate deeper draught vessels.

Through the morning mist, they saw the eerie sight of four medium-sized merchant ships burning silently, still secured to their buoy moorings in the water. The freighters had been riddled with cannon shells, clearly the work of the IAF which by now roamed unchallenged over the skies of Bangla Desh.

The task force encountered no resistance except for a short burst of small arms fire from an unknown source when the ships entered the bay-shaped anchorage. The force responded by firing LMG bursts in that direction. And then all was quiet.

The *Panvel* pulled up alongside Mongla port. Commander Samant hopped off onto the jetty, the soil of a free country. Bangla Desh had been recognized as a sovereign nation first by Bhutan and then by India just days before, on 6 December. A large crowd of locals cheered as they saw the Bangla Deshi flags on the *Padma* and the *Palash*. Pakistani forces had retreated from there and had sabotaged the shore defences by taking the breech blocks away from the six shore-mounted 40/60 Bofors guns. Locals told him that the Mukti Bahini had already taken two Pakistani naval officers as prisoners of war (POW) and left.

On that day, the war in the subcontinent was at a key inflexion point.

General Niazi had fortified the towns and cities of East Pakistan to hold out for as long as he could before a ceasefire would force the Indian withdrawal. The Indian Army, however, moved in like a monsoon torrent, bypassing Niazi's fortresses. The IAF's Mi-4 helicopters flew waves of sorties, airlifting brigades to reach all three key points on the Meghna river – Ashuganj, Daudkandi and Chandpur – and secured the Meghna bulge. Dacca was now cut off from Chittagong and the road to the capital was now exposed to the Indian Army from the east.

At Mongla, Samant saw more evidence of a mass escape of the Pakistani garrison from Bangla Desh. The identities of several Pakistani merchant vessels had been changed to help in their seaward escape – the *MV Makran* became the *MV Dora*, the *MV Ocean Enterprises* was painted over as the Panama-registered '*Ceandente*'.

Samant ordered Kapil, Chiman Singh and the naval commandos to form a boarding party to inspect the burning ships. They boarded four merchantmen to locate the ships' logs, registration documents and ciphers, anything that could prove valuable for Indian intelligence. They conducted quick systematic searches, carrying plastic explosives, plugging detonating cords and blasting down locked doors of communication compartments and safe cupboards of the bridge of each ship. They found nothing. The ships' crews had either spirited them away or destroyed all the important documents.

With no sign of the enemy in Mongla, Samant decided to sail north to Khulna, the heart of Bangla Desh's industrial heartland, over thirty kilometres away up the Rupsha river. Khulna was close to the jute plantations, well connected by air, road, rail and waterways, and had a plentiful supply of fresh water and cheap labour. The country's sole newsprint supplier, the Newsprint Mill of Pakistan, was located here. Three major jute mills were located in Daulatpur, within city limits. Khulna was well defended. Not only did it have gunboats, but since 1970, housed the province's second naval base PNS Titumir.

Samant left the *MV Chitrangada* behind at Mongla with his staff officer, Lt Cdr Mukherjee. His instructions were to render assistance to the local population and search for any survivors or prisoners of war and await Force Alfa's return.

As the *Palash* chugged upstream behind the *Panvel*, a worried Raizada traced his finger over the long, narrow channel on the map. 'We are going up a single channel,' he told Roy Choudhury. He was worried that the boats could be ambushed on their return. 'Nonsense,' Roy Choudhury scoffed. 'You've just got cold feet.'

Villagers on both banks of the river cheered the boats as they sailed up the river. The channel was silent with the quiet that only death or the threat of it brings. No boats sailed on that morning and there was no sign of the Mukti Bahini or of Pakistani forces.

The Pussur was a broad, muddy ribbon, around 500 metres wide. Khulna had developed on the inside of the river's meander bend as the province's jute hub. The three major jute mills in the city were located close to the jute plantations, and were well connected by air, road, rail and waterways, and had access to abundant fresh water and cheap labour.

Khulna's eastern riverbank was empty marshland with a fishing village and ferry point where wooden country craft took people across the river. The port city had borne the brunt of two major NCO(X) operations – Operation Jackpot's assault swimmer attack on 15 August and the mines laid by the *Padma* and *Palash* over a hundred kilometres downstream.

Force Alfa approached the city's landmark – the west German-built Khulna shipyard – along the river. The shipyard constructed commercial craft like tugs and workboats, apart from repairing ships. One of the ships lying alongside for a refit was the Somaliaregistered *SS Lightning*. The merchant ship had been hit by NCO(X) limpeteers, twice, in August and October. After the October attack, the ship had been refloated and towed upstream. The force was on the lookout for the Pakistan Navy's 'town-class' gunboat, the *PNS Jessore* and four other improvised gunboats that they knew guarded merchant ships in Khulna. Samant didn't know that on the first day of the formal declaration of war, six IAF Gnats had strafed the gunboats, destroying one and killing three crewmen on the other, the *PNS Jessore*.[57] Soon after the air raid, Commander Gul Zarin, the naval officer in charge of Khulna, had fled in a merchant vessel along with the chairman of Khulna port.[58]

Force Alfa sailed up the river in a single column, *INS Panvel* in the lead, followed by the *Palash* and the *Padma*, three interrupted dashes moving in a straight-line formation roughly 400 metres from each other. They were at action stations. The commanding officers were in the enclosed bridge, the guns were cocked, fingers hooked on triggers, and feet on gun pedals. There was complete silence. Chiman Singh had by then joined BSF Constable Chintan Sharma on the LMG position above the bridge. In the enclosed bridge below, Mitter scanned the horizon for signs of trouble. The vessel was being steered by his quartermaster Haq.

'Joy Bangla!'

It was Sub Lt Natu. He had grabbed the *Padma*'s loud hailer and was lustily shouting across the water. A scattered chorus responded from the riverbank. The force had neared the bungalow of the local superintendent of police, about 400m south of the railway bridge which spanned the Rupsha.

---

57 Gunboats being destroyed source: Siddiq Salik, *Witness to Surrender* (New Delhi: Lancer Publishers), 1977

58 Gul Zarin fleeing source: Interview with Vice Admiral Taj M. Khattak, *ISPR Hilal English Magazine*, December 2015

Then the firing started. Pakistani military, paramilitary forces and razakars dug into the bunkers along the western riverbank, barely 200 feet away, and started firing at the flotilla.

The firing increased as the task force approached Khulna. A hail of machine gun and rifle bullets whistled and cracked across the channel, kicking spouts of water around the ship. On the *Palash*, Chiman Singh had borrowed the LMG from the BSF trooper to blast away towards the shore.

From the bridge of the *Padma*, Mitter shouted at his gun crews to engage the bunkers. The gun captain, Jalal, turned his L-60 to the left even as his crew lowered the gun barrel to around five degrees above horizontal and stepped on the firing pedal.

Thud! Thud! Thud! Thud!

The first clip of four shells disappeared into the breech and the gun spat out the brass empties onto the deck. In the distance, the shells began exploding against the buildings. A three-man relay team of ammunition suppliers ran a relay of spare clips from the focsle hatch, handing it over to the loader, who continued pushing down shells. Jalal continued to peer through the twin sights and shoot. Onshore, soldiers leapt off bunkers as the 40 mm shells chewed off chunks of brick, sandbags and concrete. All three boats were firing. The channel reverberated with the crackle of small arms and cannon fire.

Three IAF Gnats had been circling high above at nearly 10,000 feet, distant predators looking for prey, and seemed to have noticed the shooting party. They decided to join in. A few minutes later, they reappeared. Right behind the Force Alfa boats, a three-jet formation line astern.

The longest seven minutes in the lives of the Force Alfa personnel began at around 11.40 a.m.

Mitter, hearing the sound of the approaching jet engines, poked his head out of the *Padma*'s bridge. His face darkened as he saw the lead Gnat flip in and line up directly behind his boat until its silhouette was a neat circle. The pilot hunched behind the controls, wings drooping with rocket pods.

'Oh my god!'

The lead Gnat spat out two 76 mm rockets. Two fiery streaks headed towards the *Padma*. The first punched through the engine room and exploded. The second rocket penetrated the bridge, where Mitter and Natu were standing, and exploded. The blast instantaneously killed BSF trooper Chintan Sharma and grievously wounded Chiman Singh on the LMG position above the bridge, and knocked out Mitter, Natu and Haq who were inside the bridge.

The *Palash* and the *Panvel* quickly realized what was going on and broke formation.

On the *Panvel*, Lt Cdr Noronha shouted out orders: 'Helmsman full ahead.'

Lt Cdr Roy Choudhury on the *Palash*, a gunner trained to recognize aircraft outlines, had identified the IAF Gnats as 'friendlies'. The feeling, alas, was not mutual. The anguished CO now worked to save his ship and crew. He ordered his helmsman to steer towards starboard just as the second Gnat lined up to fire. The first rocket missed and went straight into the water. The second penetrated the engine room and exploded. The vessel shuddered like it had been hit by a giant sledgehammer.

The third Gnat headed for the *Panvel*, sprinting up the river at over 20 knots. Noronha had already steered the ship away from the centreline. The Gnat's first rocket missed the boat. The Mukti Bahini guide who saw the jet thundering in decided to leap into the river. The second rocket caught him mid-air, before he touched the water. He died instantly.

The IAF Gnats had made a terrible mistake. They hadn't recognized the yellow cloth panels and now relentlessly pursued what they thought were Pakistani gunboats.

For the next few minutes, the only sound over Khulna was the roar of three Orpheus aero engines as the jets flew in low, pulling up, their afterburners making an ear-splitting noise.

On the *Padma*, Mitter momentarily blacked out after he felt a violent jerk on his right arm. He shook his head and struggled to open his eyes. He couldn't see. The boat's engines were silent. He stumbled around, blinded. And then as he blinked rapidly, his vision returned. The blood pouring down his forehead had entered his eyes. The return of his eyesight boosted his confidence, but what he saw next mortified the young officer. He had been showered by shrapnel. A piece of flesh had been gnawed away from above his right elbow. His quartermaster, Haq, lay next to him, weakly gasping 'Pani, Pani…' (Water, water.) Haq's right leg had been severed by the shrapnel and lay some distance away from him. Lieutenant Natu lay at the back of the shattered bridge, cradling his stomach with both his hands. He was bleeding profusely. The *Padma* was dead in the water and drifting aimlessly. The forward gun had lost three ammunition handlers. The aft gun was completely incapacitated and the gun crews scattered. The smell of diesel was all-pervasive. Wisps of oily black smoke had started coming out of the engine room. The magazine for the rear gun was behind the engine room. If the fire spread, it would ignite the shells stored there. He feared for his crew.

'Abandon ship!'

Mitter barked his orders out in English and Bengali as he located his second-in-command, Jalal. 'Jalal, throw everyone who cannot swim overboard.'

His crew jumped overboard and started swimming ashore, some braving incredible pain. Haq winced as Jalal lifted and dropped him into the water. He then threw the helmsman's leg overboard before diving into the Rupsha. The *Padma* had begun belching thick black smoke.

Chiman Singh lay on the deck, his hip exposed to the bone, blood gushing out. He dragged his mangled leg and dived into the water. Lt Natu grabbed his wounded stomach and dived overboard. Both swam slowly towards the slipway of the Khulna shipyard.

Mitter was the last to jump overboard. His right arm was limp and bleeding. In the water, the crew of the *Padma* gathered around their injured captain. 'Get away from me, get away,' Mitter screamed in Bengali. He did not want the returning aircraft to strafe them.

The aircraft returned for a second pass, this time with their 30 mm Aden cannons. They ignored the stricken *Padma* and headed for the *Palash*.

The *Panvel*, meanwhile, was frantically weaving through the river, trying to shake the angry Gnats off its back. Noronha had ordered his gun crews to fire on the jets.

Roy Choudhury gave the order to abandon ship. He asked the crew to jump into the water as he directed the helmsman to steer the vessel towards the uninhabited eastern shore of the Rupsha. The boat's diesels were churning at full ahead. His crew began leaping off from the port side of the boat into the water and swimming into the midstream of the river. Raizada grabbed a lifejacket and leapt overboard.

Roychowdhury's leg was bleeding. He had been hit by shrapnel and hence did not want to jump into the water. He, Kapil and the quartermaster stood on the bridge, watching the riverbank rush towards them. When the boat hit the steep bank, the trio leaped off the boat and scrambled for the shore. Kapil helped the wounded CO as he stumbled ashore. A Gnat roared in for two more gun runs. Cannon shells thumped into the soft river bank, fortunately missing the two officers.

Roy Choudhury was mortified by what had happened, but didn't panic. He planned to retrieve his boat once the aircraft had departed.

Meanwhile, Mitter, who was floating close to the opposite riverbank, continued to calmly issue orders to Jalal.

'Jalal, I can't swim with my shoes on.'

The young sailor dived below the water and yanked Mitter's shoes off.

'Now, Jalal,' he said, 'leave me alone and save yourself.' Mitter knew he had a better chance of surviving the razakars than Jalal did.

'No, sir, I won't leave you.' Jalal clung to his wounded captain.

'Jalal, get out … It's an order!' Mitter gathered all his strength and kicked at his second-in-command.

'Hai Allah! Ee kee korlein!' (Oh god! What have you done!) Jalal floated away with the river.

After the jets departed, the razakars emerged. Like termites after a thundershower, they poked out of the sandbagged bunkers and buildings, surveying the sole gunboat on the river.

The Rupsha was now in flood. The waters were pushing in upriver, towards the city. Mitter saw Sub Lieutenant Bandopadhyay floating in the water. He jabbed his finger towards the shore where they would head for. They were less than 100 metres away from the riverbank when a razakar appeared. He popped out of one of the shattered bunkers that the *Padma* had targeted just minutes ago. He was in his early twenties, slightly built, and wore a khaki shirt and trouser and canvas shoes, hefting a bolt-action hunting rifle. He raised his weapon, aiming at Mitter who was closer to the shore. There was nowhere to run. The first shot rang out.

Crack!

Then, a plop.

Mitter floated on.

The razakar kept up the chase, running along the riverbank in hot pursuit. Mitter lay on his back, drifting with the current, helplessly gazing at his tormentor.

This is it, he thought. *The next one will get me.* The razakar aimed and fired again.

Crack!

Plop!

The bullet missed again. The militiaman ran along the riverbank, cycling two more rounds, and fired. Both missed. He was persistent. He reloaded. The chase continued. The razakar was furious.

'Aye, kaafir ka bachcha,' (You infidel!) he hollered as he cycled another round into the rifle's chamber.

Crack!

Mitter felt a thump on his chest. He had been hit, but he couldn't see where. That was when he decided to end the chase. There was no point risking their lives. He propelled himself closer towards the shore and emerged out of the water, barefoot and dripping wet. Bandopadhyay followed him out of the water. Anger and indignation swept through Mitter as he approached the razakar.

'Why are you shooting at me? Don't you know I'm an Indian Navy officer?' he berated the man in Bengali.

The razakar disregarded his protestations. He pointed his rifle at the two officers:

'Cholin, Cholin.'

He marched his soaking-wet prisoners towards the Khulna shipyard on the riverbank a short distance away. The two officers were led into a large assembly hall in the shipyard. Mitter asked for a place to lie down. He was offered a bench. He took his orange life jacket off. A black hole marked the spot where the razakar's bullet had entered. The bullet was lodged in his chest. He yanked the bullet out rashly. Blood spurted out. A group of civilians – shipyard workers – gathered around him and watched curiously.

'What is your qualification?' a voice in the crowd asked.

'Give me a blanket,' Mitter said.

He was feeling cold. The workers looked at him quizzically. Mitter spotted some curtains and a table cloth. He asked the onlookers to take them off and give them to him. They complied. Then, everything became faint. And he felt nothing. There was no sound.

I'm going to die, he thought to himself.

He asked the workers for a cigarette. A workman thrust a cigarette in his face and lit it. Mitter puffed on it. The smoke hit the back of his throat and woke him up. An aged maulvi wearing a green-and-white lungi and a kurta pushed his way through the crowd. He sat down next to Mitter and started reading the *Kalma*. He asked Mitter to repeat after him.

On the southern edge of the shipyard, the tide had washed Chiman Singh in. The diver dragged himself onto the bank and lay there, face down, exhausted and bleeding. The blood trickled down his thigh and into the river. His hair and beard were matted with river clay. He was drifting in and out of consciousness.

On the opposite bank, Kapil and Roychowdhury crouched low and turned back to look at their boat. The skies were silent. The engine room fire had spread uncontrollably. The *Palash* was now a bonfire. Retrieving the boat was now out of the question.

The two officers cautiously walked towards the fishing village on the riverbank, Roy Choudhury dragging his wounded leg. They spotted a few huts and boats. It took them around fifteen minutes to reach the outskirts of the village.

It was unsafe to stay there. They knew Khulna was a razakar stronghold. They were ashore and had to get to safety. But where? They were deep inside enemy territory. The *Panvel* had vanished.

11
LAST BOAT SAILING

Cdr Samant couldn't see his boats. As he looked back from the open bridge of the *Panvel* which was furiously racing upstream, he knew what the two black smoke trails spiralling upwards in the distance meant. The *Palash* was beached and ablaze, the ammunition on board poofing off in a macabre celebration. The blackened hulk of the *Padma* was adrift mid-channel. Force Alfa was finished. The ship's crew from two boats dead, wounded or floating in the water.

Noronha was determined the *Panvel* wouldn't meet the same fate. From the bridge, he barked orders to helmsman Sant Ram and the gun crews who continued firing to dissuade the Gnats. The *Panvel* flew around the bend of the Rupsha. Noronha saw the soft riverbank and turned to Sant Ram: 'Quartermaster, run the vessel aground.' The *Panvel* ran up the riverbank at a steep angle. Noronha then gave the call to abandon ship.

Samant, Noronha and the rest of the ship's company walked ashore. Samant, cradling his Sterling, looked up at the jets streaking through the skies above like hungry predators. He spotted a havildar standing on the shore and asked him for directions to the naval base PNS Titumir. The havildar looked at Samant and froze. He mouthed something unintelligible, turned around and darted away to take shelter. It was a bizarre situation in the chaos of combat. Samant hadn't reckoned with the fact that someone could have killed or overpowered him.

The adrenaline was pumping through his veins but Samant was not shaken. He was upset because of the failure of the recognition signal. He pursed his lips. The choices were stark – abort the mission or press on. An order to abort meant a U-turn back down the river from where they had come and recover his crew. Going upstream towards PNS Titumir meant continuing the fight with just one gunboat, and death or capture at the hands of the Pakistani forces. He was sure the survivors of the *Padma* and the *Palash* were still in the water. He decided to go and get them.

The crew waited till the jets had cleared the sky. They then re-boarded the beached vessel. Noronha gave the order to unbeach. With a roar of its diesels, the *Panvel* lurched free. She was now back in the middle of the river, heading down the way she came.

As the gunboat headed back into the river, the crew saw the razakars firing at the defenceless survivors in the water. Samant was enraged. He ordered the gun crews to fire.

The *Panvel* lowered its 40-mm guns and raked the bunkers on the western shore, Sub Lieutenant Ashok Kumar standing on the forward gun, directing it towards the shore targets. The gun spat out bullets and the brass empties clanked down and rolled on the deck as the relay team of loaders swiftly brought up more ammunition from the stowage area just below the bridge.

Militiamen continued to aim for the survivors. A machine gun from onshore opened fire at Raizada who was swimming towards the Khulna shipyard. The bullets splashed around him and missed. Raizada turned away and swam back towards the middle of the river, away from the range of small arms. He began hatching his escape. He should get to the shore only after nightfall. The lifejacket meant he could float for a long time. Through the rattle of firing, he ducked underwater. Then he heard the sound of a propeller churning. He looked up. In the distance, he saw the enlarging silhouette of a gunboat heading towards him at full speed.

Raizada was sure it was a Pakistani gunboat. He began swimming away. The boat was heading directly for him. Finally, he spotted the Sikh gun crewman on the ship's forward 40/60 and a wave of relief washed over him.

'Raizada, we have seen you…' Samant's voice boomed through the ship's loud hailer. 'We're coming for you.'

The *Panvel* approached the floating officer who kicked with both feet at its hull. He didn't want to be sucked in by the propellers. Noronha took a circle and came back as his crew lowered a ladder for Raizada to climb on board.

On the eastern shore of the river, Kapil and Roy Choudhury crouched low and spotted their getaway vessel. It was a fishing canoe with a single oar. A small knot of fishermen stood at the edge of the steep, narrow riverbank, peering at the action on the river. One of fishermen spotted the two Indian officers boarding the boat. He yelled and ran towards them. Kapil picked up the oar and hit him with the flat side. The fisherman fell back screaming.

Roy Choudhury hopped on board and Kapil cast off and swiftly began paddling the boat to the centre of the river.

Just then, another three-Gnat flight appeared over the Rupsha. The lead aircraft dropped low over the *Panvel*. Noronha was not going to take chances.

'Quartermaster, run the vessel aground.'

Helmsman Sant Ram once again manoeuvred the vessel towards the riverbank; this time, the Rupsha's desolate eastern shore. The beaching drill was repeated. The crew jumped off their ship and headed for the cover of the mangroves. The Gnats disappeared.

Perhaps, Samant thought, they had recognized the yellow cloth display panels.

A few minutes later, the crew reboarded the *Panvel* and a relieved Lieutenant Commander Noronha manoeuvred his patrol boat towards the channel.

In his closed confinement in the Khulna shipyard, an incapacitated Mitter heard Noronha's voice over the *Panvel*'s loud hailer: 'Any survivors from the *Padma* and the *Palash*, we are here to pick you up ... *INS Panvel* standing by.'

The shore defences continued pouring fire at the *Panvel*.

Kapil had by then rowed to the middle of the river. Four of the *Padma* and *Palash* crewmen were still in the water. He gestured for them to hold on to the sides of the boat.

Noronha spotted the group of survivors huddled around the canoe and lowered its ladder. Kapil and Roychowdhury scrambled aboard. They also spotted the *Padma*'s quartermaster Haq floating in the water. He was fished out, grievously injured and semi-conscious.

Noronha was on board the open bridge from where he could look for more survivors and direct the gun. The *Panvel* picked up fourteen survivors from the water. When Noronha was sure there were no more survivors in the water, he resumed the attack on Khulna. The river echoed with the report of the *Panvel*'s twin 40-mm guns engaging shore targets. Stray bullets from ashore peppered the *Panvel*'s hull like light rain.

In the melee, Ashok Kumar saw 'Generator Raju' emerge from his position below decks, pick up a rifle and fire at the shore targets. A light machine gun rattled at the gunboat from ashore, but missed. Kumar secretly thanked the boat's designers – its sleek profile meant that the machine gunners ashore had trouble hitting the moving vessel – their shots going either over or below the *Panvel*. Just then, a bullet whizzed in and hit Sant Ram on the open bridge. He winced and held his right hand. Blood poured down. He was evacuated below deck for treatment. Lt Kapil who was standing on the bridge took over the wheel. He would be the *Panvel*'s quartermaster for the rest of the journey, steering the vessel back to Indian waters.

The *Panvel*'s gun engagement made an impact on the local population. They broke into cheers and gathered to watch on the riverbank. The *Panvel* made two circular passes on the Rupsha, traveling a distance of ten kilometres, shelling the Khulna shipyard and government offices in the vicinity even as Samant, Noronha and Kapil stood on the bridge, scanning the waters for survivors. When they were certain there were no more survivors, the *Panvel* turned and headed back towards Mongla. They passed the smoking hulk of the *Palash* and later, the *Padma* which had drifted up onto the eastern riverbank.

They turned the guns and fired at the riverside home of Sabur Khan, a notorious Muslim League leader of the city. They aimed a few rounds at the Qureishi Steel Mill on the west bank, south of the city, too.

The *Panvel*'s 40/60 guns were now red hot. Sub Lieutenant Ashok Kumar could feel the heat of the barrel near his hands. The deck was covered with brass empties. Ashok Kumar counted them. The vessel had fired nearly 300 shells in Khulna. They were now dangerously low on ammunition.

On the riverbank near the Khulna shipyard, Chiman Singh didn't hear the gunfire. But he became aware of the khaki shadows lengthening around him. He stirred. There was a crack of a rifle. He felt like a searing hot rod had entered his back. There was another shot. The soldiers approached when they were satisfied Chiman Singh was completely incapacitated. One of them stripped the Omega diving watch off his wrist. The other one grabbed at Singh's wedding ring. His hand was swollen; the ring would not come off.

The soldier tried to hack his finger away, but seemed to have a rethink. He didn't want his trophy damaged.

Chiman Singh was taken to a Pakistani officer. The officer, who did not identify himself, looked at him reproachfully. 'Chiman Singh, we are doing so much to help your cause ... we are helping your Sikhistan.' He had mistaken Singh to be a Sikh.

In the shipyard, Mitter overheard a razakar chattering excitedly on the phone in Urdu. 'I have captured two Indian officers.' Within half an hour, a military pickup truck came and took Mitter and Bandopadhyay away. Mitter was lying on the floor at the back of the pickup. Bandopadhyay in the front, behind the driver, along with their razakar captor. They entered Khulna city. At every crossing, the razakar stopped to boast about his trophies. From the window, people spat at Mitter. A few hit him. He was escorted to the lawn of a military building. It was the brigade headquarters of Khulna. Mitter saw a senior officer in khaki pacing the corridor of the barrack-like building. It was Brigadier Muhammad Hayat, whose 107 Brigade was defending Khulna. He had a lot weighing on his mind. On 6 December, Brigadier Hayat's forces had withdrawn from Jessore, over sixty kilometres away, abandoning the key fortress to the Indian Army without a fight.[59]

A smart young army captain in khaki marched up to Mitter.

'I am Staff Captain Aziz. Identify yourself, please.'

'Suvesh Kumar Mitter. Lieutenant, Indian Navy.'

Captain Aziz was incredulous. Mitter, however, did not have a shred of identity on him.

'You are not in uniform. The Geneva conventions don't apply to you.'

---

59 Hamoodur Rahman Commission Report, July 1972 (https://web. archive.org/web/20120304011310/http://www.pppusa.org/Acrobat/ Hamoodur%20Rahman%20Commission%20Report.pdf)

A truck brought in another load of prisoners. They were the crew of the *Padma* and *Palash* captured by the razakars as they swam away from their burning vessels. Mitter was sure they were all going to be shot.

Staff Captain Aziz then admonished Lt Bandopadhyay who introduced himself.

'Why aren't you in uniform?'

Bandopadhyay reached back into his hip pocket and fished out a soggy wallet. He opened it and extracted a wine bill of the INS Hooghly.

'He's an officer and so am I.'

The wine bill convinced Captain Aziz.

Two vehicles came and Captain Aziz ordered them in. The brigadier stopped pacing the corridor. 'Aziz, separate the officers.'

They plan to shoot us separately? Mitter wondered.

He had no idea where they were taking them. Bandopadhyay was taken away. Captain Aziz escorted Lt Mitter into a truck. He rode in front. Mitter lay at the back in the stretcher.

'What is your religion?' Aziz turned around to ask.

Mitter fumbled for the first time that day as he weakly clutched at a lie: 'I'm a Christian.'

The vehicle stopped after travelling a distance. Mitter was taken in a stretcher into the Khulna Sadr Hospital. The hospital, run by the city administration, was located on the riverbank. Half of it had been taken over by the army and being run as a military hospital. There was a rush of people. Medical personnel were running about, shouting for medicines for the personnel streaming in from the battlefront. In the hospital, Mitter saw a clock. It was ten past four. Then, everything started becoming faint. The way it had before he smoked the cigarette.

Not everyone got the same treatment. After Roychowdhury's *Padma* had been abandoned, Ruhul Amin, ERA in charge of the engine room and a few of the *Palash* crew had been captured and killed by the razakars. He was later awarded the Bir Shreshto, Bangla Desh's highest military award.[60]

On the west coast, the navy was hunting for the *PNS Hangor*. At around 5 p.m. that day, an Alizé took off from the Air Force station at Jamnagar and steered north-west towards the Arabian Sea off Jakhau. The Alizé was part of Operation Falcon, a massive air and sea hunt to locate the *Hangor* which had sunk the *INS Khukri*. The sinking of the *Khukri*, the navy's single biggest loss of life, led to grief and then rage. Vice Admiral S.N. Kohli threw all available aircraft and helicopters into the hunt. Two Alizés from the naval air detachment operating out of the Santa Cruz airport and four newly arrived Westland Seaking Mk 42 anti-submarine helicopters were moved up to Jamnagar. Operation Grand Slam, the final massed missile boat attack on Karachi , was postponed, as it later emerged, indefinitely.

The Pakistan Air Force, meanwhile, was looking for the tormentors of Karachi, the Osas. On 10 December, one aircraft from each mission crossed paths. An F-104 Starfighter flown by Wing Cdr Arif Iqbal armed with 20 mm cannons and two Sidewinder air-to-air missiles flew out of Masroor airbase, and caught sight of an Alizé with the tail number 203 off Jakhau on the Saurashtra coast. It was an unequal contest. The Alizé pilot flung his aircraft at wavetop height, jinking his aircraft low over the water to prevent Iqbal from getting a clean shot as the Starfighter tried to settle behind him. It was all over in seconds. Alizé 203 tumbled into the sea, leaving the Starfighter pilot clueless to the very end as he raced past the

---

60 Banglapedia   (http://en.banglapedia.org/index.php?title=Amin,_Birsrestha_Mohammad_Ruhul, by Lt Col Qazi Sajjad Ali Zahir)

wreckage. Was it his gunfire or did 203's wingtip graze the swells, causing it to crash?[61]

The *INS Panvel*, meanwhile, made its solitary voyage down to Mongla which it reached by 4 p.m. The *MV Chitrangada* was waiting. The grievously wounded Haq did not survive the passage. The bodies of Haq, Lance Naik Chintan Sharma and their local Mukti Bahini guide killed by the Gnats were handed over to the local Awami League leader. The mood on board was gloomy. At least a dozen men, including three officers, one sailor and many of Mukti Bahini crew were missing in action. Samant tuned into a transistor radio for the news. At 8 p.m. Radio Pakistan announced the names of the captured men: 'Lt Suvesh Kumar Mitter ... Lt Natu ... Sub Lieutenant Bandopadhyay and Leading Seaman Chiman Singh.'

They had been attacked by their own aircraft and taken prisoner and were being taken to the military hospital for treatment. Samant heaved a sigh of relief.

INS Panvel and *MV Chitrangada* then left Mongla anchorage separately, arriving at Garani Khal at midnight on 10 December. After anchoring in the Khal for the night, the boats reached the Border Security Force Post at Hasnabad at 6 p.m. the following day.

Mitter woke up the following morning in a large medical ward with a dozen beds. He was lying on a white iron cot with both hands immobilized. His right hand was in a heavy plaster cast and the left one was propped up on an arm rest, hooked to a saline drip. The single door in the ward was guarded by two Pakistani army soldiers in black dungarees. They were from the armoured corps. There was a knot of people huddled together in one corner on the floor. Mitter smiled weakly. He was relieved his crew was alive.

---

61 Air Commodore Kaiser Tufail's blog, 29 December 2010 (http://kaiser-aeronaut.blogspot.com/2010/)

There was a murmur outside the ward. And then the sound of footsteps in the corridor. A voice outside asked the sentries to open the door. Two Pakistani officers in khaki strode towards Mitter's bed. They were doctors. Colonel Lutfur, the officer-in-charge of the military hospital, was accompanied by a surgeon, Major Qureishi. To them, Mitter was just another officer in need of medical attention. Major Qureishi examined Mitter and nodded disapprovingly.

'I was not here yesterday. Your operation was done by civilian doctors. Shell wounds are not to be sutured or bandaged … there's danger of gangrene …I'm going to operate on you again.'

After a second operation the next day, Mitter woke up to two new ward mates. There was Chiman Singh to his right and Lt Natu to his left. All of them were recovering from serious injuries. The shrapnel had been taken out of Natu's stomach and it had been sewn shut. Chiman Singh was heavily bandaged and winced at the pain of his wounds. 'They ought to have killed me … the pain is unbearable,' he moaned.

All of them had a close shave. No one believed Mitter would survive, not even Staff Captain Aziz, who had queried Mitter regarding his religion – and seen through his lie – in order to be able to give him an appropriate funeral. Once the crew recovered, they were spared any harsh treatment or torture by the Pakistanis. They were clearly more worried about their own survival. Khulna was still holding out against the Indian Army, but it was only a matter of time before it fell.

By 11 December, the Indo–Pakistan war had reached a decisive turn. Pakistan's strategy of defending its eastern half by using diversionary tactics on the western front lay in shambles. The Indian Army parried the Pakistan Army in Punjab and thrust into Sindh through Rajasthan. The Indian advance into the Shakargarh bulge had drawn Pakistani troops away from Chhamb.

In the East, Tiger Niazi had turned into a nervous, whimpering wreck as he watched the Indian Army bypass his strongholds and pour down towards him in the thinly defended Dacca.

It was only when the general found himself gradually encircled by the enemy, which had successfully managed to bypass his fortresses and reached Faridpur, Khulna, Daudkandi and Chandpur (the shortest route to Dacca) that he began making frantic efforts to get the troops back for the defence of Dacca. It was too late by then. The ferries necessary for crossing the troops over the big Jamuna river from the area of 16 Division had disappeared and the Mukti Bahini had invested the area behind, making vehicular movement impossible.[62]

NCO(X)'s war on the waterways had played a crucial role in the land battle. There was still some hope of a face-saver for Niazi – the possibility that India would heed to a United Nations ceasefire, hand over the administration of East Pakistan to the UN and allow the Pakistan Army and its supporters to withdraw from the East.

On 11 December Samant reached Fort William for his debriefing on the Force Alfa mission. He was to report to Major General Jacob. The chief of staff was elated, but for different reasons. Lt General Aurora had asked him to prepare for Lt General Niazi's surrender. Jacob was unperturbed by the friendly fire incident. The Eastern Command's troops were now at the gates of Dacca. As far as he was concerned, the Force Alfa raid was just one skirmish with an unfortunate twist in a war that India was about to win decisively.

On the thirteenth of December the *USS Enterprise* Carrier Battle Group entered the Malacca Straits. That night, General Niazi spoke to the Pakistani C-in-C General Hamid and asked him to expedite

---

62 Hamoodur Rahman Commission Report, July 1972 (https://web. archive.org/web/20120304011310/http://www.pppusa.org/Acrobat/ Hamoodur%20Rahman%20Commission%20Report.pdf)

the ceasefire. On 14 December, General Yahya Khan sent a cryptic signal to Lt General Niazi, asking him to stop fighting.

> You have now reached a stage where further resistance is not humanly possible, nor will it serve any useful purpose. It will only lead to a further loss of life and destruction. You should now take all necessary measures to stop the fighting.

However, the Pakistan Army was not done yet. On 14 December, the army and its razakar collaborators carried out the final macabre act in its nine-month–long campaign of genocide. They abducted the cream of Bengali society from across the country. Nearly 1,000 Bengali writers, artists, lawyers, professors, physicians, journalists, lyricists, doctors, engineers, educationists, mathematicians and musicians were brought to several detention centres around Dacca and executed with gunshots to the head.

The following day, on 15 December, Radio Pakistan announced that the carrier battle group headed by the *USS Enterprise*, was heading northwards and might establish a base in East Pakistan. The glimmer of hope was quickly extinguished. The task force despatched by Nixon and Kissinger turned back without intervening. They were trained in the Indian Ocean by Soviet naval ships sent in from Vladivostok. The IAF bombed the Pakistan governor's meeting in Government House at noon that day. Later that day, Lt General Niazi and Major General Rao Farman Ali handed over their ceasefire proposal over to Herbert D. Spivack, the US consul general in Dacca. Niazi offered to cease hostilities and hand the administration of East Pakistan over to the United Nations. The collapse was complete. But it needed one final act.

12
JOY BANGLA

'Joy Bangla! Joy Bangla!' the locals hugged Atharuddin Talukder and Syed Abdul Basher. They cried and wept. It was 16 December. Talukder's team leader Basher had broken the news of the Pakistan Army's surrender in the safe house and asked him to join in the victory celebrations. They crossed the Kirtonkhola by boat, and then ran for six kilometres at full pelt towards Basher's house in Bot-tala, breathing the air of a free country as they ran towards a place where they awaited a hero's welcome.

At 4.55 p.m. on Saturday, 16 December 1971, 92,208 Pakistani personnel – regular army, paramilitary and police elements – surrendered across Bangla Desh. Five Indian Army brigades closed in on Dacca. Thousands of jubilant Bangla Deshis converged in on the surrender ceremony at the Ramna Race Course to witness history unfolding. There, with flashbulbs popping and sound recorders whirring, a glum Lt General A.A.K. Niazi signed the Instrument of Surrender, with Lt General J.S. Aurora seated to his right. Standing behind them were C-in-C East Vice Admiral Krishnan, the Air Officer Commanding-in-Chief Eastern Command Air Marshal Hari Chand Dewan and the 4 Corps Commander Lt General

Sagat Singh. Major General J.F.R. Jacob stood just behind Niazi's left shoulder, beaming into the distance, supremely pleased at his crucial role in converting the ceasefire into the only public military surrender ceremony after World War II. The moment was an eerie metaphor for the encirclement and capitulation of the Pakistan Army, one that would haunt them for a long time.

Admiral Krishnan recounted in his memoirs: 'Niazi choked with emotion and, near tears, unbuttoned his epaulettes, unloaded his revolver and handing them over to Aurora, touched his forehead to the general in total submission and the ceremony was over.'[63]

Among the officers who surrendered in Dacca were Rear Admiral Shariff and his staff officer Captain Zamir Ahmed. Shariff, who was there at the race course, handed over his Chinese-made Type 54 pistol and lanyard to Vice Admiral Krishnan.

The wheel had turned a full circle. It was on this ground, nine months ago, that Sheikh Mujibur Rahman had declared a free Bangla Desh. Now, hundreds of thousands of Bengalis basked in the afterglow of his dream. A dream for which India had paid a heavy price – 1,421 soldiers killed, 4,058 wounded and fifty-six missing, presumed killed.

All Pakistani prisoners, including Lt General Niazi, were shipped to forty-nine POW camps in thirteen military stations in the states of Uttar Pradesh, Madhya Pradesh and Bihar, where they would spend the next twenty-eight months.

That evening, all the military establishments in Calcutta exploded in celebration. Vice Admiral Krishnan partied with the officers and men of INS Hooghly. At Fort William, a short distance away, the stone corridors echoed with the cries of 'Hurrah! Hurrah!' The Eastern Army Command Officers' Mess had opened its reservoir

---

63 Vice Admiral N. Krishnan, *No Way But Surrender: An Account of the Indo-Pakistan War in the Bay of Bengal, 1971* (Ghaziabad: Vikas Publishers), 1980

of liquor, which splashed among a sea of olive green. There was, as one participant put it, 'Scotch and nothing else.' Samant was at the party too. It was one of his rare visits to the mess. He was still in his shikar boots and full-sleeve shirt, fresh from an inspection of the border.

The mood was jubilant, the air thick with celebration as the eastern army celebrated its well-won victory. People were shouting, yelling, laughing. Many of the generals were still in their headquarters on the frontlines, but the principal actors of the army's war in the east – Lt General Aurora, Lt General J.F.R. Jacob – and their staff officers were there. They spoke little, drank copiously and laughed a lot.

In his hospital ward in Khulna 250 km south-west of Dacca, Mitter heard loud bangs in the distance. A nursing assistant explained what was happening – sappers were blowing off signal communication towers in the city. The Pakistan Army had begun executing their denial plan, destroying military infrastructure and torching currency in the banks. It was what militaries did when faced with defeat. Deny the enemy any advantage. The hospital staff had tuned in to Radio Pakistan to hear an update. President Yahya Khan's gravelly voice addressed his countrymen in chaste Urdu, thanking the world for their assistance, railing against India's aggression and promising a war, a jehad that would be fought not on the battlefield but in fields, in factories and in households. 'Victory will be ours,' he declared. There was no mention of the surrender: 'On 20 December, a ceasefire will be declared; the eastern province will be given greater autonomy.'

It was a denial plan of another sort. The general was numbing his countrymen with an anaesthetic. He was preparing them for the terrible reality that their eastern limb had been cut away.

'Looks like the war will continue,' the nursing assistant whispered.

The POWs were crestfallen. Mitter tried to cheer up his gloomy wardmates: 'It's my birthday tomorrow. I'll give you all a present.'

On the morning of 17 December, Lt Mitter's twenty-sixth birthday gift arrived. The doors of the ward opened to throaty roars of Joy Bangla. Crowds of exuberant civilians had entered their hospital ward, past the trembling Pakistani guards, and made a beeline to touch and see the Bengali Indian naval officer they had heard about. Later, Colonel Deshpande, the 9th Infantry Division's assistant director, medical services, strode in. The Khulna garrison had surrendered. Colonel Deshpande was accompanied by Colonel Lutfur and Major Qureishi. He enquired about Lt Mitter's injuries and praised the Pakistani doctors for their operative and post-operative care, and directed that the Indian officers be shifted to Jessore for the flight to India. The Force Alfa trio were given a change of clothes, brought down in a stretcher and put in an ambulance and driven to Jessore. They were finally going home.

That morning, an IAF transport plane brought an unusual visitor to Dacca. It was Captain M.K. Roy, architect of the naval commando operation, bearing a personal message from Mrs Gandhi for Begum Fazilatunessa Mujib. Her husband, Sheikh Mujibur Rahman was safe, the Indian prime minister informed her.

What the DNI saw during the special military flight and upon disembarking in Dacca left no doubt in his mind about the righteousness of his covert war. To him, the Pakistan Army had lost its morality and military discipline before it had lost the war. 'The bunkers around the airport resembled brothels, with condoms and other sex items littering the military fortifications – a damning indictment of Pakistan's military norms and that too against its own citizens,' he wrote.[64] 'Torture and murder were the order of the day. The looting of provisions and stores by the Pakistan Army invariably had a note – send the bill to Indira Gandhi.'

---

64 Vice Admiral M.K. Roy, *War in the Indian Ocean* (New Delhi: Lancer Publishers), 1995

News of the humiliating defeat of its army and dismemberment of the country soon filtered back to Pakistan. The anger spilled out into street protests. Their target was the man who divided Pakistan – Yahya Khan. On 20 December, General Yahya Khan stepped down from all posts and handed power over to Zulfiqar Ali Bhutto. Pakistan's new president swiftly placed his predecessor under house arrest. Stripped of his service honours by the army, the former dictator spent the last decade of his life in ignominious confinement.

In Delhi, Admiral Nanda's office and residence were flooded with messages of congratulations. He was the father of a modern Indian Navy and had pioneered its transformation from a defensive force into an offensive arm that fought ferociously, using available resources. From towing short-legged missile boats into combat to launching air strikes from a carrier with a broken boiler and, above all, waging an unprecedented covert maritime war to paralyze the adversary even before the first shots had been fired, the Indian Navy had proved its mettle.

The greatest achievement of the navy during the war, Nanda noted,[65] was that it had established its relevance. 'The government understood its role, i.e., of denying the enemy use of its sea supply routes whilst giving our own logistic suppliers complete freedom and of having a moving airfield with powerful strike aircraft that could wreak havoc on the unsuspecting enemy. The question of the navy being irrelevant or redundant in the national security matrix never arose again. For our service, this was indeed a great milestone; the navy ranks could walk the streets with their heads held high.'

Major General Jacob was equally appreciative of the role of the naval commandos who had captured, sunk or damaged fifteen Pakistani ships, eleven coasters, seven gunboats, eleven barges,

---

65 Admiral S.M. Nanda, *The Man Who Bombed Karachi* (New Delhi: HarperCollins *Publishers* India), 2004

two tankers and nineteen river craft. 'These were, in fact, the most significant achievements of the Mukti Bahini,' he noted.[66]

The men who had carried out these missions at great peril to their lives, basked in the glory of their newfound freedom even as they sought out the families they left behind. There were tearful reunions. At a refugee camp in Kalyani, Dr Shamsul Huda Chowdhury met his son 'Abu', Abdul Wahed Chowdhury, whom he had last heard from in Toulon. There were heartbreaks. In Khulna, Humayun Kabir discovered that his father Sheikh Abdul Mazid had been taken away by razakars on 15 August. His body, like those of thousands of Bangla Deshis, was never found.

On 27 December, eleven days after the surrender, Samant sent his staff officer Lt Cdr Mukherjee to the naval POW camp in Bonani, Dacca. Barring the crew of the gunboat *PNS Rajshahi*, which had slipped away to Burma, the entire 1,047-man Pakistan Navy command were detained in this Indian Army camp. Samant wanted Mukherjee to enquire after his old Dartmouth course mate, Captain Zamir Ahmad. The captain was pleasantly surprised. He shared what many of the Pakistani garrison in Dacca believed was a close call: 'Go tell Sammy that it's great that he captured me. Had the Bengalis got hold of me, I would have been in serious trouble.'

The Indian Army prepared to march them to Narayanganj, twenty kilometres south. From here, they would embark passenger ships for the journey to Calcutta. The twenty-kilometre walk through what would be a hostile civilian area clearly worried Captain Zamir. He had one favour to ask of his course mate. 'Please tell Sammy that the navy is not used to long marches,' he told Lt Cdr Mukherjee. The news was relayed back to Samant, who arranged for army trucks to transport the Pakistan Navy personnel to Narayanganj. Zamir spent

---

66 Lt Gen J.F.R. Jacob, *Surrender at Dacca, Birth of a Nation*, (New Delhi: Manohar Publishers & Distributors), 1997

the next two years in an Indian POW camp before being repatriated to Pakistan in 1974. Samant never met him again.

In late December, Samant typed out his final report to Naval Headquarters. In the forty-five–page report, he appreciated how a small force had performed feats that were out of proportion to their numbers and against heavy odds. The Indian navy's diving branch had come of age.

C2P had trained 457 commandos and had carried out deep-penetration naval raids inside enemy-occupied territory to sink and cripple over 1,00,000 tons of shipping – the largest operation of its kind since the Second World War. Left unstated was the fact that the Indian state had proved it was not entirely a stranger to irregular warfare, which it had been at the receiving end of since 1947.

The naval commando force's casualty rate did not exceed the 20 per cent mark he had estimated. Between 15 to 20 per cent of the commandos, however, did not perform tasks assigned to them. He was willing to overlook the fact. He reasoned that it was possibly because of the increased vigilance, lack of targets, and also the fear of capture or the safety of the families they had left behind in Bangla Desh. He noted the sound and steady quality of personnel at the student level and among the Pakistan Navy escapees, recommending several of them for officer training. He marvelled at how college students-turned-soldiers had performed heroic deeds. Based on the inputs he received from Lt Cdr Martis and Lt Kapil, he made one final recommendation: for the Indian Navy to immediately create a special forces unit to carry out such clandestine operations.

EPILOGUE

NCO(X) wound down just as it had begun. Quietly. The operation outlived its utility soon after Niazi's capitulation and the joyous birth of Bangla Desh. C2P and C2H were shut down; the tents and vehicles, Havildar Mane and Sepoy Maninder Singh went back to the 2 Sikh LI. The divers were repatriated to their parent cadre, the Indian Navy. The remaining limpet mines and explosives were sent back into naval stores. All secret correspondence was either destroyed or filed away in the steel cupboards of Naval HQ, their doors painted with a red X. It was the unit that had never existed. Commander Samant was appointed to the eastern army command. Later that month, he was in Dacca, appointed the first chief of staff of the Bangladesh Navy under General M.A.G. Osmani.

The Indian Navy was content with the Mukti Bahini naval commandos taking all the credit for the entire operation. It was, after all, a plausibly deniable mission in support of a struggle for which hundreds of thousands of Bangladeshis had died.

One December day after the war, the one person but for whom Bangla Desh would have remained a dream, dropped by to meet the navy's war wounded at the INHS Asvini naval hospital in Colaba,

Bombay. Indira Gandhi, flanked by her aides and naval brass walked into the general ward which also housed the survivors of the *INS Khukri*.

Chiman Singh, his wounds still raw, sat up cross-legged and erect on the bed. His hair had been cut and his Plassey beard shaved off. The prime minister stopped by his bed. He had been a POW, she was told.

'How did the Pakistanis treat you?'

'Very badly. They were all talking about Sikhistan,' the young sailor replied.

The prime minister smiled.

'Aapne jo kiya, kiya. Hum aapke bahut aabhari hain. Aap aa gaye hain, aage hum dekhenge…' (You did what you had to do. For that, we are grateful. Now that you've come back, I will handle the rest).

The prime minister smiled, folded her hands in a namaste and moved on.

Roy, the enigmatic naval spymaster, revealed little about NCO(X) or its personnel. It was a secret he would carry with him to the grave and he expected the same of the men on the mission.

If there ever was a memory-erasing tool, Micky Roy would have used it on the X-men, Lt Kapil joked with one of the Air Force personnel he met as he landed in Dacca airport on 19 December. Kapil was on a stopover to Agartala.

He was being transported for one last mission – to close down the covert naval unit in Brigadier Shabeg Singh's Delta Sector, Tripura. It was a unit he had been informed about only recently. Four days later, he had had finished the mission and was back in Calcutta with all the remaining limpet mines, explosives and weapons.

He boarded another flight to Bombay, heading for a predictable life in Room 411. The war was finally behind him.

And so, on a pleasant December morning, he shot out of the black-and-yellow Bombay taxi that had driven him up to the porch of the command mess. Room 411 had been sealed by the Western Naval Command, the steward at the reception informed him. A board of inquiry was on because an officer staying there had died.

'What? In my room?'

'Nahin, saab...' the steward drawled. 'Woh Roy saab thchre they ... pilot. Unka casualty ho gaya.' (The pilot, Mr Roy stayed here. He died during combat.)

Lt Commander Ashok 'Aku' Roy had been the pilot of the Alizé engaged by the Starfighter over the Arabian Sea on 10 December, just hours after Force Alfa's blue on blue. Roy had escaped the drudgery of Delta Sector to get back to the Cobras. He had signed off exactly as he would have wanted to – in the left seat of the Alizé, in combat. Kapil become contemplative. The war had returned to haunt him.

TIMELINE 1971

12 January: Pakistan President and military dictator General Agha Mohammad meets Sheikh Mujibur Rahman in Dacca, heralding him as the president. On 7 December 1970, Sheikh Mujib's Awami League won a landslide in the country's first general elections. General Yahya undecided on convening national assembly.

30 January: Two Kashmiri separatists hijack an Indian plane to Lahore and incinerate it after offloading the passengers. India suspends overflights by Pakistani aircraft over its territory.

27 February: Pakistan army infantry battalions, 22 Baloch and 13 Frontier Force flown into Dhaka by PIA via Sri Lanka. Movement completed by March 1.

1 March: Yahya Khan postpones meeting of national assembly, *sine die* appoints Major General Yakub Khan as new governor of East Pakistan.

1–10 March: Indian General Elections held.

4 March: Mujib launches civil disobedience movement. Announces plan to run a parallel government in defiance of martial law. Alleged atrocities committed on non-Bengalis.

5 March: Lt General Yakub Khan resigns as governor and commander Eastern Command, replaced by Lt General Tikka Khan on 7 March.

15 March: General Yahya Khan arrives in Dhaka for talks with Sheikh Mujibur Rahman.

17 March: Indira Gandhi forms government after an electoral landslide win of 352 seats out of the total of 515 Lok Sabha seats.

22 March: Yahya indefinitely postpones meeting of National Assembly. Mujib declares 23 March, Pakistan National Day to be observed as 'Resistance Day' in East Pakistan. Asks Yahya to transfer power.

23 March: Resistance Day in East Pakistan sees demonstrations, parades, students marching in military formations with the Bangladesh flag fluttering and crowds trampling the Pakistani flag.

25 March: Yahya secretly leaves Dacca via Colombo. Operation Searchlight, the suppression of civilian protests, begins. Troops begin to move into the city from cantonment. Over 50,000 Bengali civilians killed. Radio message from Sheikh Mujib announces independent Bangladesh, calls on the people to expel Pakistan Army of occupation.

26 March: Lt General Tikka Khan imposes martial law in East Pakistan and executes military action to 'reinstate public order and central authority'. The Awami League is banned, and Sheikh Mujib is arrested and flown to Karachi three days later. Across East Pakistan, East Pakistan Rifles, East Bengal regiment and police units rise in mass revolt. Major Ziaur Rahman, 2-I-C of East Bengal regiment takes over command of forces in Chittagong, seizes transmitting station and broadcasts his declaration of independence.

29 March: Leading Telegraphist A.W. Chowdhury, and seven other crew members from the submarine *PNS Mangro* escape from Toulon, France, seeking asylum in the Indian embassy in Madrid. Given travel documents to fly to India.

31 March: Chittagong falls to Pakistani army. Major Ziaur Rahman falls back towards Belonia, blows up strategic Feni road bridge connecting Dacca with Chittagong. Bengali refugees start pouring into India. At the same time, the Indian parliament passes the resolution calling on Pakistan to 'transfer power to the legally elected representatives of East Bengal'.

Government of India resolves to help Bangladesh's armed liberation struggle. (Confirmed publicly by foreign minister Swaran Singh, later on July 29).

10 April: Lt General A.A.K. Niazi takes over Eastern Army Command from Lt General Tikka Khan and issues five-phase operational directives for 'the elimination of infiltrators' to be implemented by 15 May.

Bangladeshi resistance leaders Tajuddin Ahmed, Nazrul Islam Qamaruzzaman, Mansur Ali, Col MAG Osmani and Wing Cdr Khondkar arrive in Calcutta. Bangladesh's government in exile forms and houses itself in a bungalow on Theatre Road.

11 April: Lt general Tikka Khan is made governor and martial law administrator of East Pakistan.

Tajuddin Ahmed, Prime Minister of Provisional Government of Bangla Desh announces setting up of liberation army with trained personnel from the EBR, EPR, police and volunteers. Seven regional commands announced under Colonel MAG Osmani, new Commander-in-chief of Bangla Desh Liberation Army.

*Early April: 8 Pakistan Navy submariners from the *PNS Mangro* reach Delhi. They are introduced to a week-long training schedule in swimming and clandestine water-borne warfare on the Yamuna river by Lt Samir Das and M.S. Gupta.

*Early April: Captain M.K. Roy, Director Naval Intelligence drafts concept note for 'Jackpot–underwater guerilla forces', a plan to train 600 Bengali naval commandos. Strategic objective to completely paralyse ports, harbours and inland waterways of East Pakistan. Lists the training team– Indian naval diving specialists, officers and men.

*Early April: Samir Das returns to diving school. Asks clearance diver training staff to volunteer for a confidential assignment in Calcutta.

14 April: Colonel M.A.G. Osmani is appointed as military adviser and commanding in chief of the Bangladesh Forces.

* Date range based on recollection of interviewees.

*Mid April: Seven clearance divers from Cochin arrive on temporary duty for unspecified duration to *INS Hoogly* in Calcutta. They are joined by divers from different commands.

*Mid April: Lt Kapil meets DNI Capt Roy and Lt Das in Calcutta. Kapil and Das identify location for C2P on the grounds of a sugar mill in Plassey, Nadia district. Clearance divers reach C2P the following week.

17 April: Declaration of Independence by the Bangladesh government-in-exile at Baidyanath Tala, renamed Mujibnagar, inside East Pakistan.

29 April: Eastern Command officially given the responsibility of assisting Bangladesh forces in their liberation struggle. BSF units on the border placed under Eastern Army Command. Army sets up camps to train Mukti Bahini land forces.

*End April: Camp C2P established in tents pitched by Indian Army on banks of Bhagirathi River. Recruiting teams, headed by Lt. Kapil and Lt. Das, select about 70 volunteers.

*Early May: Training of Mukti Bahini naval commandos begins with physical training, swimming and endurance runs of five to six kilometres.

*End May: Commander M.N.R. Samant appointed in-charge of operations and training of the covert unit. He names it Naval Commando Operations (X) or NCO(X).

*End May: Maj Gen Jacob draws up draft plan for capture of East Pakistan. Final objective to be Dhaka, the geopolitical, geostrategic heart of the province.

*Early June: Lt Cdr George Martis reports to C2P as Officer-in-Charge.

13 June: 'Genocide', 9000-word story in UK's *Sunday Times* by an embedded Pakistani journalist Anthony Mascarenhas details military atrocities in East Pakistan.

1 July: Eastern Army Command launches 'Operation Steeplechase' to suppress activities of Naxalite activity in rural West Bengal.

9–11 July: Henry Kissinger's embarks on a secret visit to Beijing via Islamabad to meet Chairman Mao Zedong signalling US-China thaw.

17 July: Bangla Desh government in exile switches over to guerrilla warfare. Divides country into 11 operational sectors for guerrilla warfare, each under a sector commander. Maritime segment, Sector 10, placed directly under Colonel M.A.G. Osmani.

*Mid-End July: Cdr Samant drafts operational orders for 'Jackpot', coordinated attacks on ports of Chittagong, Chalna/Mongla, Chandpur and Narayanganj

*End July: Lt Cdr Ashok Kumar 'Aku' Roy deputed as Officer-in-Charge, Naval Detachment, Delta Sector, Tripura.

31 July: 7.2 million Bangladeshi refugees have entered India since end March. Of these, eighty per cent are Hindus, seventeen per cent Muslim and less than one per cent Buddhists and Christians.

3 August: C2P resited one kilometre inland after Bhagirathi floods.

9 August: Soviet Foreign Minister Andrey Gromyko and Indian Foreign Minister Swaran Singh sign Indo-Soviet treaty of peace, friendship and cooperation in New Delhi.

10 August: Prime Minister Indira Gandhi writes to world leaders expressing fear Sheikh Mujibur Rahman could be handed after a secret trial in a Pakistani prison.

Aku Roy launches Mukti Bahini Naval Commando team Task Unit 54.1.1 under AW Chowdhury from Delta Sector towards Chittagong port. Task Units 54.1.2 under Badiul Alam, 54.1.3 under Ahsanullah and 54.1.4 under Rahamtulla launched from Charlie sector.

15–16 August: First coordinated attack by 176 assault swimmers against Chittagong, Chalna/Khulna and river ports of Narayanganj, Chandpur and Barisal sinks 44,000 tons of ships and disables 14,000 tons of shipping.

3 September: Dr AM Malik replaces General Tikka Khan as Governor of East Pakistan.

September: Mukti Bahini operations begin to affect Pakistan army morale. Raids and ambushes were carried out, culverts and bridges blown up. Government authorises Indian army to occupy areas across the border to prevent Pakistani shelling.

*September: Second wave of 160 assault swimmers launched into Bangladesh this month. Ports of Chittagong, Khulna, Chalna, Barisal, Chandpur targeted. 6,000 tonnes of shipping sunk and 17,000 tonnes damaged.

20 September: Pakistan Navy in Dacca issues detailed anti-saboteur instructions. Instructs personnel to shoot swimmers and frogmen.

21 September: 21st session of the United Nations General Assembly begins in New York. Continues until 22 December.

22 September: Cdr Samant hands over Calcutta Port Trust general supply craft *Padma* and *Palash* to GRSE for a month long refit and conversion into gunboats fitted with two 40/60 mm Bofors guns and two mine rails each.

23 September: Cdr Samant asked DNI Captain Roy for a lieutenant from the executive branch for the gunboats.

*Late September: Lt Suvesh Kumar Mitter is deputed from *INS Darshak*, Bombay, to Calcutta. Takes over as CO *MV Palash*.

27 September: Lt Samir Das is killed in a road accident.

14 October: All BSF battalions in eastern command placed under operational control of eastern command.

25 October: Indira Gandhi begins tour of Belgium, Austria, UK, US, France and West Germany to raise awareness about the Bangla Desh refugee problem and to avert war. Tour lasts until 12 November.

*End October: *MV Padma* and *MV Palash* are ready. After post refit trials, vessels declared ready for operations, shifted to newly established Camp C2H at Haldia.

*End October: Naval commandos sink one ocean going ship and four coasters. 250 commandos launched this month.

30 October: Patrol craft *INS Panvel* departs Vizag, reaches Calcutta two days later.

1 November: Leading Seaman Chiman Singh crosses into enemy territory with Mukti Bahini naval commandos.

November: Eastern Command allows troops to go into East Pakistan to a depth of ten miles to silence enemy guns shelling their positions.

4 November: Prime Minister Indira Gandhi meets President Richard Nixon in the White House. Meeting marked by mutual suspicion and even outright hostility.

8 November: *Palash* and *Padma* escorted by the *INS Kavaratti* to execute 'Operation Hot Pants', the mining of the entrance of the Pussur river and shipping channel. *Palash* and *Padma* attack the Khulna-bound British merchantman *MV City of St. Albans.*

9 November: *MV Berlian* disabled after triggering a mine at the mouth of Pussur river.

13 November: Pakistan Navy gunboat *Tufail* destroyed by a mine at Pussur river. Intercept of a teleconversation between Khulna port and Karachi reveals port director Khulna has suspended all ship movements that day.

Mid November: Strategic and tactical mobility of Pakisitan army's eastern command reduced to the minimum due to extensive guerrilla activities targeting bridges, ferries, river–craft and ships which were the sole means of transport for shifting troops and logistics from one place to another and from one geographical compartment to another across river obstacles.

20 November: Eastern command's 9 infantry division launches preliminary operation in Boyra area.

22 November: Chiman Singh and his naval commandos stumble upon the battle line position of 22 Rajput. The team witness the battle of Boyra where IAF Gnats shoot down two Pakistani Sabre jets. Fourteen Pakistani tanks destroyed.

23 November: Pakistan government declares emergency. All Pakistan naval units except two minesweepers proceeded to sea and control of Pakistani merchant shipping is taken over by the C-in-C of the Pakistan Navy. Both Indian and Pakistani fleets put out to sea.

30 November: NCO(X) tally for operations between 1–21 November reads sinking four coasters and one barge. One gunboat, ocean-going ship and coaster each damaged. A total of 271 naval commandos launched this month, highest since operation began in August.

1 December: Eastern command intercepts signal from East Pakistan informing them of the decision not to send Pakistani shipping into the Bay of Bengal.

3 December: Pre-emptive strike by Pakistani air force. Prime Minister Indira Gandhi announces declaration of war.

Indian air force, army and navy attack on both eastern and western fronts. Objectives are to hold Pakistan offensive in the West, capture Dacca in the East.

PNS Ghazi explodes and sinks off the Vizag harbor.

4 December: Indian missile boats *INS Nirghat, Nipat* and *Veer* attack Pakistan navy off the coast of Karachi and sink a destroyer, minesweeper and merchant ship.

Vikrant's aircraft strikes Cox's Bazar and Chittagong. At the same time, US moves for an emergency meeting of the UN Security Council and sponsors a draft resolution calling for ceasefire. The resolution is vetoed by Soviet Union.

5 December: Naval divers locate wreck of *PNS Ghazi* off Vizag. The submarine is positively identified by former crewmen A.W. Chowdhury and Rahmatulla At the United Nations, Soviet Union vetoes the second UN resolution calling for immediate ceasefire and withdrawal by India.

6 December: Vikrant launches sustained air strikes sinking merchant ships, small craft, gunboats. IAF jets wreck PAF base in Dhaka, grounding the PAF until the end of the war. After Bhutan,

India becomes the second country to formally recognise Bangla Desh as an independent country.

7 December: Niazi's "Fortresses" *Jessore* and *Brahmanbari* fall to the Indian army.

8 December: Force Alfa–patrol boats *INS Panvel*, Mukti Bahini gunboats *Padma*, and *Palash* join BSF boat *Chitrangada* at Hasnabad. All sail for Khulna.

8–9 December: Pakistani naval tanker *Dacca*, and two merchant ships in Karachi hit by missile boat *INS Vinash*.

9 December: *INS Khukri* is sunk by Pakistani submarine *PNS Hangor*, south of Diu, a loss of 18 officers, 176 men. *INS Panvel* picks up radar contacts of merchant ships *MV Anwar Baksh* and *MV Baqir* leaving Mongla port with Pakistan army personnel and families. The ships are captured by Eastern naval fleet warships

9 December: Governor East Pakistan Dr A.M. Malik sends signal to Yahya Khan advocating immediate cease fire. Yahya replies he would leave the decision to Malik, instructs Niazi accordingly. Yahya refuses to entertain thoughts of ceasefire when he hears of the Enterprise carrier battle group.

10 December: Force Alfa reaches Chalna port on Pussur River, abandoned by Pakistani authorities. They resume voyage upstream towards Khulna. An attackby IAF Gnats results in destruction of the *Palash* and *Padma*. Some of the survivors are taken prisoner. The *INS Panvel* picks up survivors and returns to Mongla.

10 December: Pakistan's strategy of defending East Pakistan from the West collapses as its land offensives grind to a halt. Indian army advances into Shakargarh and draws Pakistani troops away from Chhamb. Pakistani pressure in Punjab resisted. Indian army thrusts into Sind through Rajasthan. TheIndian Army reaches the banks of the Meghna less than 40 air kilometers from Dacca and cuts off the capital city's access to the sea. Eastern naval fleet establishes total blockade. Vikrant air group damages Chittagong airfield, sinks three merchant ships and one Pakistani Navy gunboat. All sea and river traffic in East Pakistan grinds to a complete halt.

10 December: President Nixon orders deployment of the Seventh Fleet's Task Group 74, consisting of the USS Enterprise and escorts to the Indian Ocean. Enterprise task group departs Gulf of Tonkin for Singapore.

Kissinger urges China to intervene against India, assures US support if Soviet Union intervenes.

11 December: *INS Panvel* and *MV Chitrangada* reach BSF post in Hasnabad.

12 December: Third and final Soviet veto on UN resolution calling for immediate ceasefire and withdrawal by Indian forces.

13–14 December: Enterprise carrier battle group enters the Malacca Straits.

13 December: Gen Niazi speaks to Pakistani C-in-C General Hamid and asks him to expedite the ceasefire.

13 December: Soviet Pacific fleet sails out from Vladivostok for Indian Ocean to tail Seventh Fleet.

14 December: Yahya Khan sends Niazi a signal asking him to take necessary measures to stop the fighting and preserve the lives of the armed forces personnel.

14 December: Massacre of over 1000 Bengali intellectuals, writers, intellectuals, artists, professors, lyricists, musicians, and doctors by East Pakistan army and Al Badar death squads.

15 December: Radio Pakistan announces that Task Force 74 is heading northwards and may establish a base in East Pakistan.

16 December: Lt General Niazi signs instrument marking the surrender of 92,208 army, paramilitary and police elements at Ramna Race course, Dacca. This is the largest surrender after the Second World War. The surrender results in the birth of Bangla Desh. Prime Minister Indira Gandhi tells India's parliament 'Dhaka is now the free capital of a free country.'

17 December: At 8 p.m. all hostilities on both fronts cease following Pakistan's acceptance of India's unilateral ceasefire offer.

ACKNOWLEDGEMENTS

I wish to express my sincere thanks to my wife Nirmala and to many of my friends and well wishers who constantly urged and encouraged me to write this book. I am sure that, but for their encouragement, this book would have never seen the light of day.

My thanks, of course, to our daughters Ujwala, Natasha and Meghana, who took effective charge of my periodic trends of lethargy and ensured I worked with minimum interruptions till completion! I am grateful to my co-author Sandeep Unnithan and to my former colleague Cdr VP Kapil. Lastly, my thanks to Vice Admiral A.K. Chawla, commander-in-chief, Southern Naval Command, for his assistance in completing this book.

Captain M.N.R. Samant
Maha Vir Chakra, Indian Navy (retired)
Mumbai, October 2018

Among my most precious books is a copy of *War in the Indian Ocean* autographed by its author Vice Admiral M.K. Roy on the flight deck of the

INS Vikrant, soon after its decommissioning on 31 January 1997. In his insightful account, Admiral Roy revealed, for the first time, the existence of Mukti Bahini naval commandos. His book planted a seed in my mind for a book I tentatively called 'The Fighting Frogmen'. How did Bengali college students learn to blow up merchant ships?

The question lingered, and after Admiral Roy's tragic demise in 2013, I thought it would never be answered. Then, one Saturday afternoon two years ago, my old navy friend 'Mr White' introduced me to Captain M.N.R. Samant. He was a diminutive, bespectacled veteran who spoke very little. He, in fact, reminded me of the wise Yoda from the Star Wars saga. Our meeting was extraordinarily fortuitous. Captain Samant not only needed someone to co-author his book, he was in fact one of the principal architects of an operation which had piqued my curiosity many years ago.

When he spoke, and it took him a while to, he opened a window into another world – the secret world of Naval Commando Operations (X). A story whose full contours had never been revealed for nearly half a century. My Yoda impression, it seems, was more than spot on. Captain Samant was indeed the last of a secret order who had trained and raised a unique naval guerrilla army to fight a righteous war. After pronouncing the mission accomplished, these white knights melted back into the shadows. It was an almost unbelievably operatic, truth-stranger-than-fiction tale, down to the fact that one of his principal adversaries was his former roommate. Indeed, this book would never have materialized if Captain Samant didn't believe it was finally time to talk about what is arguably one of the world's most unusual covert military operations.

I spent several days over the past two years with Captain Samant and learnt something new each time we met. He opened up his notes, photographs, letters and of course racked his crystal-clear memories of years gone by for his last project, the culmination of a glorious and extraordinary sixty-year career. He approved the final draft but, tragically, did not live to see its release.

Captain Samant's deputy, the tireless Cdr Vijai Kapil, Nao Sena Medal, Vir Chakra and my father's old friend from the navy, hand-held me through the entire project, answered all my persistent queries and infected me with his quiet enthusiasm. He spent a memorable week with me in Bangladesh, criss-crossing the country and working all his old contacts to fill up the book. Thanks to Mrs Vijaya Kapil, who I discovered was my mother's old hostel mate from Benares Hindu University, for looking after us through our book discussions.

'Mr White' introduced me to the right people and acknowledged that while this story would not figure in an official account for various reasons, it needed telling in order to inspire future generations.

So many people have been key movers in this two-year odyssey that I would be remiss in not thanking all of them. So here goes.

Vice Admiral Anil Kumar Chawla, C-in-C Southern Naval Command and the officers and men of diving school, Kochi. My friends in the diving branch – the silent service – and their progeny, the Marine Commandos.

Moti Aai, Nirmala Samant, who stood rock-like behind Captain Samant for sixty years. Ujwala, Natasha and Meghna Samant, custodians of the legacy of a naval legend. Chris and Pascal, Captain Samant's son-in-laws. Ujwala, thanks for filling in the final pieces of the book. Meghna and Ashish Kapur, I am grateful for your hospitality through our long discussion sessions in Gurgaon. Thanks to Ashok and Neelam Kapur for hosting our meetings in Defence Colony.

Thank you Probir Roy, a visionary in his field, for allowing me to access the photographs and papers left behind by one of our country's most far-sighted naval leaders, Vice Admiral Roy.

Thank you, Neha Kapil, for your hospitality in Dhaka and facilitating our travel through the country.

My deepest appreciation for our tireless defence adviser in Dhaka, Brigadier (now Major General) J.S. Nanda who facilitated access with the military authorities.

To the freedom fighters who built what is now a thriving, vibrant democracy. One of its key figures – the indefatigable Commodore A.W. Chowdhury, Bir Bikram,[67] Bir Uttam, Bangladesh Navy. I sometimes

67 Bangladeshi military decorations; equal to the Maha Vir Chakra and Vir Chakra in India

wonder how history would have been if he hadn't raised a flag of revolt in distant France in 1971. My grateful thanks to Lt Cdr Mohammad Jalaluddin, Bir Uttam, Bangladesh Navy, his comrades Humayun Kabir, Atharuddin Talukder, Farhad Hussain, Badiul Alam and Anil Baran Roy of the Naval Commando Association, Dhaka. Farhad Hussain, for helping to arrange his brother Humayun Kabir's interviews. Murad, for his assistance in interviewing his father Baidul Alam. Lt Colonel Quazi Sajjad Ali Zahir, Bir Protik,[68] a war hero who continues his selfless mission to honour the Indian figures of the Liberation War. Captain Nurul Haq of the Bangladesh Navy for his precise recollections of the tumultuous events in the run up to 1971.

Naval commando historian, the late Khalilur Rahman, whom I could not unfortunately meet, for documenting the biographies of his comrades in three insightful books – *Shaagor Tole Muktijoddho, Muktijoddho Noucommando O Naabikder Jeebonkosh* and *Muktijuddher Ujjol Nakkhatra*.

Major Rafiqul Islam, Bir Uttam, freedom fighter and member of parliament from Chandpur for permission to use extracts from his wartime account *A Tale of Millions*.

Moinuddin Khanbadal, freedom fighter and member of parliament, Chattogram. Mir Mushtaque Ahmed Robi, former naval commando and now member of parliament, Satkhira for sharing their experiences.

I am grateful to Farid Hossain, minister (press) in the Bangladesh High Commission, New Delhi. The staff and organizers of Bangabandhu Memorial Museum in Dhanmondi, the Liberation War Museum in Dhaka and the Genocide Museum. Without these visits, I would never have known as much as I do about the horrors which led to the heroic people's war. Saleem Samad, freedom fighter and journalist, for his support. Mahmud Hossain, for the photography at the Liberation War Museum. Mahfuz Anam, editor of the *Daily Star*, Dhaka, for permission to use a picture of the *MV Akram*.

The naval commandos – too many to individually thank here– who came out to meet us in Bangladesh to prove age hadn't dimmed their enthusiasm from the days of struggle.

---

68 Bangladeshi gallantry award; equal to the Vir Chakra

The Bangladesh Navy, for opening up their ships and personnel to us, and allowing us to retrace Force Alfa's gun battle in Khulna. Thanks to our young liaison officer, Lt Abrar Hasan – grandson of Mohammad Ruhul Amin, Bir Sreshtho.[69] Abrar, you have a huge legacy to live up to.

Lt Suvesh Kumar Mitter, for diligently filling in the details of events of nearly a half-century ago. Lt Cdr J.K. Roy Choudhary, Commanders Vijaygopal, Ashok Kumar and V.K. Raizada, for sharing their Force Alfa experiences. Chiman Singh, MVC,[70] for recounting his incredible story and for his hospitality in Gokulgarh. Lt Cdr JPA Noronha, MVC, and his wife Teresa Noronha, and Anandi Martis, wife of the late Cdr George Martis, for contributing to the narrative.

To the family of the late Admiral S.M. Nanda. Thank you, Suresh Nanda and Commander Arun Saigal, keen maritime history raconteur and my omnipresent guide to the naval veteran community.

Lt General Abhay Krishna, GoC-in-C Eastern Army Command, for his help with details of the history of Fort William. General Shankar Roychowdhury, former chief of the army staff and brigade major Charlie Sector during the 1971 war, for his detailed recollections.

Commodore Rajan Vir – president of the Indian Maritime Foundation, for sharing his photographs and memories of his Dartmouth course mates Captain Samant and Vice Admiral Zamir Ahmed.

Gurdip Bedi for recounting his amazing role in the flight of the eight *Mangro* crewmen from Madrid in 1971.

Major 'Delta', a long-time friend who began his covert service of the state in 1971 and who continues to render selfless service in other arenas. Another untiring legend and institution builder, Brigadier B.K. Ponwar who, after fighting with the Mukti Bahini in 1971, runs the College of Jungle Warfare, Kanker.

My friends Brigadier Xerxes Adrianwala, Brigadier Kuldip Singh and Lt Colonel Rohit Aggarwal for their comments and suggestions. My gratitude to Lt Colonel Ashok Sarkar and the Lt General B.N. Sarkar family, the late Rear Admiral Subir Paul and Sumita Sen.

---

69 Bangladesh's highest military honour; equal to the Param Vir Chakra

70 Maha Vir Chakra

My friend Major General Ajay Das for his help in locating the Sikh LI veterans. Lt Colonel GS Sharma of the 2 Sikh LI for his wartime reflections. Another dear friend Colonel (Dr) D.P.K. Pillay, a remarkable soul who inspired me to document the 1971 war. Colonel Vivek Chadha of the Institute of Defence Studies and Analyses (IDSA) for his insights on the Indian Army. Mr 'Red', my friend from the IAF, for help with military aviation-related inputs.

Vinit Kumar, Chairman, Kolkata Port Trust, and Captain J.J. Biswas, director Marine Department (KoPT), for their help in tracing the history of the Flower-class boats. Bisakha Ghosh for her memories of tending to the Mukti Bahini refugees in Calcutta. Arati Mukherjee di for her wonderful encore of Jackpot's mission song – 'Amar Putul Aajke Pratham'.

Grateful to my friend Captain Sanjay Parashar, managing director of V.R. Maritime Services, for putting me in touch with stalwart Captain Ashok Mahapatra, former director, Maritime Safety Committee, at International Maritime Organization. Captain Mahapatra for helping me re-verify the ship casualty lists with Lloyds London. Sanjay Bhattacharjee of Abee Divecorp Pvt Ltd for retelling his family's tryst with the Liberation War.

Vice Admiral Ahmad Tasnim and Vice Admiral Taj Muhammad Khattak of the Pakistan Navy for their wartime reminiscences.

My dear friends Anuj Dhar and Chandrachur Ghose, who helped me translate the biographies of the naval commandos, documented by the Bangladeshi freedom fighter and historian, the late Khalil-ur-Rahman. Priyanka Sarkar for helping out with translations of other key letters and documents. Devishankar Mukherjee, former Deputy Farm Superintendent of the (now) Khaitan India Ltd sugar mill, for his vivid recollections of C2P in 1971 and for the maps of the plantation. Brigadier Prashant Ghosh for his war time stories of fighting with the Mukti Bahini.

Former navy chief and 1971 war hero Admiral Arun Prakash, Vice Admiral R.P. Suthan, former vice chief and navigating officer of the INS Kavaratti for their wartime reminiscences. Navy veterans Vice Admiral K.N. Sushil, Vice Admiral J.S. Bedi, Rear Admiral Sudhir Pillai and Commodore Rajesh Sarin, for their help and guidance at key junctures. My friend the remarkable navy spokesperson Captain D.K. Sharma, for never being more than a phone call, email or SMS away, and for filling in the gaps.

Vice Admiral Vinod Pasricha, naval historian, the moving spirit behind the Kursura submarine museum in Vizag and former INAS 300 pilot, for linking me up with his INAS 310 buddies. Commodore Bipin Bhagwat, 310 Squadron historian, for explaining the workings of the Alizé and the A Mark VII. Commodore Patwardhan , Commodore Medioma 'Mike' Bhada, Commodore Richard Clarke and Commander S. Gopalakrishnan for recounting stories of the fascinating Lt Cdr Ashok 'Aku' Roy. Rana Banerji and Dr Niila Ghosh, family members of Lt Cdr Roy for remembrances of this unsung naval hero. To another old friend and naval history raconteur, Commodore Srikant Kesnur. for his constant encouragement through the project.

Major General Ashok Narula, ADGPI, Brigadier Manoj Kumar, DDG (MC) and Colonel (now Brigadier) Abhijit Mitra, director, media, of the Indian Army, Colonel Aman Anand, spokesperson MoD. My friends Captain Aarunikant Sinha and Anjana Gupta – Babuji, truly indebted for your friendship and for chipping in with the interviews, translations and suggestions. My friend Nadim Haider who helped me source a missing piece of the puzzle. Thanks, Shikher, Sunanda, Zhenya, Neera, Manju and Abhay, for being such great friends. My agent Mita Kapur of Siyahi, for encouraging us at every step and watching this book grow over the months.

My editor-in-chief Aroon Purie, for being a beacon of inspiration. Group editorial director Raj Chengappa for his support. S. Sahaya Ranjit, Vikram Sharma, Jeemon Jacob and Romita Datta and all my colleagues at *India Today*, where I have spent close to two decades of my professional career.

My grateful thanks to T.K.A. Nair, former principal secretary to the PM. Dr Unnikrishnan S.M., Associated Vice President HLL Lifecare, Thiruvananthapuram.

My immensely talented artist friend Saurabh Singh for his cover design and graphics. Army historian Mandeep Singh Bajwa for background information on some key figures in the book.

My father, Cdr G.V.K. Unnithan, old sea salt, naval history buff and 1971 veteran, whose books, journals and photographs helped recreate the navy of years gone past. He now knows why all his Bengali-speaking comrades vanished before the formal declaration of war.

My mother Dr Saraswathy Unnithan for her anecdotes of meeting Vice Admiral Roy on the *Vikrant*. My brother-in-law Krishnakumar for his helpful suggestions in making the book more reader-friendly. My wife and worst critic Lakshmi Iyer for living in a book-strewn house and putting up with my long, two-year absence. To my in-laws Dr Sridevi Iyer and Dr Subramonia Iyer who allowed me to convert a room in their Delhi home into my writing redoubt, romba nandri.

Sandeep Unnithan
April 2019, New Delhi